T0204646

URBAN REGENERATION, COMMUNITY POWER AND THE (IN)SIGNIFICANCE OF 'RACE'

For my wife Lynne Maginn-Greenaway
and
my parents Joseph and Catherine Maginn

Urban Regeneration, Community Power and the (In)Significance of 'Race'

PAUL J. MAGINN

Edith Cowan University, Western Australia

Routledge
Taylor & Francis Group

LONDON AND NEW YORK

First published 2004 by Ashgate Publishing

Reissued 2018 by Routledge
2 Park Square, Milton Park, Abingdon, Oxon OX14 4RN
605 Third Avenue, New York, NY 10017

First issued in paperback 2021

Routledge is an imprint of the Taylor & Francis Group, an informa business

A Library of Congress record exists under LC control number: 2004012584

Notice:
Product or corporate names may be trademarks or registered trademarks, and are used only for identification and explanation without intent to infringe.

Publisher's Note
The publisher has gone to great lengths to ensure the quality of this reprint but points out that some imperfections in the original copies may be apparent.

Disclaimer
The publisher has made every effort to trace copyright holders and welcomes correspondence from those they have been unable to contact.

ISBN 13: 978-0-815-39880-6 (hbk)
ISBN 13: 978-1-351-14360-8 (ebk)
ISBN 13: 978-1-138-35856-0 (pbk)

DOI: 10.4324/9781351143608

Contents

List of Tables and Figures

Tables

Figures

Acknowledgements

I would like to thank, first and foremost, Professor Michael Ball, now at the University of Reading, for being an encouraging and thought-provoking mentor and friend who put up with my ideas and arguments over numerous lunches at the local 'greasy spoon' (Max Café) on the Wandsworth Road. I am also extremely grateful to Professor Philip Leather (University of Birmingham) for believing in my initial research proposal and awarding me a scholarship that enabled this research to be undertaken in the first place.

A note of sincere thanks is also extended to former colleagues and friends. First, Professor Chris Paris and Paddy Gray (University of Ulster, Magee College) for giving me my first research job, extending my initial contract beyond eight months and encouraging me to further my academic career. I had a wonderful 2½ years working *and* living in (London)Derry. Next, I would also like to thank Dr. Paul Connolly and Dr. Brendan Murtagh (Queen's University of Belfast), who also employed me during my time at Magee College. They may not realize it but they were sources of knowledge, inspiration and encouragement, despite our ideological differences.

When I moved to London to commence my research I was fortunate to meet Dr. Keith Jacobs (formerly at the University of Westminster and now at the University of Tasmania) via Chris and Paddy. Keith and, latterly, Tony Manzi were kind enough to employ me as a part-time Visiting Lecturer for three years on their undergraduate and postgraduate Housing Studies degree courses. It was within this arena that I was able to test out some ideas and emerging evidence from my research with the many students I thoroughly enjoyed teaching.

On the personal front, thanks also to a number of close friends – Werner Tschiesche, Will Lam and Geoff Henson – who helped in numerous little ways throughout my research and made London such a fantastic place to live in.

Last, but by no means least, this book would not exist if it were not for the generosity of the many tenants and officers who granted me access to their personal and regeneration worlds and gave up their time to take part in my research.

P. J. Maginn
Edith Cowan University
Joondalup (Western Australia)

Chapter 1

Introduction: Urban Regeneration, Community Power and 'Race'

Bringing the community into the practice of urban regeneration is a demonstrably more fraught exercise than governments have assumed it to be. In the more top-down forms of participation employed to discover opinions on an urban planning proposal (for example), involving the community might be little more than an exercise of tokenism. [...] The incorporation of community participation in urban regeneration in... Britain... has been on a much ambitious scale than is represented by the single public meeting designed to gain local reaction to a land-use change affecting the neighbourhood. (Paddison, 2001:202)

Introduction

This book is based upon an ethnographic study of 'community power' and the significance of 'race' within urban regeneration partnerships (URPs) and local community forums in three ethnically diverse neighbourhoods in London – *Northside, Southside* and *Westside*.[1]

The 'ethnographic story' presented herein paints a generally positive, but complicated, picture of the nature of power wielded by local communities over decision-making within URPs. This is contrary to the thrust of most of the British academic literature on urban regeneration policy, community participation and 'race' (Atkinson and Cope, 1997; Brownill and Darke, 1998; Brownill and Thomas, 1998; Munt, 1991). This is not to say that local communities have become 'more powerful' than their other partners on URPs. Rather, local communities are shown to be extremely resourceful agents capable of deploying a range of tactics and strategies to exert varying degrees of influence within the decision-making process at the local level.

More controversially, the findings from the three case studies bring into question the significance (i.e. prevalence) of 'race' and racism within URPs, community forums and the regeneration process in general. Hence, the playful use of the term '(In)significance' in the title of the book. It is important to stress that readers do not (mis)interpret this as a denial of the significance, historically and contemporaneously, of 'race' and racism within urban regeneration policy. Instead, it should be interpreted as an indication of the socially and politically

---

[1] The real names of the three neighbourhoods have been changed to afford anonymity and confidentiality.

contested, contextual and temporal (in)significance attached to 'race' within policy arenas.

URPs have become the major policy vehicle directed at resolving the myriad of problems that bedevil those localities now known as 'socially excluded neighbourhoods' within the UK urban policy discourse (DETR, 2001; DoE, 1997; SEU, 1998). Simultaneously, community involvement has become *de riguer* in urban regeneration and is seen as a prerequisite, by policymakers and many academics, for both policy and policy outcomes to be deemed successful (Atkinson, 1996; Foley and Martin, 2000; McArthur, 1995; Smith and Beazley, 2000; Taylor, 2000b, 2002; Wilks-Heeg, 2003). Relatedly, policy-makers have placed increased emphasis on the need for black and minority ethnic (BME) communities to be more involved in decision-making. The Conservative government's (1990-1997) approach on this front in relation to its key regeneration programme, the Single Regeneration Budget (SRB), could be best described as implicit and incremental (DoE, 1995). In comparison, the 'New Labour' government's (1997-) approach has been relatively more explicit and pro-active (DETR, 2000; SEU, 2000).

Whilst there is a vast literature on urban regeneration, partnerships and community participation (for an overview, see Imrie and Raco, 2003; Roberts and Sykes, 2000), relatively little has actually focused on the nature of power and power relations within URPs and local communities, particularly ethnically diverse ones. It, consequently, is difficult to discern whether the trend of greater democracy and pluralism within urban regeneration policy, argued here to have (re)commenced with the City Challenge initiative in 1991 under the Conservatives and galvanized by 'New Labour' in 1997, is actually influential on policy outcomes at the local level. This book seeks to contribute to this gap in the literature. It does so by focusing on the locus of 'community power' as expressed through the formal and informal relationships between partners on local URPs based in multi-ethnic neighbourhoods. Specifically, it focuses on relationships at two levels. First, it considers power relations between 'institutional partners' (i.e. local councils, housing associations, private developers and voluntary organizations) and the 'local community' partner. And, secondly, it looks at relations within community forums, the governance structure that enables local communities to participate officially within the regeneration process.

The Multi-agency Partnership Approach to Urban Regeneration

Urban regeneration policy has historically been the preserve of the state. Central government has primarily been responsible for setting the strategic policy agenda and providing funding. And, local government has assumed operational responsibility of policy programmes. As urban problems have become more entrenched and multi-faceted, a wider range of agents has been brought to the policy arena to work alongside the state. The logic behind this move is simplistic: urban problems can be addressed more effectively via the relevant agents pooling their resources and developing a comprehensive policy framework (Healey, 1997).

Carter (2000) has noted that there is now an 'emerging consensus' within urban regeneration, and other policy fields, in the need for a multi-agency approach to tackle the problems within socially excluded neighbourhoods. Partnership, along with community participation, has thus become synonymous with urban regeneration policy (Bailey *et al*, 1995).

Partnerships and Partners

Contemporary urban regeneration policy is implemented on the ground via local URPs that comprise representations from a variety of 'partners' or 'interest groups'. These partners are readily identifiable in the broad sense. They include the public, private and voluntary sectors and the local community. These four groups should not be assumed to be homogenous in structure and outlook. It is more likely that difference of opinion and fractures will prevail within each grouping. Within the local community interest group, for example, there may be divisions along racial, gender or age lines. Such divisions invariably give rise to questions about representativeness, discrimination and exclusion and agenda setting within community forums and URPs. Similarly, within the local government sector there may be inter-departmental conflicts between town planners, housing officers and regeneration officers for example. And, there may also be policy differences between elected members on a local authority's regeneration committee. Ultimately, such conflicts point to the question of who has power within and between interest groups on local URPs.

The general consensus within the academic literature is that partnerships are essentially a positive thing and are here to stay. Yet, there are some major concerns about URPs, especially in relation to the empowerment and power of local communities within such formal policy arenas (Atkinson, 1999; Colenutt and Cutten, 1994; Cooper and Hawtin, 1997b; Stewart and Taylor, 1995; Taylor, 1995, 2000a, 2002).

Mackintosh (1992) has been particularly enthusiastic about the potential benefits of multi-agency partnerships. Whilst acknowledging that partnerships are conflictual policy arenas, Mackintosh has argued that partnerships realize three key benefits for those who participate within them. First, she claims that partnerships are *synergistic* structures. That is, when the different partners combine their various resources they are able to realize more than if they worked alone in trying to resolve urban problems. Secondly, partnerships help to enhance the *budgetary capacity* of individual partners as a result of financial resources being pooled. In particular, those with the least amount of financial resources will have access to monies that would normally be out of their reach. And, lastly, it is contended that working in partnership has a *transformative* effect on partners. That is, through being exposed to one another, the various partners learn about and, ultimately, incorporate elements of each other's values and practices into their own behaviour patterns. This process of mutual learning helps to bind the various partners together and, ultimately, reinforces the synergistic qualities of partnerships.

The various benefits identified by Mackintosh have been challenged. In overall terms, Mackintosh's standpoint on the benefits of partnerships are seen as being too positivist. Hastings (1996), in particular, has argued that the synergistic and transformational benefits are likely to be unevenly re-distributed within URPs. Specifically, she has expressed concerns that local communities are the agents least likely to benefit from participating in partnerships. This is a function of being the last group invited to the process, and being denied full access to pooled resources on account that they tend to bring comparatively few resources, especially financial, to URPs. Mayo (1997) is also cautious of the benefits of partnerships to local communities. She argues that the transformational impacts of partnerships are more likely to result in the 'transformation of the community sector's interests, by those of the private sector' (p.13). In other words, communities will be rendered relatively powerless in their ability to influence the policy agenda or decision-making within URPs. For Mayo, a major reason for this is that partnerships are inherently market-oriented policy arenas that favour the interests of institutional agents from the private and public sectors. Ball *et al* (2003) have recently challenged this generalized view noting that 'the results of [our] survey of property developers... does not generally support the hypothesis that URPs provide synergistic benefits' (p.2251).

Ultimately, URPs are ladened with positive and negative attributes for all that participate in them. What seems clear is that central government, whatever their political hue, now see the partnership approach as the best and, possibly, the only way to tackle social exclusion.

URPs: Democratic and Pluralistic Governance Structures?

The existence of four broad interests groups within URPs points to the existence of a political dynamic. For sure, local URPs are portrayed as pluralistic and democratic policy arenas by central and local government. That is to say, the various partners are notionally deemed equal to one another with decisions arrived at via a process of negotiation and bargaining. Whilst the different agents that participate within URPs may be equal to one another, in the sense that they have a 'right' to participate in decision-making, they invariably come to the policy arena with varying resources. This, consequently, has implications on their ability to influence decision-making. Normatively speaking, agents with access to the most (and best) resources may be expected to command greater power than those with few or no resources. Local communities generally come to URPs with comparatively fewer resources than their institutional partners do. They, consequently, are often cast as the least powerful agent. But, is this *always* the case? As will be seen later in Chapters 5, 6 and 7, local communities are far from rendered powerless. In fact, they are able to draw on a range of resources and deploy various strategies to influence decision-making, albeit with varying degrees of success, within URPs.

Community Participation

Central government's commitment to partnership has also been complemented by a 'turn to community' in urban regeneration policy (Duffy and Hutchinson, 1997). In short, government has advocated that local communities should play a more instrumental role in URPs (DETR, 1997, 2001; DoE, 1994, 1995, 1997; ODPM, 2000). Burns and Taylor (2000) have argued that community participation is essential within URPs for a number of inter-related reasons. First, local communities have different perceptions as to their own needs, problems and solutions than policy-makers. Next, local communities' lived experiences and knowledge of urban problems is a valuable resource that can help to enhance the overall expertise within URPs. Third, participation provides an opportunity for communities to become empowered in their own struggle against social exclusion. And, lastly, 'active participation of local residents is essential to improved democratic and service accountability' within regeneration policy (Burns and Taylor, 2000: 50).

In order to participate formally within URPs local residents must generally do so by becoming members of a recognized community forum or steering group. Community forums are organizations set up, normally by the local authority, to enable the local community to come together and articulate their concerns and needs and have input into the decision-making process. Such forums, therefore, are supposed to act as the representative voice and negotiating agent of the wider community around the partnership table. This institutionalization of the local community legitimizes their participation within URPs. Some members of a local community, for whatever reasons, may not wish to participate in the regeneration process via formalized structures and processes. Instead, they may seek to influence decision-making from the outside by engaging in radical activities. Institutional agents, especially local authorities, within URPs may see such courses of action as obstructive and, perversely, undemocratic. Such radical reactions are to be expected, particularly when members of local communities see certain decisions as controversial. Moreover, informal participation by some members of the local community is arguably as legitimate as formal modes of participation. A radical course of action may be the only option open to certain groups, especially minorities, who feel that they and their interests have been excluded from community forums and URPs.

To reiterate, when local communities enter URPs they tend not to be endowed with the types of resources, for example, bureaucratic decision-making structures, a hierarchy of employees and funding streams, held by their institutional partners. This obviously has implications on their ability and capacity to participate effectively in decision-making. To compensate for this, local authorities have tended to assume responsibility for providing community forums with particular resources (e.g. office space and equipment, capacity-building training and tenant advisors). Funding for these resources tends to be derived from a mix of local authorities' own revenue streams and regeneration monies secured from central government. Arguably, the level and type of resources provided by local authorities (and other institutional partners) gives an indication of their commitment to community participation and empowerment. In short, the more resources provided the greater the commitment to community participation and vice versa.

Community Power

The active participation of local communities in URPs raises questions about the nature of their power or influence within URPs. Atkinson and Cope (1997) note that the academic literature on community participation and urban regeneration has been disappointing on the issue of power. Indeed, discussion has tended to focus on several key issues directly related to the concept of community participation but which fall short of the issue of community power *per se*. These include:

- defining who or what is meant by the 'local community' (Hill, 1994);
- outlining the various levels of community participation in decision-making processes via drawing on Arnstein's, (1969) seminal work on citizen participation (Burns *et al*, 1994; Burton, 2003);
- arguing that community participation is an essential prerequisite in order to realize successful outcomes in urban regeneration programmes (Taylor, 1995); and
- advocating that tenants need to be empowered in order to participate in the regeneration process (Craig and Mayo, 1995; Skelcher, 1993).

It is clear from the literature that local communities are seen as comparatively less powerful than their counterparts within URPs. They are often portrayed as the 'junior' partner within partnerships (Brownill and Darke, 1998; Hastings, 1996; Smith and Beazley, 2000). It is contended here, however, that there is a lack of clarity within the literature as to whether power is a process or the ability to influence policy outcomes. Furthermore, power is a relative concept. This relativity leads to confusion within the literature as to who is the most, or least, powerful within URPs.

The primary focus of this book is policy outcomes. In particular, it seeks to explore the impacts communities have on decision-making within URPs. Power is defined herein as the ability to initiate change, no matter how small, within the decision-making processes of URPs. Hence, if a local community is successful in altering a particular policy, either incrementally or significantly, it can be said that they have exercised some degree of community power. It is important to stress that in considering the issue of community power the aim here is not to assess the actual amount of power wielded by a local community or to prove that they are the least powerful agent within the three URP case studies. Rather, the objective is to determine and explain the overall nature of the *pattern* of power within each URP.

The (In)Significance of 'Race'

On the issue of 'race' the dominant paradigm within the British urban policy and sociology literature is that racism is institutionalized and endemic. In essence, 'race' is *always* a problematic matter. The dominance of this paradigm is grounded in a complex and inter-related mix of a body of empirical research that has 'proven' racism permeates British society and the politically oriented 'anti-racist' position of many, if not most, urban sociologists and policy researchers. Combined, these two factors have helped to reify the position that Britain is an institutionally and endemically racist society.

A number of commentators have argued that BME groups and issues have been systematically discriminated against and marginalized within national and local public policy arenas (Atkinson and Moon, 1994; Ben-Tovim *et al*, 1986; Brownill and Thomas, 1998; Munt, 1991; Ratcliffe, 1992; Thomas, 1994, 1995, 1997; Thomas and Krishnarayan, 1994). Other commentators have expressed concerns that, during the 1980s and early 1990s, 'race' tended to be given cursory acknowledgement by policy-makers (Brownill *et al*, 1996; Burton, 1997; Young, 1983). In relation to the SRB, Hall *et al* (1996) and Nevin *et al* (1997) have argued that BME issues have been given a low priority within local partnerships. Furthermore, BTEG (1995; 1997) have claimed that there has been a lack of involvement of BME organizations within the SRB process in general, and regeneration partnerships in particular:

> Regrettably the impact of [the Urban Programme, City Challenge and the SRB] on black communities have been short term and marginal. There have been some successes but they have been the exception rather than the rule. This is because black communities have been the *invisible partners* in regeneration programmes to date. Indeed there are still black communities struggling to access City Challenge and SRB programmes operational in their communities.   (BTEG, 1995:1)

Similar concerns have been expressed within the field of housing and tenant involvement. Cooper and Hawtin (1997a), for example, have outlined that the lack of participation by BMEs within tenant organizations has been a function of discriminatory practices at structural and interpersonal levels. The McPherson Report (Home Office, 1999) into the death of the 'black' teenager Stephen Lawrence, which resulted in the reintroduction, but with a new emphasis, of terms such as 'unwitting', 'unconscious', 'unintentional' and, most importantly, 'institutional' racism, have helped to galvanize claims that Britain is an endemically racist society.

In light of the above, it is difficult, if not impossible, to imagine that there may be anything positive to say about the issue of 'race' within the UK. Indeed, research claims that racism is not as problematic as is often claimed, or that challenge the notion that Britain is an institutionally and endemically racist society are fairly uncommon within the British academic literature. This differs considerably from the situation in the USA where academic debate on 'race' is arguably more provocative and dynamic (D'Souza, 1995; Sowell, 1994; Thernstrom and Thernstrom, 2002; Wilson, 1980).

There have been a few provocative British examples, mainly within the field of the sociology of education, but these are now rather dated. Foster (1990), for example, claimed that he found little evidence of racism within the multi-ethnic inner city school he studied. Similarly, Palmer *et al* (1986) argued that the claims and demands of the anti-racist movement in relation to educational practice and the existence of racism within schools (and British society) were misplaced, incoherent, over-exaggerated and motivated more by politics than empirical facts. More recently, the Institute for the Study of Civil Society has sought to challenge the notions that the Police and Britain are institutionally and endemically racist respectively (Dennis *et al*, 2000; Green, 2000). Not surprisingly, those that have challenged the dominant anti-racist paradigm have been summarily dismissed and essentially branded racist for advocating such views in the first place (Hammersley, 1995).

Interestingly, Lo Piccolo and Thomas (2003) have recently highlighted positive examples of the roles played by 'minorities' within the domain of urban regeneration. First, they seek to highlight the 'efforts of a number of workers [and institutions] to produce progressive results in difficult circumstances' (p.1). And, second, they hope to break the 'popular stereotypes of [minorities] as (passive) victims and a social problem' (p.1). The stories herein add to these objectives. However, unlike Lo Piccolo and Thomas who seem very much wedded to the notions that 'race' and racism always matters and that racism is so embedded within British society, the significance of 'race' and racism within and across *Northside, Southside* and *Westside* was very much a contested one.

Methodology and Theory

In order to ascertain the nature of community power wielded by local communities within URPs it is important to examine the outcomes of their (re)actions within decision-making processes. In simple terms, communities may be defined as having power if they manage to effect any change in policy within a regeneration project. As Scott (2001) notes, '[p]ower, in the pluralist view, is the ability to initiate alternatives that actually get to be adopted or to veto alternatives that are initiated by others' (p.53). The sense and nature of power exerted by community forums may be 'measured', albeit subjectively, via eliciting the views and experiences of the different agents actively engaged in URPs. Where community agents have exercised influence within URPs, it is important to identify what resources and strategies they have utilized to understand how they effected change within the regeneration process.

An appropriate research methodology, methods and strategy are necessary in order to be able to empirically test whether or not and how local communities exert power within URPs. Furthermore, a theoretical framework is needed in order to be able to explain the nature of power and power relations within URPs at the localized level.

Ethnography: Developing an Insider Account of Community Power

In considering what research methodology to use to study 'community power' within local URPs, particular attention was paid to the need to identify an approach that would enable the exercise of community power to be readily observed and measured. It was decided that an ethnographic approach would be suitable. Ethnographic research allows researchers to 'get under the skin' of social phenomena, such as URPs, and make sense of their complex structures and processes. Furthermore, by spending an extended period of time in the field collecting data via interviews and observing the regeneration process evolve, this enabled a thicker description and understanding of community participation, power relations and the significance of 'race' to be developed.

It is important to note that community forums, the formal governance structure that enable local communities to participate officially within URPs, form the locus of analysis of 'community power' and the significance of 'race'. Such sites afford the opportunity to observe, from the inside, how local communities' interact and relate with their institutional partners and themselves and, ultimately, influence decision-making. In addition, it is also possible to ascertain what significance is attached to the issue of 'race'.

A further reason for deciding to adopt an ethnographic methodology was that researchers are free to utilize a range of methods to collate data. Of course, this is not to imply that this will produce superior data, than, a singular method, such as a large-scale survey. It is enough to say at this stage, that, qualitative and quantitative approaches produce different types of data and are appropriate for addressing particular types of research questions. Empirical data for this book was collected via three primary research methods. These included: (i) in-depth semi-structured interviews with a diverse range of agents within each case study area; (ii) non-participant observations of community forum meetings and other events associated with the regeneration process in each case study; and (iii) focus groups. These various methods were selected on the basis that they complemented one another and would thus enhance the reliability of data collected.

In-depth interviews were designed to elicit tenants', and other agents', views and lived experiences of the nature of consultation, community power and the significance of 'race' within the regeneration process. Non-participant observations were conducted in order to observe interactions and relations between partners. Focus groups were used to triangulate the data collected by the first two research methods.

In terms of a research strategy, a multiple case study approach was adopted (Yin, 1984). This strategy was adopted in order to facilitate a comparative analysis. Three broadly similar case study areas were identified and secured, thus providing the opportunity to develop some 'analytical generalizations' (Yin, 1984) about the nature of community power within URPs.

Theorizing the Nature of Power within URPs

A number of key theories may be used to explain the nature of power within policy processes. These include: elite theory (Hunter, 1953), Marxist or structuralist theories (Pickvance, 1995), regime theory (Stoker, 1995) and pluralist theories (Waste, 1986). Each of these theoretical approaches 'makes very different assumptions about the nature and meaning of power, and each claims to be 'correct' in its conceptualisations and measurement of power' (Judge, 1995:4). Notably, in recent years, urban regime theory has come to dominate theoretical discussion within British urban policy and politics (Davies, 2001, 2002, 2003; Dowding *et al*, 1999; Smith and Beazley, 2000; Stoker, 1995; Ward, 1995, 1996, 1997).

Elite theory, for example, defines power in the policy process as the ability to exercise change via an agent asserting their reputation. Furthermore, power is argued to be concentrated in the hands of a small number of noble or elite individuals. Within Marxist or structuralist theories, power rests within ephemeral structures that underlie all observable phenomena, which individual agents are argued to have no 'real' influence over or resistance against. In contrast, pluralists define power as, the ability of an individual or group to effect some observable change, via the application of pressure, within the policy process. Since this book is concerned with observable outcomes in URP decision-making, pluralist theory has been 'regenerated' in order to develop an understanding of the nature of power relations within URPs at the neighbourhood level. In doing so, this book takes up the challenge set by Harding (1996) who argued that 'there would appear to be a great deal of mileage still to be gained from a combination of the three forms of analysis used in community power studies: reputational, positional and decisional' (p.652).

Through using ethnography and pluralism this book provides an intensely rich empirical and theoretical insight into the how local communities are consulted and participate in decision-making at the local level. The book challenges general perceptions about the nature of power and the significance of 'race' within URPs and local communities. The findings raise a series of dilemmas and more questions than answers for policy-makers and local communities. On the academic research front, the findings will hopefully provoke more critical discussion about community power and the significance of 'race' within urban regeneration policy and public policy in general.

Structure of the Book

The book is structured in the following way. Chapter 2 (*The 'Pluralistic Turn' in Urban Regeneration*) provides an overview of the evolution of British urban regeneration policy since the late 1960s through to the election and re-election of 'New Labour' in 1997 and 2002 respectively. The central argument is that there has been a 'pluralistic turn' in regeneration policy over this period. On the one hand, URPs are socially pluralistic policy arenas in that they comprise a diverse range of partners or 'interest groups'. On the other hand, URPs are politically pluralistic in that decision-making within such structures is (supposedly) premised on a process of negotiation and bargaining between the various partners.

Chapter 3 (*Regenerating Pluralist Theory and Community Power*) outlines the theoretical framework underpinning the empirical research. It is argued that pluralist theory (Dahl, 1961; McLennan, 1995, 1997; Polsby, 1980; Waste, 1986) provides an appropriate framework to analyse and understand the nature of community power within URPs. It is important to note that historically pluralism has been applied to analyzing political processes and structures at the national, regional and city level. This book departs from focusing on these spatial levels and instead applies pluralism at a more micro level - the neighbourhood. The chapter highlights that communities may exercise power through engaging in pressure and/or protest politics. Pluralist theory is defined and is shown to be a heterogeneous theory, not a homogenous one as it has so often been (mis)perceived.

Chapter 4 (*An Ethnographic Approach to Urban Regeneration and Community Power*) focuses on the methodological framework for the empirical analysis, providing justification for the use of an ethnographic methodology and a multiple case study approach. A number of salient methodological issues (e.g. research methods, negotiating access, generalizability and sampling within case studies) are discussed.

Chapter 5 (*Northside: Pragmatic Pluralism and the Declining Significance of 'Race'*); Chapter 6 (*Southside: Hyperpluralism and the Fragmentation of the Local Community*); and Chapter 7 (*Westside: Paternalistic Pluralism and the (Over)Significance of 'Race'*) each provide a detailed empirical narrative and analysis of the community regeneration experience. A range of issues are discussed, including: the sense of community within each neighbourhood, the composition of community forums, the nature of community power within URPs and community forums and the significance of 'race' within community forums, URPs and the regeneration process in general.

Chapter 8 (*Conclusions: Reconsidering Community Power and the Significance of 'Race'*) provides a summary of the key findings. It is argued that communities are not as powerless as has often been suggested. Yes, there was a general degree of consistency in the way in which local communities were initially informed and consulted about regeneration proposals for their neighbourhoods. Post-consultation, however, communities in the three neighbourhoods studied (with the exception of *Westside*) were found to be engaging in a variety of strategies and deploying various tactics in order to resist and/or alter a range of policy decisions. In much the same way that the pattern of power varied across each case study, so too did the significance of 'race'. Ultimately, a 'new' typology of the overall pattern of power identified within *Northside, Southside* and *Westside* is constructed.

Chapter 2

The 'Pluralistic Turn' in Urban Regeneration Policy

There must be effective arrangements to ensure that those sections of the community intended to benefit do so. This will normally entail continuing consultation and involvement with the intended beneficiaries (those who live and work in the area, local employers, businesses and traders, community and voluntary organisations) and providing means for them to have a continuing say in the management, further development and implementation of the scheme.   (DoE, 1995: 1)

Too much has been imposed from above, when experience shows that success depends on communities themselves having the power and taking the responsibility to make things better. And although there are good examples of rundown neighbourhoods turning themselves around, the lesson haven't been learned properly.   (SEU, 1998: 7)

Introduction

The preceding abstracts highlight a policy commitment, by Conservative and Labour governments respectively, to the ideas of partnership and community participation. Partnership and community participation, it has been argued, were becoming the orthodoxy of urban regeneration policy in the 1990s (Taussik and Smalley, 1998). Similarly, Hastings *et al* (1996) commented that 'it would be unthinkable to discuss regeneration without referring to partnership and community involvement' (p.1). The 'truth' of the matter is that partnership has always been a key aspect of urban policy. Community participation, albeit often in the form of resistance from outside the policy process, also has a long tradition in urban and housing policy (Brindley, 1996; Cairncross *et al*, 1994; Hague, 1990). It is only in the last 30-35 years that local communities have been able to formally participate in decision-making. This was due largely to the recommendations of the Skeffington Report into public participation in planning (Ministry of Housing and Local Government, 1969).

Ordinary citizens could be forgiven, in light of the intense academic debate and policy promotion of partnerships and community participation over the last 10-15 years, for thinking that these structures and processes only emerged in the late 1980s and early 1990s. Partnerships, in one form or another, have been a permanent feature of urban policy (broadly defined) since the mid-19th century at least. Malpass and Murie (1990), for example, in their review of the evolution of housing policy point to the various partnering arrangements that existed between central government, local government, private builders and philanthropic organizations between 1848-1914 in the pursuit by eradicating public health and housing problems. These same broad sectoral interests *and* the local community now constitute the key partners in contemporary urban regeneration partnerships.

This chapter focuses on the evolution of urban policy dating from the 1960s. This period denotes, for want of a better word, the commencement of 'modern' urban policy wherein government was slowly coming round to the realization that the 'urban problem' was a multi-faceted one. It was also a time when partnership and community participation in urban policy began to emerge as explicit policy aims and objectives.

The Wickedness of Urban Problems

Urban areas in the UK, and throughout the world, continue to be bedeviled by a swath of physical, social, economic and environmental problems. Such problems persist despite the historical efforts of policy-makers to cure the city of its various ills. The discovery of a policy panacea remains as elusive as ever. The primary reason for this is that urban problems are multi-dimensional and dynamic phenomena, constantly manifesting with varying degrees of intensity across space and time. In short, urban problems continue to remain at least one step ahead in the game of problem diagnosis and policy prescription. It may sound fatalistic, but the 'reality' of the situation is that urban problems will never be solved.

The fundamental reason for this is that urban problems are 'wicked problems' (Rittel and Webber, 1973). That is, since urban problems are so complex in structure it is impossible to gather *all* the information necessary to understand them fully. If a problem can only be partially understood then it is impossible for a definitive policy solution to be constructed and implemented. Policy-makers, consequently, find themselves engaged in successive rounds of policy-making wherein a particular policy, or set of policies, benefit some people more than others. In other words, there are no solutions to urban problems only resolutions. For sure, despite over one hundred years of formal housing, planning and regeneration policies and billions of pounds of public (and private) expenditure, policy-makers are no nearer to solving what was once called the 'inner city problem' (Lawless, 1988, 1989, 1996).

Despite this apparent 'failure' to solve the problems within inner-city areas, or socially excluded neighbourhoods as they are now referred to, policy-makers have doggedly pursued this policy problem. Why has this been the case? Mossberger and Stoker (1997) suggest that policy-makers have persisted with urban policy because they somehow feel morally compounded to do so:

> Inner city policy in Britain has carried a range of symbolic messages that have been considered important by government ministers. In addition, it provides a platform for a moral crusade – an arena in which politicians and civil servants can convince

themselves and a wider audience that they are moral beings with appropriate other-regarding intentions (p.399).

Moral crusading by policy-makers is not the only reason why urban policy has prevailed for so long in the UK. Ball and Maginn (*forthcoming a*), for example, have suggested that the political process remains competitive due to conflicts over land use and as a result this also exerts a strong influence on the decisions made by policy-makers. A policy may well have some form of moral foundation to it. For example, a council may seek to increase the supply of affordable housing units within its jurisdiction by planning gain via the use of Section 106 (Town and Country Planning Act, 1990) with private developers. Reaching agreement on this matter is often a prolonged and protracted process and the gains made by local authorities have been relatively small (Crook *et al*, 2002).

Since the mid-1940s successive British governments have introduced various policies and programmes in an attempt to (re)solve the problems that bedevil urban areas. The diverse approaches adopted over this period has led some commentators to view urban policy as an experimental adventure (Atkinson and Moon, 1994; Gibson and Langstaff, 1982). It, however, would appear that urban regeneration has been following a pragmatic evolutionary trajectory. Roberts (2000), for example, has identified five broad phases: 'reconstruction' (1950s); 'revitalization' (1960s); 'renewal' (1970s); 'redevelopment' (1980s); and 'regeneration' (1990s). These reflect variations in policy emphasis and aims, governance structures, spatial focus and attitudes to 'race'. A sixth phase, 'renaissance' (2000s), commenced under the auspices of Labour government since its general election victory in 1997, can be added to this evolutionary trajectory. Table 2.1 presents an overview of each of these phases since the 1950s.

Governance and Urban Regeneration Policy

A common thread running through the various phases of regeneration policy outlined in Table 2.1 is that their governance has been underscored by the concept of 'partnership'. In short, regeneration policy has always been implemented by at least two agents, for example, central-local government (1960s) and central government-private developers (1980s). It, therefore, is not unreasonable to state that 'modern' urban regeneration policies have, in effect, been a pluralistic venture as well as an experimental one.

Historically, urban regeneration has largely been a partnership between central and local government. But, as regeneration policy has evolved a broader range of agents have been brought to the centre of decision-making. Four broad interest groups now occupy the urban regeneration policy arena at the local level: public, private, voluntary and community sectors. This increase in the number of active interest groups, combined with their various internal sub-divisions, gives rise to a political dynamic within local URPs. This situation points to the proposition that there has been a 'pluralistic turn' in urban regeneration policy.

Table 2.1 The Evolution of British Urban Regeneration Policy 1950s-2000s

Characteristic	ERA					
	1950s	*1960s*	*1970s*	*1980s*	*1990s*	*2000s*
Policy Emphasis[a]	Reconstruction	Revitalization	Renewal	Redevelopment	Regeneration	Renaissance
Government in power[b]	Conservative (1951-64)	Labour (1964-70)	Conservative (1970-74)/ Labour (1974-79)	Conservative (1979-90)	Conservative (1990-97)	New Labour (1997)
Key Policy Aim(s)	Slum clearance-redevelopment and suburban growth	Slum clearance-redevelopment and social welfare	Housing renewal and improvements	Flagship property and economic development	Comprehensive regeneration	Social exclusion
Key Policy Programme[c,d]	New Towns	Urban Programme	Community Development Projects and Inner Area Partnerships	UDCs and EZs	City Challenge and SRB	National Strategy for Neighbourhood Renewal
Nature of Governance	Central/local government and private developers	Public and Private sector	Private sector and decentralized local government	Central government and private sector	Multi-agency Partnerships	Multi-agency/ Local Strategic Partnerships
Spatial Focus[a]	Local slum housing areas	Regional	Regional and local	Site specific and local	Local and regional	Neighbourhood and regional
Attitude to 'race'	'Non-issue'	Reactive	Ambiguous	Antagonistic	Pragmatic	Pro-active

Sources: [a]Roberts (2000); [b]www.politicos.co.uk; [c]Malpass and Murie (1990); [d]Hill (2000)

The Urban Programme: A Central-Local Government Partnership?

The rediscovery of poverty, its spatial concentration, the politicization of 'race' and the subsequent adoption of an area renewal approach to tackling housing renewal and socio-economic deprivation in the late 1960s mark the commencement of 'modern' urban regeneration policy. The Urban Programme (UP) was started in 1968 and was the government's response to the myriad of problems that prevailed within urban areas. On the face of things, it appeared that 'race' and education were central themes of the UP programme. This was because resources tended to be directed to areas with significant 'black' populations and many of the initial projects had an educational dimension to them.

Yet, the racialized aspects of the UP tended to be downplayed however. Atkinson and Moon (1994) argue that this was because the government feared a political backlash from 'white' voters, if public policies were seen to be favouring 'black' communities. The logic behind this was that 'race' and immigration had become highly politicized issues at the national and local political level. Some politicians, most notably, Enoch Powell and Peter Griffiths, had engaged in racialized politicking in an effort to galvanize political support amongst 'white' voters (Smith and Hill, 1992; Solomos, 1993). The inclusion of 'race' within the policy agenda highlights the historical role and significance of this issue within urban regeneration policy.

In terms of governance arrangements, the UP was based upon a rather loose partnership between central and local government. The Home Office assumed a strategic role, providing up to 75 per cent of costs of special social needs projects, normally inferred to mean 'race'-based initiatives. Meanwhile, local councils were responsible for drawing up and implementing projects on the ground. Ultimately, the primary objectives of the UP programme were unclear and ill defined initially. Towards the end of the 1960s a rash of area-based policy initiatives began to emerge and complement the UP programme. The Government scaling down of slum clearance programmes was compensated for by the introduction of General Improvement Areas and Housing Action Areas in 1969 and 1974 respectively. The policy emphasis shifted to the systematic rehabilitation and improvement of the existing housing stock as opposed to demolition and redevelopment (Malpass and Murie, 1990).

Furthermore, the setting up of the Community Development Projects (CDPs) and the Inner Area Studies (IASs) set in motion the demise of the 'culture of poverty thesis' (Lewis, 1968) which had played a significant role in informing policy thinking at the time. This thesis held that poor people's poverty was their own fault and self-perpetuating. The CDPs and the IASs helped to bring about a more sophisticated understanding of the causes of deprivation within inner city areas. Both of these area-based programmes were premised on a contested partnership arrangement however. Central government assumed the role of strategic co-ordinator and funding agent whilst local government was responsible for policy implementation. In addition, other non-governmental agents played important roles. In the CDPs, for example, largely academic research teams were responsible for monitoring the work of the *action teams* which were comprised of central and local government officers, and feeding information back into the policy process.

Ultimately, this tripartite partnership arrangement proved too conflictual. This was primarily due to ideological differences between central government officials and academicians. The latter group advocated neo-Marxist solutions to the eradication of inner city poverty, calling for the abolition of capitalism and an end to area-based policies. These, however, were far too radical for central government. The research teams, informed by ideas from within the advocacy planning movement (Arnstein, 1969; Davidoff, 1982), called for local communities to have a much greater role in decision-making processes. Local government resisted this call for a more democratic and pluralistic model of decision-making. It was felt that such a move would undermine the power base of local politicians and representative democracy. Interestingly, the CDPs were wound up in 1978 following the withdrawal of government funding (Atkinson and Moon, 1994; Hill, 2000).

In contrast, the IASs proffered a more pragmatic approach and retention of area-based policies in order to alleviate deprivation within inner city areas. Notably, the IASs were evaluated by 'carefully selected teams of consultants' (Atkinson and Moon, 1994). In light of this latter point, it is arguably not that surprising that the government favoured the recommendations of the IASs as opposed to the more radical proposals suggested by the CDPs. In the 1977 White Paper (HMSO, 1977), *Policy for the Inner Cities*, the government drew quite extensively on the findings of the IASs:

> This White Paper is the outcome of a major review of inner city policy... It draws on the experience of earlier initiatives, including the Urban Programme, and owes a great deal to the studies and experiments of recent years: the Educational Priority Areas, Community Development Projects, Area Management trials, development work on Comprehensive Community Programmes, the studies of London Docklands *and above all* the three Inner Area Studies. (*My emphasis*)   (HMSO, 1977:1)

The 1977 White Paper denotes the highpoint of the next phase in the evolution of urban regeneration policy and is discussed in the next section.

The 1977 White Paper: The Conception of Pluralistic Urban Policy?

Up until the early 1970s urban policy had predominantly been a physically deterministic activity. The primary objective was slum clearance and redevelopment. By the late 1960s, it had become increasingly apparent to central government that it could no longer sustain this policy approach. Greater emphasis was subsequently placed on housing renewal and improvement. Economic crisis in the early 1970s heightened the government's inability to continue with new house building. Demolition and redevelopment was simply too costly an exercise.

An increasingly sophisticated understanding of the structure of urban problems emerged in the late 1960s and early 1970s. This was mainly due to the work of the CDPs and IASs and, in part, developments in US urban policy. This period of enlightenment was incorporated into the 1977 White Paper wherein the government acknowledged that inner city deprivation was a structural problem and a function of economic decline, physical decay and social disadvantage. This also contributed to the demise of physical determinism that had dominated urban policy since the late 1940s.

A further indication that urban policy had become more socially enlightened was the recognition in the 1977 White Paper that 'race' and racism were components of the urban problem and explanatory factors as to why certain ethnic groups faced particular disadvantage. The government subsequently advocated that policy resources should be directed towards assisting ethnic minority groups. Ironically, however, 'race' issues remained within the remit of the Home Office, and the then recently formed Commission for Racial Equality, as opposed to the Department of Environment (DOE) who had assumed full responsibility for 'inner city' policy. The failure to incorporate 'race' within the remit of urban policy is seen by many commentators as a function of political expediency, and ultimately, a lost opportunity (Brownill and Thomas, 1998).

One of the most defining aspects of the 1977 White Paper was that it explicitly advocated the need for a broader partnership approach in tackling inner city deprivation. The government was of the clear view that local government, the private sector, voluntary bodies *and* local communities all had a crucial role to play in the regeneration process. In essence then, the recognition of the significance of 'race' and the need for a multi-agency partnership approach to regeneration may be viewed, as initial evidence of the 'pluralistic turn' in urban regeneration. In relation to the issue of community participation, the White Paper was quite emphatic about what role local people should play in the regeneration process. It stated:

> Involving local people is both a necessary means to the regeneration of the inner areas and an end in its own right. Public authorities need to draw on the ideas of local residents to discover their priorities and enable them to play a practical part in reviving their areas (p. 8).

Similarly, the White Paper's recognition of the need for the private sector to be more explicitly involved in urban regeneration can be viewed as a radical proposition for the then leftist Labour government. Nevertheless, local authorities were still seen to be in the best position for taking the lead in urban regeneration. The White Paper described councils as:

> ... the natural agencies to tackle inner area problems. They have wide powers and substantial resources. They are democratically accountable bodies; they have long experience of running local services, most of which no other body could provide as effectively or as sensitively to local needs; and they have working links with other bodies concerned (p.8).

The objectives set out in the 1977 White Paper, especially in relation to the roles envisaged for local authorities and local communities, failed to take root and flourish. This was a consequence of political upheaval in the late 1970s, that resulted in the then sitting Labour government losing the 1979 General Election to a 'New Right' Conservative administration. This change in government saw the Conservatives hold office for 18 years (1979-97) under two Prime Ministers: Margaret Thatcher (1979-90) and John Major (1990-97). For many commentators, urban policy was transformed virtually beyond recognition under the Conservatives (Deakin and Edwards, 1993; Oatley, 1998a). A similar view was held about related policies such as planning (Ambrose, 1986; Thornley, 1993) and housing (Cole and Furbey, 1994).

Whereas the Labour government (1976-79) had emphasized a greater role for local authorities in urban regeneration, the Conservatives saw the private sector taking up this mantle. In short, the governance of urban regeneration transformed, during the 1980s, from being about 'urban managerialism towards urban entrepreneurialism or privatism' (Oatley, 1998:4). This transformation provoked claims that a democratic deficit had been created within the domain of urban regeneration policy (Brownill, 1993; Brownill *et al*, 1996; Brownill and Thomas, 1998). It, however, is important to note that there were two broadly distinctive approaches to urban regeneration policy during the Conservative's reign – 'Thatcherite' and 'Majorite' (Allmendinger, 2003; Allmendinger and Tewdwr-Jones, 1997; Tiesdell and Allmendinger, 2001a). These are briefly outlined below.

Privatism and Competitive Bidding in Urban Regeneration

The Thatcherite Approach

For some, an air of uncertainty hung over the future of urban policy following the election of Margaret Thatcher in 1979. For a brief period, there was a feeling that urban policy might possibly be abandoned on the basis of the neo-liberal ideology that underpinned Thatcherism (Hambleton and Thomas, 1995). Urban policy, however, was reprieved and the Conservatives tentatively continued with the philosophy of the IAPs during the very early 1980s. Simultaneously, the Conservatives began to introduce their own distinctive brand of 'privatized' urban policy. This was essentially a two-way partnership between the private sector and central government. The local state, which had been a key partner in previous phases of urban policy, was marginalized and assigned the role of 'enabler' as opposed to 'provider' of resources (Cochrane, 1993).

The decision by a Conservative central government to put itself at the heart of urban regeneration policy would, on the face of it, seem to be a contradiction of the central tenets of neo-liberalism. Thatcherism, however, was premised on a complex mix of neo-liberal and neo-conservative philosophies, the latter being used to legitimize the centralization of (urban) policy.

For Thatcher, privatization was considered to be a more effective means of tackling the inner cities. The main thrust of Thatcherite urban policy centred on two inter-related processes: deregulation and entrepreneurship (Hill, 2000). Specifically, central government felt that local councils and the local planning system, which were perceived as being socialistic and bureaucratic respectively, was stymieing economic development. The belief was that laissez-faire practices would drive up the effectiveness of the policy process and unlock economic growth. Furthermore, as local areas drew in private investment and the national economy expanded, this was anticipated to have a 'trickle-down' effect. That is, there would be a redistribution of the wealth created from national (and regional) economic growth thereby alleviating economic deprivation in inner city areas.

The Conservatives subsequently set in motion a number of measures designed to undermine the general powers of local authorities and marginalize their involvement in decision-making. These included, for example, right-to-buy, restricting local government controlled public expenditure; deregulating the planning process; giving precedence to the private sector and setting up alternative non-democratic structures such as Enterprise Zones (EZs) and Urban Development Corporations (UDCs) to deliver and manage the urban regeneration process.

The introduction of EZs and, in particular, UDCs denote the commencement of a property-led approach to urban regeneration. Central government worked in close partnership with the private sector in an effort to breathe new life into inner city and deprived industrial areas such as the London Docklands, Merseyside, Cardiff, Birmingham, Sheffield, Plymouth and Tyne and Wear, Leeds, Bristol and Central Manchester (CUPS, 1998; Roger Tym and Partners, 1998). Regeneration within these various areas was delivered and managed via so called quasi-non-governmental organizations (i.e. Quangos) such as Birmingham Heartlands (Salmon, 1992), Cardiff Bay Development Corporation (Thomas *et al*, 1996) and, most notably, the London Docklands Development Corporation (Brownill, 1990, 1993). These structures were largely comprised of government appointed representatives drawn almost exclusively from the private sector. There was some involvement from local authorities and communities but their position within such structures was a marginal one (Deakin and Edwards, 1993). This lack of participation led to UDCs being heavily criticized as democratically deficient. It was only later on in the life of the UDCs that an increasing commitment to community consultation and participation began to emerge. However, this was seen as too little and too late (Brownill, 1993).

The fatalism expressed by many academic commentators (Duncan and Goodwin, 1988; Ravetz, 1986; SAUS, 1983) about Thatcher's attempts to 'roll back the local state' within urban regeneration, and related policy fields, has been described as 'greatly exaggerated' (Brindley *et al*, 1996:1). Furthermore, Stewart and Stoker (1995) have contended that the Conservatives, under Margaret Thatcher, had no grand plan for rolling back the local state. Instead, they contend that her approach was more pragmatic and incremental than ideologically dogmatic. That is, if a policy was successful then it was likely to be developed further. Conversely, if a policy ran into difficulties after having been implemented it would be adjusted accordingly. The abolition of the 'poll tax' in 1991 following mass protests by disgruntled interest groups is a perfect example of the pragmatic view advocated by Stewart and Stoker (1995). In addition, the resultant abolition of the 'poll tax' is reflective of pressure politics in action that characterizes pluralist theory (Scott, 2001). The manner in which pressure was applied to the poll tax issue may be described as 'hyper-pluralistic' or 'street fighting pluralism' (Waste, 1986).[1] This latter description is particularly apt given the reaction (i.e. mass revolt) the poll tax provoked amongst ordinary citizens.

A further reflection of the pragmatic and pluralistic approach adopted by the Conservatives is evident within urban regeneration policy. Although the UDCs were the flagship regeneration policy in the 1980s, they were not the sole policy. A plethora of other small-to-medium scale policy initiatives, orientated towards addressing social, economic, physical and environmental problems also existed. These included, for example, Garden Festivals, Safer Cities, Section 11 Grants, Ethnic Minority Business Initiative, Task Forces, City Action Teams (CATs), Estate Action (EA) and Housing Action Trusts (HATs) (Robson *et al*, 1994).

These various aforementioned programmes evolved as a result of pragmatic responses by the government to episodes of urban unrest that flared up in multi-racial inner city areas (e.g. Brixton (London) and Toxteth (Liverpool)) in the early 1980s and an ideological policy commitment to reduce the role of local authorities. Notably, many of these policy programmes were partnership-based. Although dominated by the private sector and central government, these different initiatives witnessed increased involvement from local government over time. Moreover, local communities were also being incrementally invited into these policy arenas. This was most explicit in the EA and HAT programmes (Evans and Long, 2000; Pinto, 1993).

The complex array of regeneration programmes that evolved during the 1980s under Margaret Thatcher and the conflictual relations between central and local government led to severe criticism from the Audit Commission (1989). It described the government's approach to addressing urban problems as 'a patchwork quilt of complexity and idiosyncrasy' (Audit Commission, 1989:1). Furthermore, the Audit Commission highlighted that local authorities felt undervalued by central government and recommended that they should be more actively involved in the urban regeneration policy process. Ultimately, the Audit Commission's report may be viewed as being catalytic in provoking the change in the emphasis of urban policy under John Major's reign between 1990-97 (Tiesdell and Allmendinger, 2001).

The Majorite Approach

Following the deposing of Margaret Thatcher and the election of John Major, as leader of the Conservative government in 1990, there was an expectation that urban regeneration policy would continue along a Thatcherite trajectory. Oatley (1998b), for example, has noted that '[w]hen John Major took over from Margaret Thatcher there was no significant divergence from Thatcherite principles' (p.27). Similarly, Thornley (1993) was of the view that whilst 'there may be a softening of the image and a certain degree of decentralization of power... beneath this

---

[1]   The concepts of hyper-pluralism and street fighting pluralism are discussed in Chapter 3.

appearance of a new start lies the deepening of some of the Thatcherite policies' (p.228). Indeed, the Major administration continued to 'privatize' urban regeneration policy, via establishing a competitive-bidding funding regime. Applying for central government funding under the two main regeneration programmes, City Challenge and the Single Regeneration Budget (SRB), introduced by John Major were akin to a 'beauty contest'. Put crudely, those who presented the glossiest and most attractive brochures outlining their regeneration proposal stood a good chance of winning funding. Of course, projects also had to fit in with central government aims and objectives.

Tiesdell and Allmendinger (2001a) note that regeneration policy under John Major was significantly more holistic and pragmatic than under Thatcher. In addition, greater emphasis was placed on addressing social and political exclusion at the neighbourhood. Moreover, there was also a positive shift in emphasis in the governance of urban regeneration policy. The City Challenge and SRB programmes, set up in 1991 and 1994 respectively, advocated a multi-agency partnership approach to regeneration. Both these programmes saw local authorities were brought back to the centre of local decision-making. Indeed, councils often assumed the role of lead body and were responsible for bringing together all relevant agents from the public, private and voluntary sectors and the local community to form a partnership. This multi-agency partnership approach may be viewed as the rekindling of democratic and pluralistic decision-making, something that the Conservatives had effectively abandoned for most of the 1980s. In many respects the overall approach to regeneration adopted by Major was reminiscent of that put forward by the then Labour Government in the 1977 White Paper.

The increased emphasis the Conservatives placed on the need for local communities to be more involved in decision-making was borne out of an increasing realization that community consultation/participation was instrumental if regeneration programmes were to be a success. This new found commitment to community participation can be seen in a flurry of policy advice documents during the 1990s extolling the need to involve tenants more in decision-making and how to set up effective partnerships (DoE, 1994, 1995, 1996, 1997). This viewpoint had been arrived at due to two key factors.

On the one hand, the government had come to the 'pragmatic realization that urban management could no longer be conceived of in terms of 'top-down' or 'command and control' model of governance' (Tiesdell and Allmendinger, 2001:324). As already noted, the revolt against the poll tax represents one of the most extreme examples of community backlash against the top-down imposition of government policy. In addition, the government had come under quite intense pressure from council tenants about its proposals, originally contained in the 1987 White Paper, *Housing: the Government's Proposals* (HMSO, 1987), to transfer council housing to alternative landlords. Elsewhere, another central government housing-based regeneration programme designed to transfer ownership of council housing, Housing Action Trusts (HATs), ran into considerable opposition from local communities (Karn, 1993; Woodward, 1991). Such was the resistance from local communities to HATs that the government acquiesced on the right of tenants to be able to vote to remain with their local authority landlord, and, extended 'tenant involvement and control through the development of housing co-operatives' (Cole and Furbey, 1994:201).

On the other hand, John Major was inherently more sympathetic, certainly in comparison to Thatcher, to the plight of the 'working classes'. In his biography, he outlined that his policy ideas were influenced by, his own working-class background and his experiences as an ex-councillor in Lambeth (Major, 1999). Major's relatively keener interest in people's needs was also reflected in his Citizen Charter programme that was introduced in 1991. The Citizen's Charter was primarily about central government exercising control over local government via evaluating their performance on policy outputs (HMSO, 1991). At the same time, however, it was an instrument aimed at ensuring that tenants, now defined as 'consumers' or 'citizens', had more choice and better quality public services at their disposal.

Despite the democratization and pluralization of urban regeneration at the local level, the Conservatives under John Major, as with Margaret Thatcher, continued to exert centralized control over regeneration partnerships and policy in general. On the one hand, the government attempted to keep a tight rein on public expenditure. And, on the other hand, partnerships were subjected bureaucratic monitoring of their programme outputs. Under the SRB, for example, partnerships had to submit quarterly returns to their respective Government Office for the Regions. Such restrictions, however, were seen as over-burdening local partnerships and preventing them from concentrating more on the task of tackling disadvantage and social exclusion (Foley, 1999; Hall and Mawson, 1999).

For many, including most academic commentators, when the Conservatives lost the 1997 General Election to 'New Labour' there were high expectations that Tony Blair's approach to urban regeneration (and public policy in general) would be radically different from that of John Major.

Urban Regeneration and New Labour: More of the Same?

Tiesdell and Allmendinger (2001b) have argued that, in overall terms, the Blairite approach to urban regeneration policy has continued along a broadly similar trajectory to that of John Major. That is, multi-agency partnerships, tackling social exclusion and empowering local communities remain at the heart of regeneration policy.

When 'New Labour' assumed government office in May 1997 it did not have its own clearly worked out urban regeneration strategy. New Labour continued to run with the SRB programme, which had just entered into its fourth round of funding. But, in an attempt to give the SRB a New Labour-feel, the government issued supplementary guidance notes for Round 4 (1997/98) of the programme, which had been initiated by the Conservatives. In the supplementary guidance notes greater emphasis was placed on the need for funding to be allocated on the basis of need as opposed to via competitive bidding. A further two rounds (Round 5: 1998/99 and Round 6: 1999/2000) of the SRB programme were held as New Labour sought to develop its own distinctive approach to urban regeneration.

In SRB Rounds 1-4 funding had been allocated on a strictly competitive bidding basis, however, under Rounds 5 and 6 it was allocated progressively on the basis of need. Furthermore, funding was restored to 1992/93 levels following the government's Comprehensive Spending Review (North *et al*, 2002; ODPM, 2002).

New Labour's own regeneration policies emerged initially from within the Social Exclusion Unit (SEU), a Cabinet Office think-tank. A number of key reports and strategy documents outlining the government's central aims, objectives and approaches to addressing social exclusion in local neighbourhoods were produced in a relatively short period of time (SEU, 1998, 2000, 2001a, 2001b). The central ethos of New Labour's approach was twofold. First, regeneration funding was to be allocated on the basis of need. Second, and arguably more importantly, social exclusion was to be eradicated via adopting a 'joined up' policy approach. This was to be achieved via 'investing in people, not just buildings; involving communities, not just parachuting in solutions; developing integrated approaches with clear leadership; ensuring mainstream policies really work for the poorest neighbourhoods; and making a long-term commitment with sustained political priority (SEU, 1998:10). The idea being, '[w]hen all the pieces of the jigsaw are put in place, good results can be achieved' (SEU, 1998:40).

In terms of attempting to operationalize this 'joined-up' policy approach, a large-scale policy audit, examining various issues contributing to social exclusion, was initiated by the SEU. A total of 18 Policy Actions Teams (PATs), with a diverse membership base, that comprised representatives from central and local government; the private sector, independent policy experts, the voluntary sector and the community sector, were set up with the overall aim of formulating a blueprint for action. The findings of the policy audit (SEU, 2001a) led to the construction of the government's strategy on neighbourhood renewal, *A New Commitment to Neighbourhood Renewal: National Strategy Action Plan* (SEU, 2001b).

Five key priorities were identified within the National Strategy: (i) work and enterprise; (ii) crime; (iii) education and skills; (iv) health and (v) housing and the physical environment. In many respects this set of priorities resembles a montage of past urban policy experiments since the late 1960s. Furthermore, despite being called a national strategy, it has not actually been applied across the entire country. Instead, just as in previous phases of urban policy, resources and funding are being targeted in specially selected localities. A total of 88 of the most deprived local authority districts have benefited from an £800m Neighbourhood Renewal Fund with a further £400,000 distributed over three years from the Community Empowerment Fund. This latter funding stream reflects the significance of community participation to 'New Labour'.

There have also been a number of institutional changes in the way neighbourhood regeneration is governed. At the supra-strategic policy level, for example, the government set up a specific unit, the Neighbourhood Renewal Unit (NRU), within the Office for Deputy Prime Minister (ODPM) to co-ordinate neighbourhood renewal. The NRU has effectively taken over the responsibility of addressing the issue of social exclusion from the SEU. At the operational policy level, a two-tier structure was set up to co-ordinate and implement policy. Local

Strategic Partnerships (LSPs), which comprise agents from the public, private, voluntary and community sector, provide strategic direction and vision for Neighbourhood Management Schemes (NMSs). In turn, the NMSs are responsible for implementing projects on the ground. In order to achieve results, effectively and efficiently, LSPs and NMSs are to be headed by charismatic policy agents.

Recent research by Johnson and Osborne (2003) has suggested that LSPs are likely to struggle in 'achiev[ing] their twin espoused goals of the more effective *co-ordination* of local services and their *co-governance* with the local community' (p.154). The primary reason for this is that the overall governance of LSPs are fraught with a number of 'paradoxical processes' (*ibid* p.154). Such paradoxes are rooted in differences in central and local government's macro and micro aims and objectives and the political rhetoric that surrounds the concepts of community and participation.

Imrie and Raco (2003) have also expressed concerns about the paradoxical and contradictory manner in which the concepts of community and community participation have been constructed and used by New Labour:

> ... communities are characterised as being beyond politics – apolitical entities – while simultaneously being the vehicle in and through which urban policy agendas are to be mobilised and delivered. [...] Communities are also an object and instrument of policy, as a key part of technocratic policy design and, at the same time, the alleged subject of programmes of empowerment and self-actualisation (p.26).

Despite these concerns about political rhetoric there does appear to be general support for the overall thrust of New Labour's approach to urban regeneration amongst academic commentators. New Labour's approach is much preferred to that off Margaret Thatcher and John Major. Regeneration at the local level has become a more democratic and pluralistic process under New Labour in the sense that URPs are now much more highly contested decision-making arenas. Decision-making has become so contested that the protestations and (re)actions of local communities, or to be more precise, community activists, have led to a number of key regeneration projects either being altered, severely delayed and even abandoned.

North (2003), for example, highlights the victories secured by community activists who opposed proposals contained in *Project Vauxhall* and *Elephant and Castle SRB* within LB Lambeth and LB Southwark respectively. In the case of *Project Vauxhall*, for example, this project was abandoned after those who were opposed to it managed to 'successfully outmanoeuvre the development consortium, the council and residents in favour of the proposals' (North, 2003:135). This was despite the fact that those in opposition had been excluded from the decision-making processes of the project. *Project Vauxhall* and the *Elephant and Castle SRB* are by no means isolated examples of local communities exerting influence over decision-making.

Another of New Labour's flagship area-based initiatives, the New Deal for Community (NDC) initiative, which also operates within a partnership framework, has similarly been subjected to major problems and delays due to tensions between partners. On the Aylesbury Estate NDC and the Shoreditch NDC, both in London, concerns amongst local tenants and community activists about stock transfers and the replacement levels of social and affordable housing have resulted in these projects grinding to a halt. Conflict between partners within NDC partnerships was so severe at one stage that the overall programme had only managed to spend one-third of its budget in its first three years of existence (Weaver, 2002). Elsewhere, government proposals to transfer council-controlled housing to Arms Length Management Organizations (ALMOs) have been met with suspicion. A number of councils, most notably Birmingham City and LB Camden, have suffered humiliating defeats at the tenant ballot phase of the stock transfer process with local tenants unanimously voting against such proposals (Bennett, 2004; Chatterjee, 2002, 2002a). For many policy-makers such community victories must make them think that community participation is the poisoned chalice of urban regeneration (Jones, 2003).

So, in spite of the rhetoric surrounding community participation and both central and local government attempts to socially engineer consultation and participation via marginalizing and, even excluding, those who object to proposals, local communities (and community activists) are still managing to exert considerable influence over and within local URPs. The fact that central and local government and other institutional partners within URPs do not have a monopoly on power it would be fair to state that urban regeneration has become a more politically pluralistic venture.

Conclusions

In conclusion, it has been shown that the emphasis of urban regeneration policy has undergone a series of transformations since the mid-1940s. Policy has switched from being concerned with trying to eradicate physically deterministic problems such as slum dwellings, to dealing with the more complex issue of social exclusion. Moreover, although the governance of regeneration policy has also been subject to change, one feature has remained fairly consistent: policy has always been implemented via some form of partnership arrangement. Notably, as regeneration policy has evolved a wider range of agents have been brought to the policy arena, and afforded the opportunity to play an active role in decision-making. In particular, increased emphasis has been placed on the need for tenants to be more directly involved in the regeneration process. All of this points to the simple conclusion that there has been a 'pluralistic turn' in urban regeneration policy. Pluralistic in the sense that local URPs are politically competitive and conflictual arenas. This raises questions about the nature of power within URPs. The next chapter considers the concept of power in more detail. Moreover, it outlines how pluralist theory can help to explain the pattern of power within regeneration partnerships.

Chapter 3

Regenerating Pluralist Theory and Community Power

In the pluralist vision, local democracy consists of the expression of and conflict among diverse views and values held by contending groups attempting to shape local government decisions to meet their ends, with all important groups having the ability to gain access to and exercise some degree of influence over decision-makers. Local government's role is to serve as the vehicle through which group conflict occurs, and through which this conflict is resolved.   (Wolman, 1996:160-161)

Introduction

It was argued in Chapter 2 that there had been a 'pluralistic turn' in British urban regeneration policy.   On the one hand, regeneration partnerships are socially pluralistic structures on account that they now comprise a range of 'partners'. These partners may be classified into four broad categories: the public sector (i.e. central and local government); the private sector (i.e. developers); the voluntary sector; and the community sector (i.e. local tenants. Furthermore, within each of these four broad groups, various sub-groups can be expected to prevail.   The presence of such a diverse range of agents represents a significant shift in the governance of urban regeneration. In the 1970s and 1980s, urban regeneration was essentially a partnership between central and local government, and, central government and the private sector respectively.   On the other hand, and, more significantly, regeneration partnerships become more pluralistic in the sense that, the existence of a diverse range of agents gives rise to a political dynamic. In other words, since the various partners are likely to have conflicting needs, decision-making is premised on a process of negotiation and bargaining. Invariably, such a scenario raises questions about the nature of power relations within regeneration partnerships. As Saunders (1986:127) notes:

... as soon as individuals [or groups] attempt to achieve transcendent goals (that is, to impose their objectives against those of others) conflict becomes inevitable and power becomes crucial.

The issue of power has been the subject of immense academic discussion within the fields of policy analysis and political studies (Dowding, 1996; Lukes, 1974; Scott, 2001). An understanding of the concepts of power and power relations is essential, in order to appreciate how policy processes operate. As Hill (2000) succinctly notes, 'policy is the product of the exercise of political influence, determining what the state does and setting limits to what it does' (p.41). Understanding the concept of power and the nature of power relations, therefore, are of central importance within any analysis of decision-making within regeneration partnerships. This is especially true of contemporary regeneration policy, which has been increasingly portrayed by successive governments, since the early 1990s, as a democratic policy arena where local communities, in particular, are an instrumental component of the decision-making process. Such involvement by local communities raises questions as to the nature (and extent) of power they have within formal policy arenas that have traditionally been the domain of well-resourced institutional agents. Atkinson and Cope (1997) have noted that the academic literature on community participating has tended to overlook the issue of power. This book seeks to make an empirical and theoretical contribution to this research gap.

The general aim of this chapter is to outline the theoretical framework, and related concepts, which underpin the empirical focus of this book. The chapter is divided into a number of sections. First, discussion focuses on explaining why pluralism was selected as the theoretical framework in analyzing local urban regeneration partnerships (URPs). Second, the concepts of power and power relations, which are central to pluralist theory, are discussed. This paves the way for the construction of a definition of 'community power'. Discussion on these various issues provides a base understanding as to the nature of power relations within URPs. Next, the central tenets of pluralist theory are outlined. Particular attention is devoted to Jordan's (Jordan, 1990) 'general pluralist model'. This pulls together the variants of pluralist thought, which have evolved through a combination of 'comparative empirical investigations – across cities, countries and time – but, in large part it also results from counter-responses to these findings by other theories' (Judge *et al*, 1995). This general model provides a framework for understanding the pattern(s) of power within local URPs. Finally, the discussion turns to an examination of Waste's (1986) typology of pluralist theories. Waste's central thesis is that all policy arenas are essentially pluralistic, in that, all decision-making is premised on negotiation, bargaining and the exercise of power in order to achieve desired outcomes. But, since different policy arenas comprise different agents, and are situated within different 'spatial, temporal and socio-economic contexts' (Judge *et al*, 1995:5), this leads Waste to assert that there are different types of pluralist theory. The typology developed by Waste provides a basis for being able to classify the patterns of power found within regeneration partnerships.

Why Pluralism?

How can power and power relations within political and policy arenas be theorized? A range of theoretical perspectives, for example, Marxist (Duncan and Goodwin, 1988; Pickvance, 1995), structuration theory (Giddens, 1990; Jacobs, 1999) and urban regime theory (Davies, 2001, 2002, 2003; Smith and Beazley, 2000; Ward, 1995, 1996) may be utilized. Urban regime theory, which Taylor

(2002) and Stoker (1995) intimate has its roots in pluralist and neo-pluralist theory respectively, has come to dominate discussion on urban policy and politics in the UK in recent years. It is argued here, that there is a case for regenerating pluralist theory (Dahl, 1961; Polsby, 1980) on the basis that it offers an appropriate means of understanding the nature of power within local urban regeneration partnerships (URPs). The decision to utilize pluralism was premised on two key factors.

First, URPs constitute a policy arena, wherein publicly funded goods and services (e.g. housing, jobs, training and community facilities) are produced for social consumption. In line with Saunders' (1986) 'dual state' thesis, the decision-making processes, associated with the distribution of consumption goods, within such localized policy arenas are, by definition, *imperfectly pluralistic*. That is to say, when the local state is deciding on how to allocate such goods, its decisions are reflective of 'the weight of popular opinion and various demands articulated by different sections of the population' (Saunders, 1986:307). This conceptualization of the policy process is premised upon observable outcomes of agents' interactions with the state. URPs are policy arenas where it is possible to observe the impacts of local communities' actions and reactions on the decision-making process. Pluralist theory provides an explanatory framework for understanding the nature of power exercised by tenants within such arenas, since it is concerned with analyzing 'observable' outcomes. And, ethnography provides a methodological framework for observing the decision-making process in action (see Chapter 4).

Second, there has been a political and academic revival of interest in pluralism. Politically, pluralism has been gathering momentum since the early 1990s with successive government's calling for a wider range of groups from the private, voluntary and community sectors to be involved in local decision-making (see Chapter 2). Local policy arenas, such as URPs, may be viewed as socially and politically pluralistic structures governed by conflict and negotiation between different partners.

Pluralism, as a popular theoretical framework, reached its peak in the 1950s and 1960s (Harding, 1996; Wanna, 1991). This was at a time when pluralist theorists, most notably Dahl (1961) and Polsby (1980) were embroiled in an intellectual duel (i.e. 'community power debate') with their elite theory adversaries Hunter (1953) and Bachrach and Baratz (1962). The popularity of pluralism began to wane however, with the growth of more deterministic and structural understandings of group interests and power relations in the 1960s and 1970s (McLennan, 1995). In particular, these schools of thought criticized pluralism for its 'ad hoc' process of defining groups, the interests they had and the means by which political outcomes were achieved (Harding, 1996). Interestingly, in response to the changing governance structures within local politics, there has been renewed intellectual interest in pluralism, mainly within political studies, in recent years (Hirst, 1990; King, 1993). To be sure, Judge (1995) has commented that 'it is now academically respectable to take pluralism seriously' (p.32). Similarly, Harding (1996) sees pluralism (and elitism) as having considerable potential in contributing to an understanding of the nature of power within decision-making structures. He contends that this can be achieved if researchers are explicit and pragmatic, about the methods and theory they adopt in their empirical studies:

The community power debate showed that any research enterprise which attempts to trace patterns of power and influence inevitably invites charges that the researcher's chosen object(s) of study are informed by his/her pre-existing understanding – or mere hunch – about where such power and influence lies. Ultimately, the realistic methodological challenge is not 'objectively' to protect research from such charges but to be explicit about theoretical foundations, thereby facilitating open and informed criticism, and to employ a research approach which is not unnecessarily restrictive in scope from the outset and allows a shift of empirical focus if the weight of evidence during the study demands it.   (Harding, 1996:652)

In concluding this section, the revival of pluralism has not occurred in the form of a Kuhnian-style revolutionary paradigm shift. Rather, interest in it has grown because of the now perceived weaknesses of the structural theories that originally replaced it in academic favour. In addition, researchers in the pluralist tradition are more aware of potential criticisms than practitioners in the 1950s and 1960s and, hence, tend to show greater care in their empirical methodologies and a heightened sensitivity to potential objections. It is interesting to note, however, that despite the 'pluralistic turn' in the governance of urban regeneration, combined with the recent academic call for pluralist theory to be revisited, there has been no explicit re-working of this theoretical framework to look at the nature of community power within URPs. Instead, discussion has tended to centre more on issues such as the meaning, purpose and advantages and disadvantages of partnerships (Hastings *et al*, 1996; Mackintosh, 1992) or 'anodyne concepts like 'empowerment' (Atkinson and Cope, 1997). Power and power relations within urban policy in general and URPs in particular have, of course, been analyzed (Baeten, 2001; Cooper and Hawtin, 1997; Hastings, 1999; Kearns and Turok, 2000; Smith and Beazley, 2000). These, however, have tended to look at power issues from a structural and strategic policy perspective. This book is concerned with the theoretical and empirical nuances of power within a more localized context – local URPs and community forums situated within ethnically diverse localities.

Power, Social Power and Community Power

Since the 1950s, power and power relations have been central issues in empirical and theoretical analyses of the public policy process (Dowding, 1996). This has been most clearly reflected in that 'old chestnut; the community power debate' (Harding, 1996:637), which raged between pluralists (Dahl, 1961; Polsby, 1980) and elitists (Hunter, 1953; Bachrach and Baratz, 1962, 1970), during the 1950s and 1960s. Such researchers focused their attentions on trying to discern 'who ruled' within city politics (Harding, 1996:637-640). Elite theorists argued that 'power' was concentrated in the hands of a small number of political elites, for example, wealthy businessmen, elected politicians and high-ranking military personnel. These various agents were deemed 'powerful' because of their notable 'reputation' or 'position' within civic society, which, in turn, was premised on the level of resources, for example, finances, property, personnel and networks they had command over or moved within. Subsequently, the methodological approach adopted by elite theorists was labeled 'reputational' and 'positional' (see Waste, 1986 and Harding, 1996 for an overview).

The perception of the type of power held by such elites may be said to be a 'static' one in the sense that it is embedded within the bodies (and minds) of so-called reputable individuals. But, as Saunders (1986) has noted, 'power is a dynamic phenomena' (p.24). And, it is dynamic in two key ways. On the one hand, the locus of power is likely to vary (i.e. move), across different groups within different policy arenas as individual or groups mobilize whatever resources they have at their disposal. And, on the other hand, since policy-making is itself a dynamic process, characterized by endless rounds of (re)negotiation and (re)formulation, so too, by default, is power. This is because policy, politics and power are inseparable phenomena. As Dowding (1996:1) notes:

> The answers to questions about power in society are answers to questions about the very nature of politics and the policy process.

This dynamism has been recognized by pluralists. Furthermore, for pluralists, power exists, and is capable of being measured, when it has been *exercised* within real decision-making structures and processes where its impacts can be observed (Harding, 1996). Notably, pluralists are in part-agreement with elite theorists, in the sense that, the degree of power wielded by interest groups is a function of the resources they have at their disposal (Dahl, 1961, 1986).

Defining Power

So, what is actually meant when it is said, for example, that someone has power or influence, or that they are powerful or influential?[1] Scott (2001) has noted that power 'in its most general sense... is the production of causal effects' (p.1). Similarly, Russell (1986) states that 'power may be defined as the production of intended effects' (p.19). In other words, and, within the specific context of local URPs, power may be viewed as the *ability* of one (or more) partners to bring about a change in the policy intention(s) or direction(s) of another partner.

For example, a developer in a regeneration project may 'convince' the local authority of the need to relax its housing density policy. If the council agrees to increase housing density from ten to fifteen units per square kilometre, then it can be said that the developer has exercised some degree of power over the local authority. If, however, the figure of 15 units per square kilometre was a compromise, from an initially desired 20 units, following objections by local tenants, then it can be equally said that this latter group has also exerted some influence on the policy process. In this simple situation, it is impossible to state categorically who is the *most* powerful agent: The developer has managed to secure a 50 per cent increase in housing density levels; Simultaneously, tenants have managed to reduce the original intentions of the developer by 50 per cent.

---

[1] The terms 'power' and 'influence' are used interchangeably.

Of course, if the developer had managed to have housing densities increased to the levels it had initially desired, then it could be said that it was *relatively* more powerful than local tenants. Moreover, if the developer was successful in altering the majority or all policies that it had difficulties with to its desired outcomes then it may be stated that it was the *most* powerful agent. Ultimately, if the developer were to usurp all other agents' ability to exercise any influence within the local URP, then, it may be described as being all-powerful within that context.

Establishing who is the most/least powerful agent within regeneration partnerships is arguably a valid research venture. But, it is not the concern here. Instead, the primary concern is to determine the overall pattern of power (relations), paying particular emphasis to the nature of influence wielded by local communities, via their participation on community forums, within local URPs.

Defining Social Power

An attempt by a particular agent to exert influence over other agents within an URP and the reaction(s) that action provokes points to the existence of a power relation. Such a sequence of events reflects an attempt to exercise 'social power'. Dowding (1996:5) defines social power as:

> ... the ability of an actor deliberately to change the incentive structure of another actor or actors to bring about or help bring about outcomes.

In other words, for 'true' social power to have prevailed, the agent seeking to exercise their power (i.e. 'the principal') over another agent (i.e. 'the subaltern') must do so consciously and with intent. Furthermore, the subaltern must be free, to resist any influence being exerted on or over them, and vice versa (Scott, 2001).

If a principal agent is able to persuade a subaltern agent to change their mind, or direction, on a particular issue then it can be stated, albeit simply, that the former is more powerful than the latter on that particular issue. This should not lead to the automatic conclusion that the subaltern is powerless. That is, since subalterns are endowed with the *potential* to resist influence from principals, this provides an opportunity for conflict to emerge within policy structures and processes. Furthermore, where subalterns are able to draw upon sufficient resources and exhibit determination, to resist the influence of a principal, it is reasonable to assume that a process of negotiation and bargaining might well be entered into in order for some form of consensus to be produced. Obviously, even within this context, one agent will triumph over the other in some way, thus leading to the same basic conclusion that one is relatively more powerful than the other. Even in this scenario the 'winning' agent will probably have conceded something to the 'losing' agent. It, therefore, may be claimed, albeit in rather simple terms, that the subaltern has exhibited some degree of power by virtue of the fact that they have resisted, and managed to alter the primary advances of the principal.

Scott (2001) argues that the exercise of social power relies on the mobilization of resources. He notes that two different, but complementary, modes of power may be deployed. First, agents may use *corrective influence*. In this situation, physical and/or other tangible resources are utilized in a 'punitive' manner, so as to force agents to alter their interests. For example, a local authority may 'threaten' a local community by intimating that plans to build a new community centre may have to be abandoned unless tenants agree to proposals to increase housing density.[2] Alternatively, a council may threaten to withdraw funding from a community forum, unless it takes appropriate action to ensure that its membership is more representative of the local community. Local communities may also use corrective influence for their own ends. A community forum, who feel particularly aggrieved about something within an URP, may threaten a council and the other institutional partners via the use of the media (i.e. local newspaper in the first instance), other political avenues (i.e. raising concerns with their local MP) and even legal redress. These latter two options were used extensively and varying degrees of success in *Northside* (Chapter 5) and *Southside* (Chapter 6).

On the other hand, *persuasive influence* may be used. In this situation symbolic or abstract resources are mobilized in order to effect change amongst agents. For example, a community forum may convince the developer partners within an URP that their political and public reputations could be enhanced if they were to donate and develop a piece of land for use as a youth centre. If the community is successful in achieving their desired outcome, it can be said that they have exercised influence within the regeneration process. Or, to be more precise, they have exercised what may usefully be termed 'community power'. This is discussed in more detail in the next section.

Community Power: Protest and Pressure

Local communities are generally perceived as being the least powerful agent within local URPs (Mayo, 1997). The primary reason for this is that tenants tend not to have the same quantity and quality of physical and symbolic resources (e.g. capital, professional experts and political nous) as their institutional partners. This, however, does not mean that local communities are rendered totally powerless within local partnerships. As noted earlier, all agents have the *potential* to exert some degree of power (or resistance) over one another. This is particularly true when agents enter into policy arenas premised on negotiation and bargaining. So, how do tenants exert influence within the policy process?

Local communities tend to be the last partner to join local URPs and, more importantly, after their institutional partners have formulated preliminary proposals to regenerate a neighbourhood. As will be seen later this was very much the case in *Northside*, *Southside* and *Westside* (Chapters 5-7). Local communities involved in URPs generally start from a position of having to resist or counteract pre-existing proposals. Communities, therefore, face a major uphill struggle from the outset. This is then compounded by the lack of resources, knowledge, access and skills they also generally bring to URPs. Despite such disadvantage, influencing

---

[2]   This is an extreme example but it helps to illustrate vividly the concept of 'corrective influence' and the complexity of power relations within URPs.

decision-making within URPs is an achievable goal. Two basic strategies are open to communities.

Legitimate Counteraction and Negotiation

Local communities may engage in 'legitimate' counteractive strategies in order influence decision-making and achieve outcomes that they desire. Legitimate counteraction entails entering into formal negotiations with other agents via mobilizing whatever resources are immediately to hand and built up over time and networking, with the intention of applying 'pressure' within the decision-making process in order to effect change. Tenants, for example, may collate data and present a counter-argument to the forecasted outcomes of a particular policy. Such evidence may be gathered and presented by ordinary tenant activists. Alternatively, a professional agency such as a planning advocacy group (e.g. Planning Aid for London) or a regeneration consultancy (e.g. PEP Consultants) may assume this task. The latter situation suggests that tenants may be fairly well resourced or networked, since acquiring the services of professional agencies, especially consultants, generally necessitates some form of financial payment to be made.

Tenants may also take the 'traditional' political route of taking their concerns directly to their local councillors. And, if they feel dissatisfied with the response from their local councillor local communities can turn to their MP for assistance. If enough people make such representations, this can lead elected representatives to champion their concerns and raise them amongst colleagues within relevant policy committee meetings. If public opposition is particularly vehement over a certain proposal, this may, at least, cause a delay in it being implemented, as it is debated within the policy committee.

A delay over a proposal before a final decision is taken provides room for tenants and community forums, to acquire greater resources and develop more sophisticated networks and political nous. This would then enable them to articulate a more sophisticated and professional counter-strategy and, ultimately, enhance their chances of influencing decision-making.

Radical Counteraction and Negotiation

Alternatively, local communities may opt for a 'radical' counteractive strategy. In other words, they may seek to bring about changes within URPs, via stepping outside the confines of the institutionalized policy process to 'protest' against proposals. Again, in order to effect change resources and networks have to be mobilized. In this context, tenants seek to initiate change via mobilizing populist support and taking to the streets, literally and metaphorically, to display their disquiet with the view to effecting change. If, such protest support is sufficient, as was the case in the poll tax revolt, this has the potential to bring about a change in policy.

At a minimum, radical actions are also likely to cause delays in the regeneration process. If, and when, this occurs the institutional partners within URPs incur unwanted political and financial costs. A prolonged period of delay and increasing costs may be enough for a developer, for example, to reconsider their proposals, role within that particular URP and, more fundamentally, the whole idea of URPs (Ball *et al*, 2003). A subsequent change in policy, even if it is not of the magnitude desired by tenants, reflects an exercise of power. Moreover, for the protesting tenants, the change in policy will be viewed as a kind of moral victory.

Local communities are free to use either pressure or protest politics within local URPs. It is not unreasonable to assume that both strategies will manifest, to varying degrees, especially within large-scale regeneration projects that affect large and diverse neighbourhoods. It is worth noting that the potential and overall nature of community power wielded by communities is placed under threat when serious divisions emerge within community forums. In other words, if one group of tenants feel that pressure politics is the more appropriate means of effecting change and another group favours protest politics, then an intra-community power struggle may ensue. This raises new dilemmas for policy-makers and local communities alike.

In concluding this section, it is important to stress that the empirical focus of this book is with overt expressions of power that can be observed within policy structures in what Clegg (1989) has defined as 'obligatory passage points' (see Cairncross *et al*, 1994; Jacobs, 1999). Pluralist researchers have devoted their attention to tracing the nature of power within such observable arenas. The discussion now turns to outlining the central tenets of pluralist theory. This will help to provide a basis to understanding of how notionally democratic arenas, such as URPs, are supposed to operate.

Pluralist Theory

Pluralist theory has traditionally been concerned with the analysis of 'power' within policy arenas operating at the level of national, regional and city politics. In fact, pluralism is most closely associated with analyses of the distribution of power within cities (Dahl, 1961, Polsby, 1980). Judge (1995) refers to this as 'urban pluralism'. It is this form of pluralism that is the primary focus of this book. As already noted, pluralism constitutes one half of the 'community power debate', that emerged between pluralist and elite theorists during the 1950s and 1960s in America. To reiterate, this debate centred on a series of claims and counter-claims about the distribution of power within city government.

The community power debate reached an impasse, and pluralist theory was rendered obsolete with the emergence of structuralism in the late 1960s and 1970s (Ricci, 1971; Waste, 1986). Despite its apparent passing, pluralism is argued by Judge (1995) to be 'the theory from which many perspectives on urban politics have developed, or against which many others have set themselves' (p.13). As already commented, there has also been something of a revival of interest, both academically and politically, in pluralism. This revival can be mainly credited to political science scholars (Hirst, 1990; Judge, 1995; King, 1993).

Core Tenets of Pluralist Theory

Pluralist theory encompasses a number of core tenets. These are reflected in Jordan's (1990) 'general pluralist model', which draws on the various strains of pluralist theory that have evolved since the 1950s. These core tenets include:

- Power is *fragmented* and *decentralized*;
- Interest groups (i.e. partners within URPs) have varying levels and degrees of resources and thus varying *potential* to exercise power within the policy process;
- The dispersed nature of power is a desirable feature of so-called democratic arenas;
- A variety of outcomes can be expected in different policy contexts due to the existence of different agents, different processes and different distributions of power within individual contexts;
- An exercise of political power involves more than simply participating (i.e. voting) in elections and other formal political structures and processes;
- 'The interaction of interests would supply a practical alternative to the "general will" as the source of legitimate authority (Jordan, 1990:293); and
- The dispersed nature of power combined with the 'instability of the pluralistic bargaining process' (Jordan, 1990:293) helps to ensure that interest groups remain a part of the process in that one day they will come out as 'winners'.

For pluralists, the policy arena is akin to a market-place. Organized individuals or 'interest groups', such as private businesses, environmentalists, homeowners, the elderly and ethnic minorities, are free to enter, and actively compete and bargain with one another in an effort to influence the policy process. These various actors enter policy arenas with a diffuse range of interests, and, more importantly, varying levels of resources that include items such as: finances, expert advisors, knowledge, information, political support, networks and personal determination/motivation. Such resources endow agents with the *potential* to exert influence within the policy process. This eclectic mix of agents, combined with their various resources bases, which are also argued to alter over time and context, precludes all decisions, and hence, power, gravitating repeatedly towards the same individuals and/or interest groups. In other words, no one has a monopoly *per se* over power.

The nature of power in the policy process, as depicted above, has been heavily criticized by elite theorists (Bachrach and Baratz, 1962; Dye, 1986; Manley, 1983). In particular, elitists took umbrage with the notion that all individuals/groups have *equal* access to the policy arena; that the policy arena was *accessible to all*; and that the state played the role of a neutral agent, mediating between different interest groups. These critics have tended to view pluralism with tunnel vision however. That is, they were unable to see beyond the 'classical pluralist' model of decision-making. This model was used as an 'ideal type', to illustrate how power should be structured within perfect democratic arenas and societies. As Smith (1990:302) has argued:

> ... [t]here is little doubt that many critics of pluralism have attacked a crude model of pluralism without taking account of the subtleties that exist in actual pluralist theory and its empirical application.

Pluralists have never contended that *all* interest groups have automatic, and unhindered, access to policy arenas. Instead, they merely have the *potential* to enter policy arenas, and their capacity (i.e. power) to influence decision-making fluctuates depending on what resources they have at their disposal at any given time. Again, as Smith (1990:303, 304) has noted:

> ... [p]luralists do not expect a free flow of groups and ideas into the policy arena, nor do they regard all groups as having equal access and power... the power of a pressure group depends on the level of its resources and variation in resources often lead to one group having greater access than another.

In simple terms, the varying level of resources held by different interest groups leads policy arenas to becoming stratified. That is, those groups with the greater quantity and better quality of tangible and abstract resources, for example, local government and developers in the case of URPs, tend tentatively to dominate the policy arena. This is primarily because they are more formally interested and wedded to the policy process *per se*. But, this is not seen as overly problematic by pluralists, in that, this dominance is inherently kept in check on a number of fronts.

First, the dominant group(s) will often turn to other interest groups within policy arenas, in order to garner their support for policy ideas and/or to retain their dominant position of power. In return for lending their support these subaltern groups can be expected to ask for concessions or a share of the power held by the principal group. A redistribution of power can be said to have taken place when this occurs.

Second, subaltern groups may form alliances with one another in order to pool their resources and thereby enhance their collective bargaining power within policy arenas. Or, this course of action may be undertaken with the ultimate aim of overthrowing the dominant group. This type of situation may arise, for example, as a result of the dominant group having failed to take account of the needs of others within the policy arena.

Finally, those who attain a dominant position of power, tend to do so within a single or a small number of policy arenas, as opposed to the majority or all of them. This prevents a particular interest group from securing a monopoly on power. In his seminal study of political nominations, urban redevelopment and public education in New Haven, Dahl (1961) observed that different groups of agents prevailed within each of these policy arenas. For pluralists, this 'epitomises a democratic distribution of power which [Dahl, 1971] calls 'polyarchic democracy' or rule by multiple minorities' (Scott, 2001:54).

A Typology of Pluralist Theory

The above leads to the assertion that all policy arenas are essentially pluralistic in character. That is, they are pluralistic, in the first instance, on the basis that they comprise a diverse range of interests groups. Judge (1995) refers to this as 'social pluralism'. URPs are a perfect example of a socially pluralistic policy arena. More important, however, is the concept of 'political pluralism'. That is, the pattern of power within policy arenas. The fact that different policy arenas are likely to comprise different sets of interest groups, with varying levels of resources, who may assert 'legitimate' or 'radical' strategies to influence the policy process, points to the existence of different forms of political pluralism. To be sure, Waste (1986) has developed a typology of pluralist theory that illustrates various patterns of power based on successive empirical analyses of the policy process. These theoretical variants included: 'classical pluralism'; hyper-pluralism'; 'stratified pluralism'; and 'privatized pluralism'.

For Waste (1986), all policy arenas are essentially pluralistic, in social and political terms. It is just a matter of how pluralistic they are. Consequently, he states with confidence:

> ... the assertion "community *x* or country *A* is (or is not) pluralist" should be followed by a second assertion... to determine what type of pluralist community local *x* (or *A*) is (or is not) held to be. The assertion that local *x* is *pluralist* is less helpful than the more precise assertion that local *x* is a *classical pluralist, hyper-pluralist, stratified pluralist* or *privatized pluralist* polity (*my emphasis*).
>
> (Waste, 1986:120)

The four key types of pluralism identified by Waste reflect varying degrees of inclusiveness by individuals and interest groups, and different patterns of power within policy arenas. The essential characteristics of the four types of pluralism are briefly outlined below.

Classical Pluralism

This form of pluralism represents the 'perfect model' of how policy processes are supposed to work in democratic societies and draws on the works of classic liberal commentators such as De Tocqueville (1955). In short, the policy arena is characterized as being 'open and free' to all citizens and groups. Moreover, all citizens actually participate in decision-making. This is made possible because of the relatively small size of the population involved. Decisions are arrived at via open discussion and debate and subsequently voted upon by the various participants. All citizens agree to abide by whatever decisions are arrived at on the basis that this is the 'general will' of the population. An unequal accumulation of power, by a particular individual or group, is avoided due to the existence of a myriad of pre-existing, and constantly forming groups with an equally complex mix of evolving interests, needs and wants.

Hyper-Pluralism

This is the most inclusive form of pluralism after classical pluralism. Within this model the policy process is also characterized as being relatively open and free, and tends to be dominated by a plethora of interest groups, who exert influence, or seek to do so, on the policy process via resorting to protest politics. This form of pluralism generally prevails within larger political settings such as city or regional government. The crucial aspect of hyper-pluralism is, the state is rendered 'weaker than the pressure group system' (Waste, 1986:123). In other words, the state balks to the various demands of pressure groups. Ultimately, if a policy arena is in a constant state of hyper-pluralism the decision-making process is at risk of grinding to a halt as anarchy takes over.

Policy arenas tend not to be dominated by such extreme situations for extended periods of time. Instead, hyper-pluralistic activity is more likely to emerge around particularly controversial policy issues. As already noted, the reactions to the poll tax, and the subsequent outcome of such action would be an example of hyper-pluralism within the policy process. Other example include The recent mass protests by a diverse range of community movements from 'the left' (e.g. the anti-road lobby, the anti-globalization movement and the anti-fox hunting lobby) and 'the right' (e.g. the Countryside Alliance).

Stratified Pluralism

If, classical pluralism and hyper-pluralism represent 'perfect' and 'radical' models of the pattern of power within policy arenas, then stratified pluralism reflects an 'imperfect' one. That is, although the policy arena is essentially open to all, those who tend to participate within it are drawn from the politically motivated, active and organized within society. Such groups, which Dahl (1961) defined as being the 'homo politicus', or interest groups in more common parlance, tend to be relatively small in number. Consequently, this leaves a significant proportion of the population, the politically inactive (apathetic and/or excluded), or, 'homo civicus' (Dahl (1961), outside the policy arena. These two broad groupings of the 'active' and 'inactive' lead Dahl (1961) to assert that the policy process is stratified (see Judge, 1995; Waste, 1986). Nevertheless, the politically active often lay claim to representing the interests of the populations they have emerged from. So, for example, tenant activists who participate in local URPs could assert that they represent the views of the wider local community or discrete communities from within the neighbourhood (e.g. 'the elderly', 'the disabled', children and young people; or some BME group).

The policy arena is stratified further, in the sense that the various interest groups that come to the policy arena possess different levels and types of resources. Whilst this may suggest that those with the most resources are likely to be more powerful, interest groups are dynamic in their membership, resource bases and network spread, hence their potential to exert influence is constantly shifting over time and from context to context.

Privatized Pluralism

Privatized pluralism represents the least inclusive form of pluralism. In this instance, the policy arena is occupied by a small number of interest groups, whose primary objective is to '[usurp] the authority and resources of public policy-making for private ends' (Waste, 1986:128). This form of pluralism tends to be found operating within supra-policy structures situated at the national and/or international governmental level. Such supra-policy arenas comprise key agents and/or large-scale interest groups that represent the interests of private (e.g. multi-national corporations) and public (e.g. trade unions) organizations. These private and public interests groups are in direct competition with one another and seek to protect the interests of their respective members. Those (i.e. 'lobbyists') acting on behalf of the multi-national, for example, will be there to protect their clients (i.e. the firm; managers; and shareholders) various interests – sustained existence of the firm and profitability. Conversely, the role of those (i.e. 'negotiators') representing the trade union is to 'protect' and negotiate the best deal, usually in relation to pay and work conditions, for their members, the employees of the multi-national corporation (or a public sector employer for that matter).

Again, the quantity and quality of resources are an instrumental factor in determining the outcomes within these high-ordered policy arenas. Yet, the pattern, or distribution, of power within such arenas is likely to be a dynamic one. In simple overall terms, for example, the trade union movement in the UK exerted significant influence over central and local government during the 1970s. In fact, as far as Margaret Thatcher was concerned, after winning the 1979 General Election, they were too powerful and were deemed to be stifling economic growth. Hence, she set about undermining their influence during her tenure in the early 1980s. The 'dismantling' of the trade union movement during the 1980s combined with the rise of globalization in the 1990s now means that the large corporations wield relatively and significantly more influence within national and international policy arenas. Whilst it may be true that corporations (and government organizations) dominate such policy arenas they do not *always* get their own way. This is because of the exercise of protest and pressure politics by alliances of 'radical' interest and campaign groups (e.g. Defend Council Housing; Reclaim the Streets; and Stop the War Coalition), trade unions and other social and community movements.

In concluding this section, the idea that pluralism is a 'homogenous theory' (Waste, 1986:133), as it has tended to be viewed, has been dismissed. The various forms of pluralism outlined above illustrate that power, in overall terms, is diffused across a variety of policy arenas operating at different spatial and political levels. Furthermore, each of these different policy arenas comprises an eclectic mix of agents wherein new relationships, networks and alliances are constantly being forged. It, consequently, is this eclecticism and dynamism that gives policy arenas their distinctive pluralistic character. The essential characteristics of the variants of pluralist theory identified by Waste (1986) and briefly discussed above are summarized in Table 3.1 to provide a schematic overview.

Table 3.1 An Extended Typology of Pluralism

Forms of Pluralism

Element	*Classical Pluralism*	*Hyper-Pluralism*	*Stratified Pluralism*	*Privatized Pluralism*
Context	village	city	city/region/ nation	city/region/ nation
Participants	individuals	individuals/ interest groups	political activists	business and commercial
Resources	votes	votes	votes	investment
Inclusion	open and free	open	selective	restricted
Process	debate	confrontation/ protest	representation	negotiation
Government	brokerage	weak	brokerage	private

Adopted from Waste (1986)

Waste's typology provides a useful template in helping to classify the different patterns of power that are likely to prevail across the hundreds of URPs within the UK. It, consequently, has been applied here to describe the nature of decision-making within *Northside*, *Southside* and *Westside*.

Conclusions

It was argued in Chapter 2 that there had been a discernible 'pluralistic turn' in British urban policy, during the early 1990s, at the local level. Specifically, local URPs, as distinct policy-making arenas, now comprise representation from the public, private, voluntary and community sectors. These various agents have been bestowed the status of 'partner' by central government and been told to tackle their local problems together.

Local communities have been brought to the centre of these policy arenas under the impression that they are 'equal' partners and that they have 'power' to effect changes within the decision-making process. Consequently, this chapter has sought to define and clarify the concepts of 'power', 'social power' and 'community power' so that a base understanding of the nature of power relations within URPs could be developed. Relatedly, it was highlighted that policy agents may deploy various strategies in order to effect change within the policy process.

Moreover, it was contended that all agents have the *potential* to influence decision-making.

In order to develop an understanding of the pattern of power within localized policy structures such as URPs this necessitates using some theoretical framework. For this book, pluralist theory was regenerated since it is concerned with the study of power as measured in the 'observable policy outcomes in specific decision-making processes (Scott, 2001:53). Furthermore, Waste's typology of pluralism provides a template for classifying the different patterns of power that are likely to be found across the many URPs within the UK.

The pluralistic framework used herein contrasts with those common within the urban regeneration literature where other commentators have tended to use more 'elite' and/or 'structural' lenses to analyse the political and policy process. Those who have adopted such approaches have generally assumed that local communities are the least powerful partner within URPs and that they are far from pluralistic, democratically speaking, structures (Anastacio *et al*, 2000; Burton, 1997; Mayo, 1997). It is argued here that the nature of community power within URPs is an empirical question that should be approached, as best as possible, from a neutral stance. That is, no prior assumptions are made about the specific nature of power within URPs save that there is likely to be some variation due to the number of URPs that exist and that they are not homogenous structures located within identical settings and comprising identical agents. This overall eclecticism virtually guarantees for a variation in the nature of power within URPs. To recap, the two questions at the centre of this book are:

- What is the nature of community power exerted by local communities within local regeneration partnerships? and
- How significant is the issue of 'race' in (i) structuring tenant participation within community forums, and (ii) regeneration partnerships in general?

These are classic pluralistic type research questions. The question, however, of how these should and can be empirically investigated remains. It is argued that ethnography is an appropriate methodological approach to use. The benefits and, ultimately, why this approach was adopted, are outlined in detail in the next chapter.

Chapter 4

An Ethnographic Approach to Urban Regeneration and Community Power

In the past thirty years, ethnography and other forms of qualitative method have moved from a marginal position in many social science disciplines towards a much more central place. Of course, in the case of social and cultural anthropology ethnography has always been the predominant method; but it now has a strong presence in sociology and social psychology, as well as in applied areas like education and health. (Hammersley, 1992:11)

Introduction

The aims of this chapter are to contextualize the research methodology, and techniques that underpin the empirical inquiry in this book. The chapter focuses on a number of key issues. First, a brief outline of the resurgent interest in the concepts of *community* and *community participation* in urban regeneration policy is presented. A critical evaluation of these concepts necessitates a methodological approach that can help construct a better understanding of them. It is argued that an *ethnographic* approach, as opposed to a *quantitative* one, is particularly suited to achieving this task. Next, a brief historical overview of ethnography is presented. This is then followed by a definition of ethnography and a brief discussion on its potential contribution to the analysis of urban regeneration. Fourth, the ethnographic research process is outlined. Fifth, the issue of negotiating and securing access to research settings is examined. Then, the research techniques associated with ethnographic research are outlined. Finally, the chapter concludes by arguing that there is much to be gained from adopting an ethnographic approach in urban studies, especially where the focus of inquiry is on local communities and their participation in policy processes and structures.

Understanding Community and Participation: The Need for Ethnography

There can be no doubt that the evolution of national urban regeneration policies from Estate Action in the late 1980s through to the City Challenge (1991-1993), SRB (1994-2000) and the National Strategy for Neighbourhood Renewal (2000-) have become increasingly community-minded. As Duffy and Hutchinson (1997) have noted, there has been a 'new turn to community' (p.350) in urban policy. Indeed, wherever one turns within the urban policy arena, the terms 'community' and 'participation' are used with great frequency and aplomb, particularly by government policy-makers. This is arguably done in an attempt by government to promote and convince communities, that urban policy arenas are now more democratic and sensitive to their needs and wants.

The concept of 'community' as used and interpreted by policy-makers is, however, in danger of losing its meaning and sense of complexity and dynamism (Cohen, 1985). This is a consequence of two key inter-related factors. First, the term community is at risk of becoming a meaningless and hollow concept due to its overuse within policy documents and public statements by politicians and policy-makers. Second, and more importantly, policy-makers have a tendency, as a consequence of their bureaucratic mindsets (Jones, 1995) and traditional 'gate keeping' roles (Pahl, 1975), to construct a narrowly defined perception of who or what constitutes *the* 'local community', and what role they should (or can) play in decision-making.

In simple terms, policy-makers seem to have constructed an image of the 'local community' with the following characteristics: (i) monolithic in structure; (ii) static in profile and nature; and (iii) bounded and attached to a particular spatial locale (e.g. council estate or neighbourhood). Policy-makers have subsequently presupposed that the people within these spatial locales can be relatively easily informed and consulted about regeneration proposals. Furthermore, local communities' incorporation as a 'partner' within urban regeneration partnerships (URPs) had been assumed by policy-makers to be a relatively easy task. A number of commentators have highlighted that involving the local community is a particularly fraught exercise (Imrie and Raco, 2003; McArthur, 1995; McGregor *et al*, 1992; Peck and Tickell, 1995; Taylor, 2002). And, whilst policy-makers now recognize the complexities associated with community participation, bad (bureaucratic) habits live long.

Quite often, politicians and policy-makers see community participation as sufficient to validate a project. Atkinson and Cope (1997), for example, note that 'the notion of community is uncritically used by... governments... that tend to assume that simply by adding 'community' it somehow legitimates a policy' (p.2). Atkinson (1999) takes this position further, with the use of discourse analysis, in his interrogation of the symbolic and practical meanings of the concepts 'community', 'participation' and 'empowerment' within the prescriptive policy guidance manual, *Involving Communities in Urban and Rural Regeneration: A Guide for Practitioners* (DoE, 1995). He comments that the manual 'contain[s] a great deal of extremely useful practical information' (p.11) in relation to engendering community consultation and involvement and makes quite considerable progress in recognizing that targeted areas contain a plethora of dynamic communities. Yet, the overall discursive nature of the policy language and intentions within the manual leads Atkinson to note that, 'who constitutes the community is by no means self-evident' (p15). The manual states:

> For the purposes of this manual... the community can be defined very simply. Virtually all DoE sponsored regeneration programmes... are intended to benefit areas. Those people living or working within those target areas are, in general, the

people intended to benefit from regeneration initiatives. They constitute the
community.   (DoE, 1995: 7)

Drawing on the work of Bourdieu (1991), Atkinson argues that those who 'possess the symbolic authority to make performative utterance... which give certain individuals/groups the right to be heard and listened to' (p.16) define who, from the community, should be *included* or *excluded* from the regeneration process. In regeneration practice, those with the 'symbolic authority' may generally be inferred to mean the 'accountable body' within URPs – normally local authorities. Rhodes *et al* (2002) have shown that local authorities were the accountable body for an average of 53 per cent of all successful SRB bids over Rounds 1-6 (1994-2000). Hall *et al* (1996) found that during Rounds 1 and 2 of the SRB voluntary and community groups often '[felt] excluded from the process and [were] frequently seen as the junior partners in terms of power, influence and size' (p.80).

Atkinson's analysis suggests that policy-makers actually construct a simple binary classification of local communities. That is, local communities are differentiated in terms of those who are *supportive* and *co-operative*, as opposed to those who are perceived as *problematic* and *antagonistic* towards regeneration proposals. Consequently, those who fall into the former classification tend to be readily invited onto partnership boards and community forums. This involvement by local community members is then used to portray a commitment to community consultation and participation. Conversely, antagonistic community members may find themselves held at arms-length, or possibly even excluded, from the regeneration process. This is because they are perceived as posing a threat to parts, or all, of a regeneration programme. If, and when, such exclusion occurs this throws into disarray the notion that policy-makers are *fully* committed to community participation.

The notion of 'community', therefore, is highly contested both conceptually and in regeneration practice (Cohen, 1985; Hill, 1994). This contestability has major implications for regeneration policy where 'community' and 'participation' are now fundamental issues. Put simply, policy-makers need to be more aware and informed about the profile, relations and dynamics *within* and *between* the various communities that co-exist within regeneration areas. A failure to map and take account of the diversity and dynamism within communities may produce serious negative reactions. A community backlash to regeneration proposals may result in, at best, a short delay in the programme or, at worst, an abandonment of parts or all of a regeneration scheme.

The renewed policy emphasis on community participation, combined with a lack of critical understanding of the notion of community on the part of policy-makers, raises the question of how can a greater understanding of both of these concepts be developed. What seems to be needed is a methodological approach that recognizes and emphasizes the complexities of the concept of community and is able to develop an insider account of the complexities and dynamics of community participation and governance structures such as URPs. Qualitative research or inquiry, as opposed to a quantitative approach, provides an ideal opportunity to undertake such a task. Ethnography, one form of qualitative inquiry, offers the best way forward on this front. The reason for this is straightforward: Ethnography is concerned with analyzing and making sense of the 'culture' (i.e. structures, processes, groups, agents, and social relations) within social settings.

Ethnography: A Historical Overview

Walsh (1998) has noted that ethnography has an established history within anthropology where it has been the 'primary and almost exclusive method' (p.218) of social investigation that has traditionally been used to study *less developed, inferior* and/or *exotic* societies and cultures (also see Denzin and Lincoln, 1994). During the last three decades, however, ethnography has become increasingly associated with a wide range of social science disciplines including social anthropology (Wallman, 1982, 1984), human geography (Crang, 2002, 2003; Jackson, 1985, 1999; Lees, 2003) and educational research (Fetterman, 1984; Hammersley, 1990a). In Britain during the late 1980s and 1990s ethnographic methods were increasingly applied within the sociology of education, where the issues of 'race' and racism were a central concern (Connolly, 1998; Connolly and Troyna, 1998; Foster, 1990; Troyna, 1991, 1992). Notably, within an 'urban studies' context only sporadic attention has been devoted to the role of ethnography within research, scholarly or applied, in recent times (Franklin, 1986; Greed, 1994; Jacobs, 1993; Maginn, 2003). This seems somewhat peculiar in light of the rise of ethnography more generally.

Ethnography, however, has an established history within urban sociology, mainly within an American context but also a British one (Savage *et al*, 2003). Ethnography and ethnographic techniques were used quite extensively by the 'Chicago School' of sociology and human ecology, who dominated sociology from the 1920s through to the early1940s, within their studies of community life in Chicago. Notably, the human ecologists concentrated quite a lot of their research on trying to explain racial and other socio-cultural relations amongst 'minority' groups within Chicago (Anderson, 1961; Park and Burgess, 1967; Thomas and Znaniecki, 1958; Thrasher, 1963; Wirth, 1956; Zorbaugh, 1929). As Saunders (2001) has recently noted, 'much of the inter-war output of the Chicago School... took the form of ethnographies which provided detailed accounts of 'ways of life' of different urban [ethnic] groups' (p. 40). However, the ideas and theoretical perspectives of the human ecology movement, especially those ideas on ethnic relations (i.e. assimilation, acculturation and amalgamation) were continually criticized during the post-war era. Parks' conceptualization of America as a racial melting pot were seen as naïve, over-ambitious and misguided (for an overview, see Vidich and Lyman, 1994). Additionally, sociological analysis and debate during this period had increasingly turned to structuralism (Saunders, 2001) and quantitative techniques to explain social phenomenon (Hammersley, 1995). Arguably, this eclipse of the Chicago School resulted in the relegation of ethnographic methods within urban studies/sociology.

Within a British context, Hammersley (1990b) and Franklin (1989) have both noted that ethnographic techniques enjoyed a degree of popularity during the

1950s and 1960s. In particular, the Institute of Community Studies (ICS) conducted a series of 'community studies' in an effort to explore various aspects of British working-class life. Moreover, these community studies focused very much on the family, exploring issues such as kinship networks, relations and structures (Townsend, 1957; Young and Wilmott, 1957), class (Wilmott and Young, 1960), and education (Jackson and Marsden, 1962; Marris, 1964). Platt's (1971) critical evaluation of the ICS's work is a testimony to the ethnographic content and commitment of the community studies movement. She highlighted that the aims and objectives of the ICS, as set out in the preface of their reports, emphasized that 'the Institute had tried to bring some of the strengths of *anthropology* to sociology, combining *personal observations* and illustration with statistical analysis' (p.1) (*my emphasis*).

The community studies movement eventually suffered the same fate as the Chicago School due to the dominance of structuralism and statistical analysis within sociology (Bell and Newby, 1971; Platt, 1971). As Savage *et al* (2003) observe:

> Research into communities became bogged down in a series of intractable problems of a conceptual and methodological character. These problems finally undermined the use of the term 'community', as it was recognised that its use was ideological – that is to say, that it reflects widespread cultural assumptions and biases, rather than reality. [...] By the 1970s the community studies were denounced as scientifically flawed, though they were appreciated as interesting ethnographic accounts (p.116-117).

To reiterate, ethnography has not been used to any great extent in urban and planning-related studies in recent times – but there is evidence of a quiet revival. Franklin (1989) has argued the absence of ethnography within housing studies has been a consequence of it being 'too closely identified with one theoretical position and theoretical tradition [i.e. the Chicago School]' (p.92). This situation has changed recently due to the rise of partnerships and a renewed policy interest in local communities and neighbourhoods (DETR, 1997, 1998a; SEU, 1998, 2001). A number of recent studies on URPs have utilized a range of qualitative research techniques and methods. For example, Hughes and Carmichael's (1998) study on partnership processes and structures in the Greater Shankill Partnership in Belfast (Northern Ireland) comprised (i) in-depth semi-structured interviews with nine representatives from the voluntary, community and statutory sectors; and (ii) 'non-participant observations of the partnership process... during a three month period' (p.206).

Similarly, Hastings *et al's* (1996) study into community participation in estate-based regeneration initiatives drew on similar qualitative techniques. They comment that 'a large number of in-depth consultations were held with current and former participants [in addition] researchers also attended meetings of the regeneration initiatives and of the local community groups' (p.51). Skelcher *et al's* (1996) study into community networks and networking within regeneration schemes used similar methods. These included: (i) one-to-one interviews with public, private, voluntary and community sector agents operating at different spatial levels; (ii) utilizing life diaries 'to record network activity within and between agencies and sectors' (p.3); and (iii) focus groups and workshops.

Further evidence of a revival in the use of qualitative methods in neighbourhood regeneration can be seen in a series of reports produced by the Joseph Rowntree Foundation (Andersen *et al*, 1999; Cattell and Evans, 1999; Forrest and Kearns, 1999; Silburn *et al*, 1999; Wood and Vamplew, 1999). And, Power and Mumford's (2003) recent study on community life in East London replicates in many ways the approach used in the old community studies of the 1950s and 1960s.

Defining Ethnography

Ethnography is a *qualitative* research methodology and technique. That is, it is a means of collecting data and also a method of presenting research data or findings about the social world.   Hammersley and Atkinson (1995:1) offer a liberal definition of ethnography, seeing it as:

> ... a particular method or set of methods. In its most characteristic form it involves the ethnographer participating, overtly and covertly, in people's lives for an extended period of time, watching what happens, listening to what is said, asking questions – in fact collecting whatever data are available to throw light on the issues that are the focus of the research.

Furthermore, Fetterman (1989) defines ethnography as 'the *art* and *science* of describing a group or culture' (*my emphasis*) (p.11). Both Hammersley and Atkinson and Fetterman's definitions highlight the *subjective* and *objective* nature of ethnographic research. Ethnographic research is subjective in the sense that what ethnographers produce is a 'thick description' (Geertz, 1973) of the social phenomena they study in the 'natural' world. Despite the 'death of positivism' ethnographic research is still viewed as an inferior methodology by many quantitative researchers, and even policy-makers. It is viewed in this way as a consequence of its subjective approach to data collection and analysis and, moreover, inability to produce statistical generalizations. Ethnography is thus seen as producing anecdotal or soft data (Hammersley, 1995). Moreover, it is considered to have a limited role in enhancing knowledge and understanding of social phenomena and contributing to the policy process (Denzin and Lincoln, 1994; Quinn Patton, 1988, 2002).

Despite these criticisms it is contended here that objectivity is inherent within ethnographic research as a consequence of triangulation being an in-built feature. That is, in making use of a range of research techniques, ethnographers are constantly and systematically cross-referencing the data they collate so as to enhance the validity and rigour of their findings.

The Aim of Ethnography

What sets ethnographic research apart from quantitative-based research is that it enables researchers to get 'under the skin' of social settings and develop an 'insider account' of the 'culture' within them. Furthermore, the range of research methods that may be used in ethnographic research enables data on an issue to be collated from a variety of perspectives. The generation of an eclectic mix of data combined with the extended time spent in the field enables the development of an in-depth account of the socio-cultural structures, processes and relations within a particular setting. Quantitative methods are unable to generate such in-depth and rich data on social phenomena. Franklin (1989), for example, has noted that survey research into explaining why council tenants decide to become homeowners manages only to 'solicit brief summary rationales rather than the specific social contexts' (p.102) of their motivations. He then contends that an ethnographic methodology would enable researchers to 'explore the relevant cultural milieu and expose potential processes of cause and motivation' (p.102) that underpins decisions to become homeowners.

This should not be interpreted to suggest that ethnographic inquiry is in any way superior to quantitative methodology. What quantitative methods lack in terms of producing in-depth data, they make up for in producing data which highlight statistical correlations, trends and patterns across much larger sample populations than ethnographic methods, which tend to focus intensively on a small number of sample cases. In short, both qualitative and quantitative methods have their advantages and disadvantages and should not be viewed as being mutually exclusive or superior to one another. Instead, they should be viewed as being complementary, in that, they may be used for different purposes and at different stages in a research project.

In essence, then, ethnography is concerned with trying to make sense of the complex 'culture' that prevails within social settings. The social worlds that qualitative (and quantitative) researchers study are constantly evolving. Furthermore, the various agents that occupy these worlds express a potentially infinite number of values and attitudes towards different issues; respond and behave differently to particular events and situations; and have fluctuating and contested relationships with other agents with whom they may or may not interact with. As a result, neither qualitative nor quantitative researchers can produce the 'whole story' of the complex social phenomena they study (Back, 1995). Nevertheless, within ethnographic research the adoption of an 'holistic orientation' (Fetterman, 1989:29), that is, observing relevant and poignant events and interviewing key agents within a particular setting, over a sustained period of time, enables the construction of a relatively comprehensive picture.

The data collated in ethnographic research through observations and interviews (formal and informal) is often quite voluminous. It is this that gives ethnographies their richness. Interview transcripts and observational field notes are used to construct 'a narratology' in order to 'take the reader through the streets and alleyways' of the phenomenon under investigation (Flyvbjerg, 1998:7). In Chapters 5-7, interview transcripts are used extensively to provide a detailed narrative of different agents' – *community, bureaucratic, democratic,* and *professional* – lived experiences and understandings of participation, racism and community power within URPs.

The Ethnographic Research Process

The ethnographic research process commences as soon as a research problem or issue has been identified. Fetterman (1989) notes that the nature of the research problem ultimately steers the entire research process. Ethnography is characterized, therefore, as progressing through a series of broad inter-related and overlapping stages, which are instructive and informative to the overall research process. That is, as the ethnographer confronts and negotiates each stage of the research process this experience helps, firstly, to guide and inform the overall research process and methodology and secondly, to generate hard data which may be incorporated into research findings. Figure 4.1 presents a simplified overview of the ethnographic research process. Of course, the research process does not progress as smoothly and sequentially as this. The 'naturalistic' character of the settings analyzed in ethnographic research means that the research process is more likely to be in a general state of flux. That is to say, the ethnographer is free to alter their course as the research process unfolds. A denial of access to use a particular setting may result in initial research questions being reformulated. Similarly, different or additional research techniques may be used once inside a setting. There may, for example, be too many relevant agents to be interviewed individually. Hence, focus groups may be used to capture data.

In general, as soon as the research questions have been formulated the ethnographer will have a broad idea as to what they would like to observe, and, whom they would like to interview. It, however, is not until access to a setting has been secured and its topography and demography mapped that it is possible to discern what and who should be observed and interviewed. It is important to note that ethnographers do not simply walk into social settings and commence their research, unless, of course they are undertaking covert research. Consideration must be given to the various practical 'foreshadowed problems' (Hammersley and Atkinson, 1995:24) associated with any ethnographic research endeavour. Access to settings is one, if not, the most significant foreshadowed problem facing ethnographers.

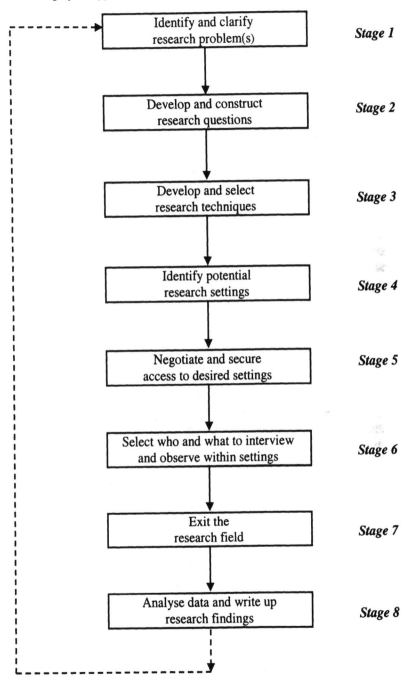

Figure 4.1 A Linear Overview of the Ethnographic Research Process

Negotiating Access

Access to settings is arguably the most fundamental aspect of any ethnographic study. This can be seen by the fact that, access, or to be more precise, the process of negotiating and securing access, pervades the entire ethnographic research process (Feldman *et al*, 2003). Furthermore, a denial of access to specifically desired settings means that research questions cannot be pursued. In general, however, it is possible for researchers to shift their gaze to securing access to other settings.

There are two broad strategies open to researchers seeking to secure access to settings. On the one hand, they may conduct their research covertly. Such an approach tends to be associated with ethnographic research conducted within 'private' or 'closed' settings such as religious or political cults. This strategy may, of course, also be used within 'public' settings (e.g. schools, offices, hospitals or neighbourhoods). Analysis of these latter types of settings tend to be more closely associated with the second research strategy – overt research – which is now more commonly used within ethnographic research, especially applied ethnography. An overt research strategy was adopted in order to negotiate access to the various neighbourhoods targeted as potential case studies and was mainly used throughout fieldwork in *Northside, Southside* and *Westside*. A very small element of covert fieldwork research was also conducted in each area.

Securing initial access to and subsequent access within settings is quite often a time-consuming process (Lyon, 1997). This is because the ethnographer needs to acquire the support, confidence and acceptance of the various 'gatekeepers' (Walsh, 1998:224) and informants who line the various 'front-' and 'backstages' within a setting (Hunter, 1993:38). Garnering the support and permission of these agents highlights that access is a relational process (Feldman *et al*, 2003). Developing relations requires what Hammersley (1995) calls 'the mobilisation of social and personal networks' (p.60). Again, researchers may deploy two broad strategies on this front: formal and informal networking. In fact, both strategies are likely to be used over the course of a research project. This was the case in efforts to secure three case studies for the empirical research underpinning this book.

Negotiating Access: Formal Networking

Letters of introduction were sent to the Directors of the Housing, Planning and Regeneration Departments in five London boroughs. These boroughs were selected on the basis of their involvement in urban regeneration, multi-ethnic population base and policy commitment to community participation. The letter also briefly outlined the nature and purpose of the research; a request for additional information about local regeneration programmes; and a request for a meeting with the view to securing a case study within their area. The letter explicitly stated that the research was concerned with 'race' issues, noting that the focus was on both 'black' *and* 'white' communities' experiences of regeneration. The decision to be explicit about the racial focus of the research was grounded in increasingly positive, albeit incremental, shifts within the wider policy arena about the issue of 'race' with BME issues being recognized as a key strategic objective within the SRB (DETR, 1997, 1998b; DoE, 1994, 1995, 1997).

Responses to the initial letter were not particularly forthcoming. A reminder letter was subsequently issued approximately six weeks later and generated a more positive response. A reply was eventually received from each council but not from all the departments that had been sent a letter. Furthermore, the replies were a mix of disinterest and veiled reluctance to participate in the research. A response from the Regeneration Department in one council, for example, simply stated that they were unable to assist with the research. The responses from two other councils were marginally more positive. One council sent additional information and provided a contact name if any further assistance was needed. The other stated that they were still considering the idea of the research and would be in touch once they had arrived at a decision. The most positive response came from the Assistant Director of Housing Management and Development in another council who agreed to a meeting to discuss the research further. A meeting was eventually secured after meeting the Assistant Director at a conference, reminding him of the letter and 'dropping' the name of a former colleague from Northern Ireland with whom he had a good relationship.

Due to the slow and guarded replies from the initial target sample of local authorities the field of inquiry was broadened. Consequently, a sixth council that had recently applied for SRB funding to regenerate a large 1960s high-rise residential and commercial development were sent a letter of introduction.

Negotiating Access: Informal Networking

In parallel to making formal approaches to local authorities, a network of contacts were built up as an additional means of trying to identify and secure access to potential case studies. A plethora of contacts, academic, governmental (local and central), professional bodies, voluntary organizations and BME advocacy groups from across London were established by the time the three case studies were finally secured. This informal networking was undertaken for two inter-related reasons. First, it was to test knowledgeable agents' reactions to the research. And, second, it was to use contacts as a lever to identify possible research settings; to reduce possible suspicions about the research, especially from local communities; and to facilitate access to potential settings.

In overall terms, the research was well received, especially amongst those contacts working in the community and voluntary sectors. Reactions from local authority contacts were also positive but erred on the side of caution. This was largely due to bureaucratic sensitivities surrounding the community participation and racial focus of the research. The degree of sensitivity towards these issues varied across and within the various settings targeted. As a result, a range of strategies and personas were adopted in an effort to reduce suspicions and win over confidence. It was stressed to all bureaucratic and community gatekeepers that the research was concerned with analyzing both 'black' *and* 'white' communities' experiences of regeneration. The policy evaluation potential of the research was highlighted to local authority officers. Community representatives were assured that the research was an independent academic exercise and they (and all interviewees) would be provided anonymity if they took part in the research. Different aspects of identity – professional (i.e. researcher), racial (i.e. 'white') and ethnic (i.e. 'Northern Irish') – were accentuated within different contexts. And, finally, a conscious attempt was made to 'mingle in the social milieu' (Hunter, 1993:44) within targeted areas in an effort to develop relations with agents.

Patience, Persistency and... Luck Pays Off

As noted earlier, negotiating access tends to be characterized as a lengthy and time-consuming process. Since URPs are multi-levelled bureaucratic structures that comprise a range of 'gatekeepers' and informants, negotiating and securing access to three case studies proved extremely time-consuming. It took a total of almost 15 months of letter writing, networking, meetings and patiently waiting for responses before *Northside, Southside* and *Westside* were eventually secured. By the time these three neighbourhoods had been secured four other neighbourhoods – *Eastville, Riverview, Uptown* and Midtown – in different London boroughs had been targeted. Despite being refused permission to conduct research within these neighbourhoods, varying degrees of access were negotiated within them.

Efforts to secure permission to use *Eastville* and *Riverview*, were quite deep access was actually secured, were particularly time-consuming and arduous. This was due to the highly politicized atmosphere and animosity that prevailed between residents and council officers and within the local community in both neighbourhoods. Nevertheless, the access secured within both of these neighbourhoods provided useful insights and data about the nature of participation, community power and the significance of 'race'. The access experience within both these settings helped to enhance awareness of what to be on the look out for in the three secured case studies.

The time and effort invested in negotiating access to the aforementioned neighbourhoods, only to be denied permission, also took a personal toll. The whole experience proved to be particularly tiring, frustrating and stressful. At one stage, the prospect of securing one, never mind three, case study seemed like a hopeless task. It, consequently, was decided to abandon the idea of doing a comparative analysis and concentrate efforts on securing one case study. Ultimately, a combination of patience, persistency and luck eventually resulted in securing three case studies.

Northside was secured following several meetings with the Assistant Director of Housing Management and Development and the Chairman of *Northside Community Forum* (NCF), who readily agreed to the research. The willingness of the NCF Chairman was grounded in the fact that the Assistant Director had sent him a letter of recommendation about the research. Ultimately, permission to conduct the research had to be obtained from the full NCF committee. This, consequently, entailed attending a full committee meeting to outline the aims of the research and to answer any questions that members may have had. The committee agreed unanimously in favour of the research to proceed.

Fieldwork subsequently commenced approximately two months later – some nine months after the initial letter of introduction had been sent to the Assistant Director. Fieldwork had begun in *Northside* before *Southside* and *Westside* presented themselves as possible case studies.

Access to *Southside* was actually secured following the receipt of an unsolicited fax from the Director of *Southside Partnership Board* (SPB). The fax was received shortly after fieldwork had commenced in *Northside*. *Southside* was located in the same council area as *Eastville* and it transpired that the Director had been informed about the research from the key council contact there. The Director indicated early on in a meeting with him his support for the research, perceiving it as a 'free evaluation'. He stressed, however, that permission would have to be obtained from the SPB and the *Southside Community Forum* (SCF). The institutional members (i.e. the local authority and two housing associations) of the SPB, the executive decision-making body, readily granted their permission. The Director facilitated the setting up of a meeting with the then acting Chairperson and Secretary of the SCF who were also members of the SPB. These two representatives, who were both elderly 'whites', were somewhat apprehensive about the research initially. It was assumed that this was due to the racial focus of the research. It later transpired that their apprehension was due to extremely serious internal conflicts within the community forum. It took a further two meetings, one with the newly appointed Chairman, a youngish Anglo-Irish male, and the other with the community forum committee before permission was eventually secured.

Access to *Westside* was negotiated through the brokering efforts of colleagues who had recently completed a community audit in the neighbourhood. It was this that provoked a request to colleagues to mention the research to key agents within *Westside* in order to ascertain their attitude towards it. In general, there was a favourable response that resulted in the setting up of two meetings. The first meeting was with the Westside Community Forum (WCF), the executive decision-making body. And, the second meeting was with the *Westside* Consultative Committee (WCC), a community-wide advisory body to the WCF. Both meetings progressed smoothly and permission was duly granted – approximately 15 months after networking had commenced! A keen interest in research and 'race' issues amongst two members of the WCF was a major factor in securing *Westside* as a case study.

Methods and Techniques

Two primary data collection techniques are associated with ethnographic research: (i) participant observations and (ii) interviewing. Ethnographers are also free to use secondary data sources to supplement their primary data. Participant observations and interviewing are interdependent on each another: It is via conducting observations that the ethnographer is able to identify and target potential interviewees. Similarly, from conducting interviews information can be elicited that can help to fine-tune observations and, more importantly, verify conclusions derived from observations.

Participant Observations

Observations in ethnographic research commence as soon as a potential setting has been identified and efforts to negotiate access are undertaken. Once inside a setting participant observations are often conducted in an unwieldy and unstructured manner as the ethnographer attempts to acquire a broad overview of its terrain. This unsystematic approach may result in the production of masses of data of varying usefulness in relation to the research question(s) being pursued. But, as the ethnographer becomes increasingly accustomed to the terrain of the setting under investigation they are in a position to narrow their focus of observation on the most relevant data sources.

In terms of conducting participant observations ethnographers may adopt a number of observational roles. The nature of the research problem will ultimately determine what role(s) should be adopted. In simple terms, observations fall into two broad types: participant observation (Atkinson and Hammersley, 1994; Hammersley and Atkinson, 1995) and non-participant observation (Adler and Adler, 1994). Within both of these contexts observational research may be conducted covertly and/or overtly. This 'simple dichotomy' (Atkinson and Hammersley, 1994: 248) suggests, however, that observational research is both polemic and static in nature. Junker's (1960) typology of fieldwork roles, however, highlights a spectrum of observational roles. On one half of the spectrum researchers play a *comparatively involved* role and may assume the identity of a 'complete participant' and/or 'participant as observer'. On the other half of the spectrum researchers play a *comparatively detached* role and may assume the identity of a 'complete observer' and/or 'observer as participant'. Furthermore, Junker's typology suggests that observational research is a dynamic process where researchers may assume different observational roles over the course of conducting fieldwork. This chameleon-like behaviour enables the ethnographer to look and get at research issues from different perspectives and generate different forms of data.

Mainly non-participant observations were undertaken in order to experience and track the regeneration process in each case study area as it evolved. The primary locus of observations was the community forums. These were selected because it is at this level within regeneration programmes, that the local community are formally consulted and participate in the decision-making process. By focusing on these arenas it would be possible to observe the nature and extent of community participation, the significance attached to the issues of 'race' and racism, interactions with institutional partners and the strategies and tactics used to exert influence within URPs.

A predominantly 'observer as participant' role was adopted in *Northside, Southside* and *Westside*. This role was assumed in an effort to minimize any direct impact on the 'natural' behaviour of community forum members and the evolution of proceedings within community forums, which were the primary locus of observations within each case study area. Clearly, the presence of an outsider, especially a researcher, will have impacts on those being researched. As a result of being located in each case study for a year, conducting mainly non-participant observations but developing positive and informal relationships with community forum members (and other agents) it was possible to gain acceptance and blend into the background. On occasion, it was necessary to interject into proceedings of forum meetings (and other settings) in order to seek more details and/or clarification on certain issues.

Additional observations were also conducted at a range of other meetings and events, such as community organization's annual general meetings; officer working groups; community open days; and conferences and seminars. Observations at these events enabled a wider picture of the complexities and dynamics of the regeneration process, the condition of participation and the significance of 'race' to be ascertained. It was in these wider arenas that covert fieldwork was undertaken.

A total of 88 non-participant observations of community forum meetings and other settings/events were undertaken across all three case study areas (see Table 4.1). Differences in the organizational structure, proceedings and frequency of meetings within each case study area help to explain the uneven distribution of observations.

Table 4.1 Distribution of Non-Participant Observations

Neighbourhood	Observations Completed	Per cent of Total Observations
Northside	39	44
Southside	33	38
Westside	16	18
Total	88	100

Interviewing

'The interview is the ethnographer's most important data gathering technique' (Fetterman, 1989:47). Similarly, Fontana and Frey (1994) state, 'interviewing is one of the most common and powerful ways we use to try and understand our fellow human beings' (p.361). As with negotiating access, interviewing pervades the entire ethnographic experience. In addition, interviewing complements observational research and vice versa. It is via asking questions of agents that the researcher is able to contextualize and develop an understanding of what has been observed. Additionally, interviews may also be used to develop a retrospective overview of the issues being investigated. This enables the researcher to develop an historical overview of the setting and agents being studied.

Interviews may assume a variety of formats. The most common and popular form is the face-to-face interview. In addition, other increasingly popular forms of direct interviewing include group interviews such as focus groups (Morgan, 1993) and telephone interviews (Fontana and Frey, 1994). Furthermore, interviews may be structured, semi-structured or unstructured in nature. Structured interviews offer limited scope for the researcher and/or interviewee to explore and/or articulate broader contextual issues. Conversely, semi-structured and unstructured interviews allow greater interaction and freedom to explore important 'off-the-schedule' issues that tend to emerge during interviews.

Within ethnographic research interviews may also be conducted under informal or formal conditions, which, in turn, determine whether an unstructured or structured interview should be used. In applied ethnographic research, informal and formal interviews tend to be used intermittently. Informal interviews tend to be spontaneous events and mainly occur within two main arenas. First, during participant observations the researcher is able to ask questions in order to clarify things that have just been observed (Lofland, 1971). Secondly, chance meetings with agents provide an opportunity to conduct interviews covertly via general conversation. In contrast, formal interviews tend to be pre-arranged events. This requires obtaining an agent's permission to be interviewed and then setting up a date, time and place for interview.

Deciding who should be interviewed generally emerges during participant observations when the researcher is able to identify key protagonists. Additionally, *invisible* agents, that is, those not directly observable within a setting, but who have played a critical role either historically (e.g. a former tenant activist) and/or exogenously (e.g. a consultant or central/local government officer), may also have to be interviewed. Such invisible agents tend to be identified through interviews. For example, a certain name may keep cropping up in interviews thus signifying some degree of importance with that person and therefore someone noteworthy of interview.

It was through observational research and informally interacting with various agents within settings that it was possible to develop positive relationships with potential interviewees. For example, by arriving early for meetings, helping to set-up the committee table and engaging in general conversation it was possible to develop relations and collect data simultaneously. The development of positive relations with agents helped to further reduce suspicions about the research and agreement to be interviewed.

Interviews were semi-structured in nature. This approach enabled agents' historical and contemporaneous experiences, understandings and attitudes towards urban regeneration, community participation and 'race' to be explored. In a further effort to encourage forum members to be interviewed they were given control over where and when interviews would take place. Community forum members were interviewed either at their homes or local community centre. The sense of security provided by their home, combined with a guarantee of anonymity and the existence of positive relations, contributed to a willingness to discuss issues quite freely. Interviewees with whom particularly strong relations existed were subsequently used as conduits to recruit some of the more reluctant members of community forums. Recruiting officers and other professionals to be interviewed was fairly unproblematic, the only real difficulty was arranging a mutually appropriate date and time. Interviews with officers and other professional agents were normally conducted at their place of work.

A total of 69 interviews were conducted across all three neighbourhoods (see Table 4.2). This comprised a total of 42 existing (and former) community forums members: (i) *Northside* (17); (ii) *Southside* (12); and (iii) *Westside* (13).[1] A conscious effort was made to interview a good mix of 'black' and 'white' community forum members and this objective was realized. The following 'black'/'white' mix of forum members were interviewed: *Northside* 9/8; *Southside* 3/9; and *Westside* 5/8. A total of 27 interviews were conducted with various bureaucratic, other professional and political agents: (i) *Northside* (n=15) (ii) *Southside* (n=10) and (iii) *Westside* (n=2). The variation in the number interviewed in this category of agents reflects the overall level of involvement of such agents within each area.

Table 4.2 Total Interviews by Neighbourhood and Type

Type of Interviewee	Northside No.	%	Southside No.	%	Westside* No.	%
Tenants	17	53	12	54	3	20
Local authority	6	19	5	23	1	7
Voluntary sector	6	19	2	9	9	60
Local councillor	1	3	1	5	1	7
Consultant	2	6	1	5	-	-
GoL	-	-	1	5	1	6
Total	32	100	22	100	15	100

* As already noted, all interviewees, with the exception of the local councillor, in *Westside* were actually community forum members and as such they have been included as being part of the community forum interview sample.

Focus Groups

Focus groups, as an interview technique, have tended to be used mainly by market researchers (Morgan, 1993) and more recently by political analysts, particularly by those within government itself. Holbrook and Jackson (1996) have noted that they have been increasingly used within the social sciences. Their popularity stems from being a 'social, synergistic, reflexive, liminal and potentially empowering' (Goss and Leinbach, 1996:117) methodological tool and arena that may help the researcher to generate both new and confirmatory data (Frey and Fontana, 1993).

---

[1]   Only three interviewees from the *Westside* Community Forum were actually members of the local community. The remaining interviewees were actually members of bureaucratic and/or professional organizations.

Focus groups were used towards the end of fieldwork for two main purposes. First, they were used as a reflexive device. That is, focus groups were used to triangulate data that had been collated during in-depth interviews and observations. Second, they were used as an alternative means of trying to access a few agents who had been reluctant to be interviewed on a one-to-one basis.

The focus groups were designed in such a way so as to engender participants to play both a primary and active role. A series of unseen questions, in sealed numbered envelopes, based on particular issues and themes identified during interviews and participant observations were devised. Participants were then invited to select an envelope and read out the question they had selected. Again, this strategy was adopted in order to give participants a sense of control over the research process and that as a group they would be more willing to respond to questions read out by their friends. A total of five focus groups, comprising between 3-8 participants, were conducted, three in *Northside* and one in *Southside* and *Westside* respectively.

Conclusions

This chapter has sought to provide both an historical and definitional overview of ethnography and outline why and how this methodological approach was adopted. It was shown that ethnography enables researchers to develop and 'insider account' of social phenomena and provides them with the freedom to use a range of strategies and techniques to collect primary data. In short, since ethnography *is* the study of the 'culture' of communities and the social settings they exist within, it is the most appropriate methodology to develop an understanding of the nuances and dynamics of urban regeneration and community power in multi-ethnic localities.

In conclusion, it is important to stress that ethnographic research is often criticized for its inability to generalize research findings to the wider population. No attempt is made here to claim that the findings from *Northside*, *Southside* and *Westside* are in any way statistically generalizable. They do, however, provide what Yin (1984) refers to as 'analytical generalizations', or what other scholars have termed 'fittingness' (Guba and Lincoln 1981, 1982); 'comparability' (Goetz and LeCompte, 1984); and 'empirical generalizations' (Hammersley, 1992). That is to say, these types of generalizations are applicable to some finite population (Hammersley, 1992). In the context of this book, *Northside, Southside* and *Westside* typify a range of socially excluded neighbourhoods from within inner-London, in that, although there are some differences, they share a number of similar demographic, socio-economic and policy orientation characteristics. Consequently, this leads to the assertion that the findings from these case studies may be generalized to other similar areas within London and throughout Britain.

Chapter 5

Northside:
Pragmatic Pluralism and
the Declining Significance of 'Race'

We recognise that the problems and opportunities facing the borough are best
addressed by everyone with an interest working closely together to a shared agenda.
[...] We are committed to working through partnerships, but the local authority
alone has the responsibility over the long-term for the well being of all the
borough's residents and businesses, and, by virtue of being democratically elected,
can speak for the whole borough.

(Urban Regeneration Strategy, Hackney LBC, 1996a:9)

Introduction

The above abstract represents a dramatic shift in policy by the London Borough of
Hackney (LB Hackney) (Jacobs, 1999; Pinto, 1993). It reflects the beginnings of a
forward thinking attitude to working in partnership with agents such as private
developers, housing associations and local communities, which was virtually
anathema during the 1980s. The council's assertion, however, that it 'alone has
responsibility for the long-term well-being of the borough's residents and
businesses' echoes of its hard-left socialist and paternalistic past. Nevertheless, the
council's new corporate slogan and strategy – *Transforming Hackney* – pointed
towards, symbolically at least, a commitment to improve service delivery and
reform its political standpoint.

This progressive transformation was particularly evident within the Housing
Department who had assumed a lead role in urban regeneration and housing
renewal through its Comprehensive Estates Initiative (CEI). As its name suggests,
the CEI was a comprehensive regeneration initiative set up to tackle the housing,
social and economic problems that bedeviled *Northside* and several other
neighbourhoods. Furthermore, the CEI was staffed by dynamic community-
minded officers at the strategic and operational policy levels. This chapter is set
within the context of this overall paradigmatic political and policy shift.

The chapter focuses on a number of key issues. First, a descriptive
overview of the *Northside* neighbourhood is presented in order to provide a
thumbnail sketch of the area. Second, the council's strategic and localized
regeneration strategy is briefly outlined. Next, the consultation processes and
participatory structures put in place to facilitate community involvement in

decision-making are examined. Particular attention is devoted to examining the impacts of the setting up of a new community structure, the *Northside Community Forum* (NCF), on intra-community relations. And, relatedly, the membership profiles of community structures, old and new, are examined in order to establish their socially pluralistic character, particularly in ethnic terms. Then, the discussion turns to an examination of the nature of community power, as interpreted and experienced by NCF members and institutional agents. Fourth, the significance of 'race' in relation to its impacts on community participation and within the overall regeneration process are considered. Finally, some conclusions are drawn about the overall pattern of community power and the significance of 'race' within *Northside*.

Setting the Scene

Stepping outside the train station onto the high street close to *Northside* the senses are immediately alerted to the areas' ethnic diversity and chaotic built environment. A broadly bi-polar demographic profile was visibly distinguishable: a high proportion of young BME and elderly 'white' cohorts. A chaotic mix of retail outlets that include a thriving local market; a panoply of low-order retail outlets plus a small number of national chain outlets (e.g. Sainsbury's, Superdrug and McDonald's) add to the eclecticism of the area. The high street is heavily congested: The footpaths are overcrowded with shoppers, workers and school children hurriedly going about their business. Cars and buses snake slowly through the high street, stopping and starting at the busy pedestrian crossings. The area is aesthetically unattractive and cluttered due to the poorly maintained condition and inconsistent form of many of the buildings. Nevertheless, the area has an intensely vibrant atmosphere.

The *Northside* estate itself lies to the south-west of the main shopping high street. It is a mainly residential area bordered on the south by a main road, and a small enclave of large Victorian houses, largely owner occupied and private rented; and to the east and west by two through-roads lined with more traditional types of housing. The 'old' estate originally comprised a mix of terraced and medium-sized Victorian houses but was designated a slum clearance area in the 1960s. The 'redeveloped' estate was completed in the early 1970s and consisted of approximately 1200 properties comprising a mix of medium- and high-rise system-built flats. At the time of its completion *Northside* was heralded as a major achievement in social planning and architecture by the local authority. The new systems-built housing were also praised by many 'established' and 'new' tenants who saw them as modern and spacious. Notably, a number of 'black' interviewees commented positively about the quality of the accommodation, the strong sense of community within the area, and the local authority's approach to housing management. As one 'black' interviewee commented:

> The place that I used to live in was too small so I was moved into the towers. I had two bedrooms and the rooms were quite big! It was a really nice place then! It was

sometimes called the 'Cream of London' or the 'Cream of Hackney' in the sense that the tower blocks were well kept and very clean, the lawns were nicely kept, the lifts were cleaned about two or three times a day!   (Interviewee 1)

By the 1980s, however, it was clear that the systems-built housing suffered from a combination of technical, environmental health and social design problems. Parallel to this, several other overlapping problems compounded the highly stigmatic and stereotypical image of the estate.

First, the neighbourhood had become highly residualized and stigmatized. Long-term 'black' and 'white' interviewees noted that an increasingly high number of 'problem families' were allocated housing during the 1980s. This led to the area being perceived as a housing 'dumping ground'. By the early 1990s over 75 per cent of tenants were on the housing transfer list – a clear indicator of the estates unpopularity. Second, crime, in the form of muggings, burglaries and drug dealing was a major problem on the estate. Both 'black' and 'white' interviewees saw criminal activity as largely being perpetrated by disaffected 'black' youth. Finally, much of the housing stock suffered from high levels of disrepair. Interviewees described *Northside* as: 'a no-go area'; 'dirty'; 'a problem area'; 'stigmatized'; and, having 'a reputation for lawlessness, muggings, break-ins and assaults'.

The *Northside* estate has undergone quite significant population restructuring during the last 20-25 years. Yes, 'whites' were the single largest ethnic group (42 per cent) but they were also the 'minority' population by virtue of the fact that BME groups constituted 58 per cent of the total neighbourhood population: Afro-Caribbeans and Africans (48 per cent); Chinese/Others (7 per cent); and 'Asians' [i.e. Indian, Pakistani and Bangladeshi] (3 per cent) (LB Hackney, 1996). The concentration of a small number of Turkish/Kurdish-owned retail outlets, mainly grocery stores and fast food restaurants, on the perimeter of *Northside* suggested that this ethnic group was a growing facet of the local population.

As well as being an ethnically diverse locality, *Northside*, as with Hackney in general, suffered from high levels of socio-economic deprivation (see Table 5.1). For example, only 3 per cent of the population were owner-occupiers compared to 26 per cent for the borough overall. Table 5.1 also provides a more detailed overview of the demographic and socio-economic profile of *Northside* by ethnic group. It can be seen that both 'white' and 'black' groups tended to suffer slightly higher levels of socio-economic disadvantage than 'Asian' and Chinese/Other groups.

As housing and socio-economic problems intensified throughout the 1980s, the *Northside Tenants Association* (NTA), the neighbourhood's primary community forum, began to campaign for change. Their efforts, however, went largely unheard as their local authority was embroiled in an ideological battle with the Conservative government.

Table 5.1 Demographic and Socio-economic Profile of *Northside* by Ethnicity (per cent)

Variable	White	Black	Asian	Chinese/ Other	All Groups Council	N'side
Population	42	48	3	7	100	100
Economically active	54	69	49	60	60	58
Economically inactive	47	29	51	40	38	42
Unemployed	32	30	22	39	28	31
Long term ill	18	10	27	6	12	15
No car	77	79	76	78	53	78
Owner occupied	3	4	14	3	26	6
Local authority housing	86	89	81	78	49	84
Housing association	4	7	-	5	12	5
Private rented	4	0.4	5	8	11	4
Density >1.5	3	12	-	-	10	8
No central heating	8	10	14	24	19	14

Source: Hackney LBC (1996b); PPCR (1996)

In an effort to confront the assault of Thatcherism on local democracy the council began to espouse and practise a radical socialist agenda. Ironically, their combative stance manifested itself in localized ideological dogma. The council effectively lost sight of its own social and democratic principles during its anti-Thatcher stance throughout the 1980s. More importantly, the council had lost a grip on policy implementation and management. This was particularly evident in education and housing, where service delivery had deteriorated significantly. In short, local councillors were more devoted to fighting an ideological battle against the Conservatives than delivering their public service duties. The following comment by the local councillor for *Northside*, provides an insight into how politically dogmatic the council was in the 1980s:

> We were open-minded! We we're not rigidly fixed to fighting a Tory government as the 1980s Labour Group was which is where we got the 'loony left' tag! […] At the end of the day it's about Mr. and Mrs. Singh at the top of that tower block or in a house that is damp and unheated, unsanitary and poor conditions. I often said: "let's go and have this debate in Mr. and Mrs. Singh's flat and see which of the arguments they would go for". Would they go for the Council leader's line of you ride the horse the way it's going? In other words, you accept that the Tories are in power. But, how can we work with them in a way that is to the full benefit of OUR people? If that means playing their game, whatever that might be, let's do it!
>
> (Local councillor)

The council's policy shift was grounded in a combination of inter-related factors. First, there was an increasing feeling that the Conservatives would win the 1992 General Election. In the event of this happening, the council knew that if it continued on its own counter-crusade then it was unlikely to win central government funding for much needed urban regeneration and housing renewal. Second, as implied in the above interview transcript, there was a shift in power and attitude within the council, politically and administratively, with the rise of a more pragmatic leader of the Labour grouping and the appointment of a new forward-thinking Chief Executive. This helped to galvanize the need for the council to be more pragmatic and work in partnership with the private sector.   Finally, councillors were re-awakening to the fact that they had become de-sensitized to the needs, wants and protestations of their local electorate throughout the 1980s especially in the borough's poorest and worst housing estates such as *Northside*.

Learning to Play the Regeneration Game

The Strategic Policy Game

The council gradually came to the realization, in the face of an increasingly competitive and diminishing public funding regime, particularly within urban regeneration policy, that it alone could not tackle its housing and socio-economic problems. There was a clear need to develop an alternative and innovative policy agenda.   The council established a 24-member partnership, with equal representation from the public, private, voluntary and community sectors, in 1991 to develop a strategic vision on regeneration for the borough. This new partnership marked the formal transition from radical to pragmatic local authority. It should be noted that the council retained the power of veto within the partnership – a measure designed to reinforce the notion that it was the most powerful partner.

The council subsequently went on to devise a borough-wide urban regeneration strategy in 1996. This strategy consolidated the aims and objectives of all existing regeneration initiatives, including the CEI, operating within the borough. The regeneration strategy had a two-pronged approach to attract much needed investment to the borough. First, the strategy sought to *place market* the borough by highlighting its comparative advantages: lower operational costs, proximity to 'the City' of London, a large supply of labour and cultural diversity. Second, the strategy sought to attract government funding by highlighting the high levels of deprivation within the council. The key objectives of the regeneration strategy included:

- building a competitive economy through attracting investment and jobs;
- getting people into jobs by identifying their existing skills and training needs;
- improving the physical environment and promoting sustainable development; and
- building a stable mixed community.

Community participation was a further key objective of the regeneration strategy. It was recognized that the long-term success of regeneration could only be achieved with full community participation. A series of community forums were subsequently set up in the various neighbourhoods being regenerated under programmes that included Estate Action, the CEI, Estate Renewal Challenge Fund (ERCF) and the SRB.

The Localized Policy Context

The CEI began in the early 1990s and was the council's flagship area-based regeneration programme. It had a total budget of almost £300m, comprised a mix of public and private sources (see Table 5.2), and operated in several neighbourhoods throughout the borough. The *Northside* CEI consumed one-third of the total budget.

    The public-private partnership approach to regeneration, proposals to revert to a more traditional form of housing and estate layout and a decision to diversify tenure signified just how pragmatic the council had become. Renewal of the housing stock was by far the largest aspect of the regeneration of *Northside*. The CEI, however, was a holistic regeneration programme that was also concerned with addressing social, economic and environmental problems. And, in an expression of its commitment to establishing a more democratic regeneration process, representatives from the NCF were granted direct access to the political (i.e. CEI sub-committee) and operational (i.e. CEI Neighbourhood Office) decision-making arenas of the CEI programme by the council.

Table 5.2 Regeneration Funding Regime for *Northside*

Funding Source	£m	%
Central Government	96	34
Housing Association	72	25
Private Investment	44	16
LA Housing Capital	40	14
Land values	20	7
LA Non-housing Capital	11	4
Total	283	100

The Long Road to Community Participation

Despite proclaiming a commitment to *full* community participation, it cannot be said that the *Northside* neighbourhood were involved from the outset of the regeneration process. Prior to the 'official' announcement of the CEI programme (i.e. the securing of government funding), the council had been engaged in 18-24 months of behind-the-scenes negotiations with central government officials, political and administrative, from the then Department of Environment (DoE) and Housing Corporation.

    Such stealth negotiations were unavoidable however. First, the competitive bidding regime and short lead-in times associated with submitting regeneration bids for government funding precluded any community involvement in the embryonic stages of the regeneration process. Secondly, there was a perception that community participation might actually jeopardize chances of securing funding. There were concerns amongst councillors and officers that the local community would vehemently object to the council signing up to Conservative government policies. It, therefore, was expedient to side step the community in order to ensure that negotiations with central government proceeded as quickly as possible.

Having secured central government funding, the council commenced setting up the necessary structures and processes to implement the regeneration programme. Figure 5.1 depicts the organizational structure of the CEI programme within *Northside*. It can be seen that there were four key decision-making arenas: central government; local government (strategic and operational); and local community. The NCF (and subsequent community forums) were mainly engaged in the operational policy arena, interacting with institutional agents responsible for managing and implementing regeneration on the ground. It was at this level that most observational fieldwork was conducted. The NCF also had direct access to the strategic political decision-making arena, the CEI Sub-Committee, within the council. Moreover, the NCF was also successful in negotiating access to the Housing Corporation at the central government level.

In terms of community forums, the primary locus of attention was on the NCF. But, it can be seen from Figure 5.1 that there were a number of community structures within the area: Northside Joint Management Board (NJMB); Northside Tenant Management Organization (NTMO); and the Northside Community Development Trust (NCDT). These forums had all evolved from various sub-groups within the NCF. The functions and purpose of the CEI Sub-Committee, the CEI Neighbourhood Office and the NCF are briefly outlined below.

CEI Sub-committee

In light of the financial magnitude and political (central and local) importance of the CEI initiative, the council set up the CEI Sub-committee, in 1991/92. The sub-committee was responsible for strategic political aspects of the CEI programme and comprised councillors and officers from the Chief Executive's Office and the Departments of Housing, Education, Economic Development and Equal Opportunities. Furthermore, two members from the NCF (i.e. the Chairperson and Vice-Chairperson) and other CEI community forums had co-opted status on the sub-committee. This meant that community forum representatives had no voting rights within the sub-committee. They, however, were entitled to table questions and debate issues about the CEI programme in their neighbourhood. The new policy culture and political regime within the council laid the foundations to ensuring that the NCF's views were both 'heard' and 'listened' to by policy-makers (Forester, 1989; Murtagh, 1999).

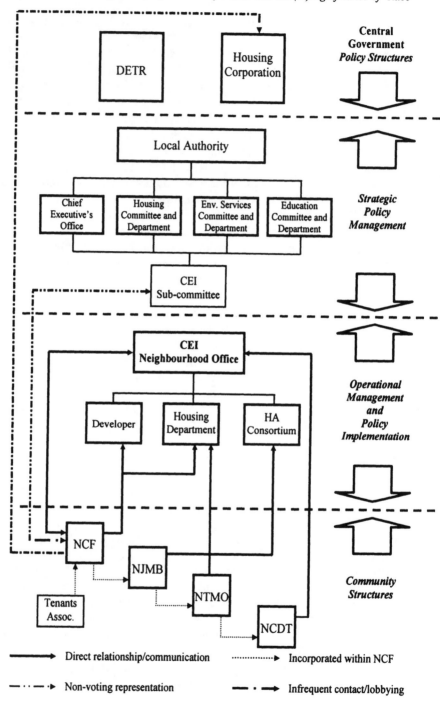

Figure 5.1 Organizational Structure of Regeneration Process (*Northside*)

CEI Neighbourhood Office

The Neighbourhood Office (NO), a decentralized unit of the council's Housing Department, was responsible for overseeing operational aspects of the regeneration of *Northside*. This included, for example: demolition of local authority housing stock; decanting and rehousing tenants; providing capacity-building training and other services for tenant activists and general project management in association with the developers and architects. Furthermore, the NO operated on generic working principles. That is, officers adopted a hands-on management approach; offered advice and information freely; and had a mutually understanding relationship with the NCF, whose Chairman had a particularly strong relationship with the council's Project Manager.

The Northside Community Forum

The council's commitment to fostering effective community participation was reflected in its gradual provision of physical, financial and human resources to the NCF. First, the NCF was provided with its own 'nerve centre', in a former council property, which comprised office space, committee rooms, telephone, fax, computer and photocopying facilities. Next, the council employed two tenants' advisors to work *with* and *for* the NCF. The first advisor, a community-planning consultant, was employed on a consultancy basis for two years. The second advisor a community development officer, whilst directly employed by the council, was based at the NCF's nerve center and worked to their direction. Both advisors were charged with enhancing wider community participation and the NCFs capacity to participate within the regeneration process. All of these resources ultimately helped the NCF to assume an autonomous identity and, more importantly, exercise influence within the regeneration process.

It would be naïve to assume that the regeneration process progressed without any problems once participatory structures and processes were established. On the contrary, conflict is inevitable within large-scale decision-making arenas with a diverse range of interest groups. It is important to stress that problems associated with community participation were not solely the fault of the actions (or inactions) of central or local government. Fieldwork data revealed that community members in *Northside* also played a critical role in creating problems within the participation process. This was also true in *Southside* where deep intra-community divisions seriously impeded community participation (see Chapter 6).

Informing and Consulting the Local Community

Community participation officially commenced with a widely publicized, and well-attended, public meeting held at the 'old' community centre. The primary purpose of the meeting was to *inform* the local community that the council had been successful in securing significant central government funding for housing renewal and urban regeneration and the often discussed intention to regenerate *Northside* was now a concrete reality. The council also announced that the local community was to be directly and actively involved in the regeneration process. Despite these proclamations the local community's initial reactions can be best described as guarded. That is, they remained unconvinced after 10-15 years experience of inadequate housing management that the council was capable of delivering the CEI programme:

> Obviously there had been a lot of work done behind the scenes before it became public that there was going to be this R-E-G-E-N-E-R-A-T-I-O-N of the estate! But even then a lot of people didn't believe it! I think that a lot of people, until things ACTUALLY started happening, around here don't believe what the council tell them! [...] I don't think it was until people actually started getting moved out and buildings being demolished that people actually believed that it was REALLY going to happen!
>
> (Interviewee 6)

> [The council] held a public meeting in the community hall and said: 'We are going to redevelop this area and you will be given a chance to vote on how much of the property you want down [i.e. demolished]. [...] I think that the tenants then knew that it was going to happen. But, "I'll believe it when I see it" used to be the attitude as much as anything.
>
> (Interviewee 7)

In light of this scepticism, compounded by pressures from central government to involve tenants more, the council embarked on a programme to stimulate wider community involvement. Traditional top-down consultative techniques – leaflet drops, newsletters, public meetings, open days and exhibitions – were used initially. In addition, surveys were conducted to measure and monitor peoples' views about the regeneration programme. Furthermore, in recognition of the ethnic diversity within the estate, information was translated into a number of different languages including Bengali, Turkish/Kurdish and Vietnamese. Additionally, interpreters were used at open days, exhibitions and community forum meetings. A local Turkish resident, and a member of the NCF, was also employed by the NO on an *ad hoc* basis as an interpreter/mediator with the growing Turkish/Kurdish community.

As the regeneration process gradually gathered momentum so too did consultation with tenants and NCF member:

> [Consultation] for the first period was VERY w-e-a-k and flimsy! BUT! As things have started to HAPPEN the NCF and the Neighbourhood Office have got their act together. Having started working together in harmony there's been more and more consultation and more and more information – because there's been more information to throw out! They're telling tenants what's happening! [...] So, NOW the information that we're getting is a lot better than what it was 2-3 years ago!
>
> (Interviewee 6)

> I would say [consultation] was GOOD! They leafleted all the blocks and there was plenty of information [when] one of the blocks was blown down! They give us information as to when land is being handed over to the different housing associations. We get information as to what stage [the regeneration process] is at

and whether land has been handed over and when plans for buildings have been approved and all that kind of thing.   (Interviewee 8)

The above comments provide a good illustration of the council's evolving commitment to community participation. Simultaneously, it became increasingly clear during fieldwork that a genuinely mutually understanding relationship prevailed between the NO and the NCF. There were often frank and intense exchanges between both parties and other interests at meetings. There were also 'behind-the-scenes' manoeuvres. Notably, the NCF Chairman had developed a special rapport with the council's CEI at the NO. Furthermore, their relationship was generally seen as a positive thing amongst NCF members.

Ultimately, the relationship that evolved between the NO and NCF was another instrumental facet in the latter's ability to participate effectively in decision-making. As with consultation, the participation process was beset with various problems during its initial phases. The NCF (and NO) overcame these problems and, in the process, it was able to carve out an autonomous identity and influential role within the CEI programme.

Involving the Local Community

From Oligarchic to Pluralistic Community Structures

Members of the local community could only 'formally' participate within the CEI programme if they were members of a recognized community forum. When the CEI programme commenced the tenant movement was oligarchic in structure. Local community politics was dominated by a single organization, the NTA.

The NTA was very much a product of 1970s tenants' activism (Cairncross *et al*, 1994; Cooper and Hawtin, 1997b; Hague, 1990). It was primarily concerned with housing management issues (e.g. repairs and maintenance, rents and refuse collection). Moreover, it was comprised almost exclusively of elderly 'white' tenants. As a result, its agenda favoured the interests of elderly 'whites'. This was reflected in the activities, for example, bingo, bowls and an OAPs luncheon club, held at the 'old' community hall. Other user-groups (e.g. a karate club and a steel band), with a mainly 'black' youth clientele also, used the community hall. There, however, were concerns amongst council officers that the NTA over-zealously managed the community centre and coveted its 'ownership'.

The control of the NTA and the community centre was rooted in deep 'socio-cultural attachments' (May, 1996) held by the NTAs founding members. These members had lived in the area for 40-60 years; had experienced the first redevelopment of the estate in the late 1960s and were involved in the campaign during the 1980s to have the estate regenerated. They, consequently, saw themselves as the vanguards of the neighbourhood.

Despite its role in bringing about the regeneration of *Northside*, the NTA was not deemed to have the necessary qualities to act as the voice of the community by the new pragmatic council. A number of council officers commented that it was an organization that was 'closed minded', 'backward looking' and 'lacking teeth'. More crucially, as an elderly 'white' dominated organization, in a neighbourhood with a majority BME population (58 per cent), it was seen as an 'unrepresentative rump' by a 'white' senior council officer. This same officer suggested that BME under-representation was largely attributable to the presence of a former senior NTA member, who was described as "nothing more than a racist bigoted git".[1] Another officer, a 'black female', was also of the view that some subtle racism was at play within the NTA. Simultaneously, however, she felt that elderly 'white' NTA members were jealously guarding what they had founded and built up:

> The ['white'] people running the TAs at the time had been there for years. Their view of things was: "This is *my* estate! My dad lived here and I've lived here"! All the time they were saying – "These people [i.e. BME tenants] don't want to join in". It never occurred to them to find out WHY BME tenants didn't want to take part! The attitude was – "Well they don't want to join! They can't be bothered"! It wasn't a nasty sort of thing! They hadn't excluded people on purpose it was just how they saw things. It was a very narrow view of life!   (Interviewee 13)

The Oligarchic Backlash

As part of its newly found pragmatism and the profile of the NTA, the council decided it was opportune to set up a new community structure, the NCF. In an effort to create a more representative NCF, a strong equal opportunities statement was inserted in its constitution.

Somewhat expectedly, the setting up of the NTA antagonized a number of established community activists on the NTA. They felt that all their efforts over the years were being overlooked. One long-standing NTA, an elderly 'white' female, was so incensed that the NTA had been superseded by NCF that she 'retired' from community activism altogether. She complained that the 'newcomers' (i.e. NCF members) had no right to be accorded power and responsibility since they had not been involved in the NTA-led campaigns against the council to have the estate redeveloped during the 1980s.

The NTA sought to frustrate the NCFs development by being uncooperative with the NO during the initial phases of the regeneration process. But, as it became increasingly clear that the council was fully committed to the NCF, the NTA reluctantly joined it, appointing its Chairman (an elderly 'white' English male) as their representative on the NCF committee. In short, the NTA had come to the realization that if it was going to retain some sense of influence within the new regeneration process it had to be on the inside of it. Interestingly, the NTA representative recounted in interview that he was actually asked to be NCF Chairman. He acquiesced, however, citing that it would be inappropriate to hold too many positions of power. Nevertheless, he did assume the post of Vice-

---

[1]   This comment was made off-air following the council officer's request to stop recording so that he could name the person he was referring to.

Chairman for a period thereby ensuring that the NTA retained a grip on the reins of community politics.

Divisions between the NTA and NCF were resolved after 6-12 months of groundwork by the NCF's first tenants' advisor who noted in interview that he had to work extremely hard to even get the 'more pro-active and forward thinking [NTA] members' to sign up to the NCF.

Community Participation: A Hostage to Policy Short-sightedness?

Despite its commitment to community involvement there were two major flaws with LB Hackney's participation vision and strategy. If these flaws had not been identified then community participation would almost certainly have been held as an unwitting hostage to policy shortsightedness.

The first flaw was operational in nature and transpired during the early phases of the regeneration process. The council seemed to be under the impression that expressing a commitment to participation and granting access to decision-making arenas was sufficient for the local community to be in a position to readily and easily participate in the regeneration process. The council, however, had naïvely overlooked that the fact that the majority of new members on the NCF had limited knowledge and experience of the nuances of urban regeneration. The NCF, therefore, was at the risk of being rendered an ineffective community structure as the regeneration process gathered momentum. The NCF's first tenants' advisor detected the council's lack of foresight on this front highlighting that sufficient time had to be made for community participation to evolve:

> ... we recognise the ease with which tenant participation in a complex, and fast moving programme can be become geared to the needs and timetables of officers rather than tenants. In such a situation it is often only the tenant activists who have the skills, energy and knowledge base to keep and exert any influence. [...] ... the critical-path timetables we had seen *assumed* rather than *planned* for tenant consultation [and] without such timetabled consultation periods... you are left with the near certainty that, when the rush is on, tenant participation is squeezed.
>
> (*Northside* Tenants' Advisor Report, 1993:12)

The second flaw in LB Hackney's participatory vision was a strategic one. In simple terms, the council's objective of creating sustainable community participation, as directed by central government, was in effect being negated by another government policy commitment, a reduction in homelessness. The council had to sign up to this latter policy commitment, known as the '70/30 Rule', in order to secure government funding for the regeneration of *Northside*. The '70/30 Rule' rule stipulated that 70 per cent of all new housing association housing on the newly regenerated estate had to be allocated to households from the councils' homelessness register. In other words, only 30 per cent of pre-existing tenants would be allocated a new home whilst 70 per cent would be decanted and re-allocated accommodation elsewhere in the borough. Both the NCF and the NTA objected vehemently to this policy.

It was actually the NCF who highlighted to both the council and the government the contradictory impacts of the '70/30 rule'. On the one hand it was argued to be a threat to the already precarious 'sense of community' within the area. And, on the other hand, it was contended that the '70/30 Rule' would ultimately result in a failed regeneration project. The NCF contended that by allocating the majority of new housing to homeless households, with no social attachments to the area or involvement in the regeneration process, *Northside* would remain a highly problematic and difficult to manage community and estate:

> When they nominated people to various phases, it would have been based on a 70/30 principle. That is, 70 per cent of new housing would be homeless people and 30 per cent would be for local people. Now, this is where we went to town. It meant that people who wanted to remain on the estate and who had lived here for donkey's years wouldn't be able to. Would that be fair that they would have to be shifted out to somewhere were they didn't want to go and be replaced with homeless people – with all sympathies to homeless people? (Interviewee 11)

Both flaws with the council's participatory vision were gradually resolved. The operational problem was offset through the actions of the tenants' advisor who secured training, facilities and other support for the NCF who through time developed the skills and political nous to engage with bureaucratic decision-makers. This manifested itself most explicitly when the NCF by-passed the council and the Housing Corporation and successfully lobbied central government to have the '70/30 Rule' overturned on the grounds that it contradicted its own policy commitments to effective community participation and creating sustainable communities.

It is also interesting to note that objections to the '70/30 Rule' came from both 'black' and 'white' NCF members. This shared objection was grounded very much in their shared housing-class experience (Rex and Moore, 1967; Saunders, 1990).

Community Participation and Representativeness

Representative Community Forum Structures?

The early development of the NCF proved to be an extremely testing period in terms of creating an organized and representative community forum. In the first 12-18 months of the regeneration process the NCF had only managed to attract 8-10 'regular' participants. Notably, the majority of these members were 'white' females. The NTA Chairman was one of only two males on the NCF. The other male was the local ward councillor who the NTA Chairman had reservations about. In terms of ethnic representation during this early period, the NCF comprised two 'black' Caribbean females, one of whom had joined when it was initially set up in 1992 and described herself as a founding member. However, both of these 'black' tenants' participation tended to be slightly erratic due to family commitments.

The NCF had two 'white' female Chairmen during the early phases of its development. Both, however, resigned during the course of 1993. Their resignations, particularly that of the second Chairman, had a serious negative effect on morale and progress within the NCF. The second Chairman was viewed as 'an active and well-informed committee member' (Interviewee 18). Her resignation was prompted by the pressures of trying to balance the time-consuming responsibilities of the post, without any financial recompense, with personal and family commitments. Both resignations compounded the problems (e.g. in-fighting between 'old' and 'new' activists, recruiting new members and developing a sense of identity, purpose and influence) within the NCF as it sought to acclimatize to the regeneration process.

Following the resignation of the second female Chairman, the NTAs representative was promoted to 'Acting Chairman'. This helped to extend the NTA's dominance within local community politics. In the intervening period, whilst nominations were sought to elect a new Chairman, the NCF temporarily reverted back to being an 'oligarchic' community forum.

A total of seven nominations were received for the post of NCF Chairman: six for the local ward councillor and one for the founding 'black' female member of the NCF. The 'black' female nominee stood down claiming that she lacked the necessary confidence and experience for the post. Her nomination, however, points to the emergence of a progressive attitude within the NCF, something that was unimaginable within the NTA. As will be shown later, by 1998 the majority of members and officer posts on the NCF, and other community forums, were held by BME tenants. The local councillor was duly elected Chairman at a specially convened meeting, attended by only eight people, where he received a total of seven votes. The NTA's representative expressed acute dissatisfaction at the local councillor's appointment as NCF Chairman:

> Our Chairman [at one stage] was a Councillor much to my disgust and I was the Vice-chair. I've never been one of those that have approved of councillors being part of tenants meetings because I don't believe [they] can wear two hats. He can't work for the Council and work for us at the same time! [He's] a nice man! BUT! I don't think he was really as effective as he should have been. To be honest, at one time he shut me up while I was really having a bash at the Chief Co-ordinator and a member of the executive from the town hall. I was really going to town on them and he cut me off. The tenants told me afterwards that they felt inclined to walk out of that meeting because of that. As I say, I'm very sceptical about councillors being involved. (Interviewee 7)

It is apparent from the above comment that the NTA representative's negative attitude was grounded in his self-perceived position of power being usurped by the local councillor. Despite these criticisms, the councillor was instrumental in nurturing a more structured, democratic and informed NCF. This was a function of his understanding of political processes and 'insider knowledge' about decision-making at the town hall. The NCF's own consultant advisor described the local councillor as being 'very dedicated to the [NCF]'. He was also highly regarded by the NCF Chairman at the time of fieldwork. And, another member of the NCF saw him as a valuable asset in terms of acquiring information:

> We had a councillor who was democratically elected as Chair of the NCF. [...] He's brought x amount of things from Council meetings to NCF meetings and put them to us. As Chair of the NCF he had to report back what was happening in the Council chambers. [...] So, I think we've been – how can I say it? – Lucky in reality to have a person like him. Cos' he lives in the area as well. He knew what was happening. He knew all about the development on *Northside* because of [his attendance] at the big council meetings and all that.   (Interviewee 12)

The election of the local councillor as Chairman loosened the NTA's grip on the reins of power within the NCF. This enabled attention to be refocused on widening the NCF's membership base and developing an understanding of the regeneration process so that it could engage more effectively in decision-making. In other words, the NCF had reverted back to having a pluralistic agenda.

Ethno-Pluralistic Community Structures?

The membership lists of the three community forums, the NCF, *Northside* Joint Management Board (NJMB) and *Northside* Community Development Trust (NCDT), revealed a total of 30 formally registered tenant activists. This was three times the number of activists involved during the first 18-24 months of the programme. Crucially, in terms of ethnic composition, BMEs constituted the majority (57 per cent) of members across all community forums. Furthermore, in terms of the gender profile of community forums, females accounted for the majority (63 per cent) of members. In simple statistical terms, the ethnic profile of community forums was virtually identical to the overall proportion of BMEs (58 per cent) within *Northside*. In comparison, females were significantly over-represented (63 per cent) across all three forums where they constituted 55 per cent of the neighbourhood's population.

Closer analysis of the membership across the different forums revealed significant variations in the representation of 'whites' and BMEs and males and females (see Table 5.3). The oldest, largest and most influential community forum, the NCF, comprised 22 members: 21 tenants and a local councillor. The proportion of 'white' (45 per cent) and BME (55 per cent) members on the NCF was broadly similar to that of the wider estate population – 42 and 58 per cent respectively.

The NJMB, set up in 1997, was the second oldest forum. Its remit was housing management issues on the new housing stock managed by the *Northside* Housing Association Consortium (NHAC).[2] BMEs and females were significantly over-represented on this forum accounting for 72 and 82 per cent of members respectively. Similar levels of over-representation were also found on the youngest

---

[2]   The NHAC was a partnership involving several mainstream and BME housing associations.

community forum, the NCDT, which was concerned with developing a community-led social and economic regeneration strategy for the area.

Table 5.3 Ethnic and Gender Profile of Community Forums (*Northside*)

Community Forum	Ethnic group				Gender			
	BME		*'white'*		*male*		*female*	
	No.	(%)	No.	(%)	No.	(%)	No.	(%)
NCF	12	(55)	10	(45)	10	(45)	12	(55)
NJMB	8	(72)	3	(28)	2	(18)	9	(82)
NCDT*	9	(82)	2	(18)	5	(45)	6	(55)
All 3 forums	17	(57)	13	(43)	11	(37)	19	(63)
Northside Pop.	-	(58)	-	(42)	-	[+](45)	-	[+](55)

* Excludes officer members (the NCDT had two officer members).
[+] Based on all males/females aged 18+ years old.

Source: Northside Community Forum Membership lists (1997, 1998); PPCR (1996).

It should be noted that despite the general ethno-plurality across all three forums, the breadth of ethnic diversity was narrower on the NJMB and NCDT. The NCF was the most ethnically diverse forum, with members drawn from a range of ethnic backgrounds: 'majority' (i.e. British/English) and 'minority' (i.e. Irish and Scottish) 'white' communities; and BMEs of 'black' (i.e. Afro-Caribbean/West Indian/Black British) and Turkish origins. Both the NJMB and the NCDT comprised mainly 'white' English/British and 'black' members, although the NJMB had a member of North African origin. Whilst it cannot be said that the various community forums were wholly representative of *Northside*'s multi-ethnic population, they were all mindful of their neighbourhood's ethnic diversity.

Symbolic Power of Authority within Community Forums

Who held the *symbolic* positions (i.e. Chairman, Vice-Chairman, Secretary and Treasurer) of authority within the NCF and other community forums? Historically, a 'white' male has always held the Chairmanship of the NTA. This patriarchal stranglehold on community leadership was broken following the setting up of the NCF which, as already noted, had two 'white' female Chairmen during its first year of operation. The Chairmanship of the NCF reverted back to being held by a 'white' male, firstly, by the local ward councillor following the resignation of the last female Chairman and then by the current post-holder who was appointed in 1995.

The establishment of the NCF also paved the way for increased participation by BME tenants thereby breaking the old ethnic homogeneity that prevailed within the NTA. As already noted, BMEs and women came to be significantly represented on new community forums, over-represented in fact on the NJMB and NCDT.

Patriarchy: A Matter of Concern?

The patriarchal leadership of the NCF gave rise to concerns amongst several senior CEI officers. Whilst it was recognized that the NCF was 'representative' of the wider community, it was felt that the Chairmanship of the NCF was still the preserve of 'white' males. Additionally, there was a (mis)perception that BMEs were being excluded from holding positions of power within the other forums on the estate. In other words, these officers were of the view that discriminatory processes were in operation. The comments of one senior officer help to illustrate the perceived notion that BMEs were denied access to positions of authority:

> I have to say truthfully that the NCF has been representative! Well, FAIRLY representative, of the community! BUT! Having said that, it's at the lower level! THEY'RE JUST MEMBERS! What I'm saying is the NCF, and most of the other groups, except for the JMB, AS IT HAPPENS, the Chairmanship has gone from 'white' male to 'white' male! There was ONE stage when there was a 'white' female who was the Chair of the NCF. But, in general, 'white' males have held the higher positions! [...] The highest position attained by a 'black' person, in my opinion, has been the current one – the Vice-chair! I've NEVER EVER seen anybody but 'white' Anglo-Saxons in the position of Chair! Rightly or wrongly, that can be taken in many ways but I'm SURE that it's almost as if – "Oh! The 'black' residents aren't interested"! But there are some very capable ['black'] people there and it's just sad that they never reach that position!   (Interviewee 13)

It, indeed, was true that the NCF had yet to have a 'black' Chairman. The claim, however, that BMEs were 'just members' was wholly inaccurate. BME tenants actually held *all* the other officer posts (i.e. Vice-Chairman, Treasurer and Secretary) within the NCF and were, in fact, into their second or third terms of office. Moreover, they were more than content with the positions they held and had no apparent aspirations to be Chairman on account of having family and work commitments. In contrast, the Chairman was retired and was in a position to devote more time to working for and leading the NCF. As his 'black' colleagues noted:

> The [Chairman's] more in touch with all that's going on! Whether it's because he's more knowledgeable about procedures or the fact that he's got more time and actually goes to either the CEI office, this person or that person and has meetings and talks with all these people. He has certain things that the rest of us WOULD NOT feel or know about!   (Interviewee 9)

I mean, being the Chair of the NCF [involves] a lot of work and you have to know so much of, not just *Northside*, but the whole [regeneration] system: Where the money's coming from! Who you go to when you think they're trying to make a fool out of us. There's so much to it. You couldn't just come along and do the job the present Chair is doing.   (Interviewee 10)

It is important to point out that the NCF Chairman was *not* part of the old 'white' vanguard that had dominated community politics during the 1970s and 1980s. In fact, he had no prior experience of community politics when he joined the NCF. Despite his lack of experience, he brought considerable enthusiasm, open-mindedness and leadership to the NCF:

The current Chairman emerged on the scene some time down the line because he wasn't an original member of the NCF! But he displayed an interest and he didn't seem to have any axes to grind! He was GENUINELY interested in it for its own sake! I eventually persuaded him that he should put himself forward and I was delighted when he was voted as Chairman of the NCF. He has done so ever since and has done really well!   (Interviewee 3)

Pragmatism and Meritocracy

Fundamentally, the elevation and retention of this elderly 'white' tenant, with no prior history of community activism, as Chairman was not premised on 'white' nepotism since BMEs constituted the majority of NCF members. Instead, his appointment pointed towards a pragmatic and meritocratic attitude within the NCF. He was deemed by other NCF members to be the best person to lead the NCF on account of his knowledge of the regeneration process, relations with the NO and his capacity to commit time to leading the NCF.

A further indication of the evolving pragmatic and meritocratic culture within community structures was evident in the experiences of a North African tenant, a relative newcomer to the neighbourhood. Despite having only lived in *Northside* for two years and speaking relatively little English, this tenant attained the positions of Vice-Chairman and Treasurer on the NJMB and NCDT respectively. He outlined in interview that he encountered no significant barriers, other than language initially, or attempts to deliberately exclude him from joining the NJMB or NCDT. As a 'newcomer' and a non-English speaker it was difficult to comprehend what was going on in meetings but other members made him feel very welcome. Moreover, he was able to make use of an interpreter at meetings and attended English language classes at the Neighbourhood Resource Centre (NRC), all of which was funded under the regeneration programme.

Crucially, the election of the North African tenant to the positions of symbolic authority on the NJMB and NCDT were premised on a combination of factors. First and foremost, he *wanted* to get involved in community politics for personal and altruistic purposes. He commented that getting involved was an ideal way to learn and improve his English and develop an understanding of localized British culture. Participation was also seen as a means of integrating into the local community. His altruistic motives were premised on the fact that he had been involved in a housing co-operative in his own country and the treasurer of a small refugee support group in London. Lastly, as a qualified accountant, albeit that his qualifications were not recognized in the UK, he was deemed by his NCDT peers to be the right person to assume the post of Treasurer. The NCDT even provided funding to cover the costs of an accountancy conversion course so that he was 'officially' qualified.

More Than Just Members?

Returning to the assertion that BMEs were 'just members' and excluded from holding positions of power, this was thoroughly contradicted by the fact that *all* officer posts within both the NJMB and NCDT were held by BMEs. This can be clearly seen in Table 5.4 below.

Table 5.4 Positions of Power and Responsibility by Ethnicity and Gender on Community Forums (*Northside*)[3]

Position	NCF	NJMB	NCDT
Chairperson	WM1	BF3	BF4
Vice-Chairperson	BM1	BM3	BM1
Treasurer	BF1	BF8	BM3
Secretary	BF2	-	BF3

Source: NCF, NJMB and NCDT Membership Lists

Profoundly, this 'BME-ization' of community structures had gone virtually unnoticed by another senior BME officer also concerned about the exclusion of 'black' tenants from positions of authority. It was brought to her attention during an interview that the NJMB was actually made up predominantly of BMEs and women. Her response was one of complete astonishment:

> NJMB meetings are predominantly female and 'black'? REALLY? OH GOOD! OH GOOD! Oh Good! I'm pleased to hear that! That's very interesting! I've missed out on that then! I would be interested to go along to a meeting were PREDOMINANTLY 'black' tenants are attending meetings which would be such a change to all the normal meetings that I've ever attended.   (Interviewee 14)

Interestingly, it never struck this officer or other CEI officers critical of the historical dominance of 'whites', that the now significant over-representation of 'black' tenants on community forums was, demographically speaking, akin to the ethnic exclusivity that had prevailed within the much-maligned NTA. The key differences between the NTA and the new community structures were that the latter

---

[3]   The letter and numbers (e.g. WM1 and BF2) refer to ethnic/racial (i.e. W = 'white' and B = 'black') and gender (i.e. M= male and F = female) identity of different individuals.

advocated and sought to actively enhance inclusivity by regularly attempting to recruit new members from across the neighbourhood.

The Over-represented and the Passive Minority

So far, it has been suggested that new community forums within *Northside* were pluralistic and meritocratic structures in terms of their aims, objectives and membership. Of course, community forums were not wholly representative of all interest or social groups within *Northside*. It would be more accurate to describe community forums as *imperfectly pluralistic* structures. Their imperfect membership profile was the function of two inter-related factors.

On the one hand, there was a 'core group' of nine tenant activists (30 per cent), predominantly BMEs, who were members on two or all three forums. Five activists (two BME males and females and one 'white' female) were members of two community forums; and, three (one BME male and four BME females) were on three community forums. The over-concentration of the same people tends to be a fairly common feature within community structures in neighbourhood regeneration. Moreover, such scenarios may also give rise to potential problems. For example, forums may lose their dynamism and creativity as a consequence of the lack of 'new blood'. Additionally, they may be perceived as 'closed shops' and the preserve of local community elites, thereby deterring normally non-active or apathetic tenants from joining (Anastacio *et al*, 2000; Hastings *et al*, 1996; Taylor, 2000). In overall terms, the NCF (and the NJMB) did not really suffer from any of these problems.

On the other hand, there were several small BME communities, Turkish/Kurdish, 'Asian' and Vietnamese, who were passively or indirectly represented on community forums. The Turkish community, for example, was closely wedded to the regeneration process. A young Turkish male graduate was in fact a full member of the NCF. His attendance at meetings was somewhat erratic however. But, as already noted, he had been employed as an interpreter by the NO and was quite *au fait* with local regeneration issues. The Turkish community in *Northside* had fairly good access to the NCF through this agent. As for the Vietnamese and 'Asian' both of these communities tended to utilize their own support networks and community organizations that would make representations to community forums, the council or NHAC. As an officer from one of the BME housing associations on the NHAC commented:

> [...] A lot of our housing association's activities in the past have come via the mosques! I still believe that there is a reluctance amongst [our tenants] to go to the council and statutory providers! The mosque is where people voice their concerns rather than the normal routes such as councillors and so on!   (Interviewee 15)

The passive or indirect representation of these various BME groups should not be perceived as being a particularly problematic issue. These communities were not being deliberately excluded from joining community structures or the regeneration process in any way. It was clear from interviews and observations of forum meetings that their lack of active representation was grounded in a complex mix of inter-related factors. These included: (i) lack of group self-confidence; (ii) lack of strong community leadership; (iii) language barriers; (iv) small population size; (v) low sense of attachment to the area; and (vi) cultural traits and group preferences. As another officer from the NHAC succinctly noted in relation to the Vietnamese and Turkish communities:

> The Vietnamese are a very shy people – very very shy people! You would need someone there who was VERY DYNAMIC, VERY CONFIDENT! You would probably get that in someone who has been born and bred here. [...] A lot of it is to do with confidence. A lot of it is just keeping themselves to themselves. And, a lot of it might also be to do with that they don't feel as though they REALLY belong. [...] I think their community also needs to get bigger! With the diverse client group here they don't feel comfortable in that because they're quite a small minority. If Vietnamese residents do have problems they have their own organizations that they to go to where everybody is Vietnamese! That's the kind of conditions they feel comfortable in! The Turkish/Kurdish are quite a large group but their problem is language! They're quite confident in putting across a viewpoint or if they feel that something should be changed. But it's the language barrier! We've tried to address that by getting translators in.   (Interviewee 16)

Although community forums meetings, especially when CEI/NHAC officers and other professionals (e.g. architects and surveyors) were in attendance, tended to be quite formal arenas, efforts were made to make them open and friendly. In an effort to engender self-confidence and facilitate more direct involvement by under-represented BME groups, a number of strategic and operational measures were undertaken. These included: leaflets, posters and newsletters in a range of languages; delivering English language classes at the NRC; and holding pre-meetings before NJMB meetings for Turkish/Kurdish tenants, in their own language, on account of being the fastest growing under-represented group within the neighbourhood.

Despite imperfections in community representativeness both community and institutional structures expressed and a high degree of commitment and, more importantly, actively sought to ensure that as broad a range of tenants as possible were informed and engaged in the regeneration process. Moreover, the lack of and/or passive participation by certain BME communities on the NCF was not premised on racist or exclusionary processes *per se* (Cooper and Hawtin, 1997b; Munt, 1991; Ratcliffe, 1992; Taylor, 2000). As will be seen later, within *Northside* 'race' was an issue of declining significance (Wilson, 1980).

Community Power and Influence

After the various problems with the council's community consultation/participation vision and strategy had been ironed out and inter- and intra-conflict within the NTA and NCF had been resolved, the NCF found itself, for the first time, ready to participate in decision-making. The NCF's accumulation of 'community power' hinged on its ability to interpret the political nuances of the regeneration process and act decisively against policies that it considered unfair. The ability to operate in this way was grounded in several key factors: the council's commitment to community participation, community cohesiveness and strong leadership within the NCF and a mutually understanding and trusting relationship between the NCF and the NO.

The various resources, especially the tenants' advisors and tenant training, provided by the council enabled the NCF to become a much more organized and focused structure. The first tenants' advisor was instrumental in setting up a series of sub-groups (i.e. Design; Training and Employment; Community Facilities; Senior Citizens; Children and Young People and Housing Management) that enabled NCF members to *specialize* in key aspects of the regeneration programme. This division of labour approach meant that that the NCF was in a position to develop a clearer and deeper understanding of different aspects of the regeneration process. With the passage of time the NCF developed a solid understanding of the nuances of the regeneration process. Moreover, the various NCF sub-groups subsequently evolved into autonomous community forums – NJMB (Housing Management and Design); NCDT (Community Facilities, Training and Employment and Children and Young People); and NTMO (Senior Citizens) – as the regeneration process unfolded and matured.

The various tenants, especially the core group of nine activists, who had been actively involved in the regeneration process, must also be credited for the community power the NCF has accumulated. These members displayed a dogged enthusiasm, determination and commitment throughout the regeneration process. The NCF managed to overcome the various problems throughout the participation process due to a strong sense of community cohesiveness, a function of members' shared housing-class experience, and the leadership qualities of their Chairman, who was elected in 1995 and was still in post when fieldwork ended in late 1998.

The development of good working relations between the NCF and CEI officers, largely due to efforts of the Chairman, helped to foster trust and mutual understanding between both sides. The 'them and us' mentality that tends to pervade many regeneration schemes had literally been eradicated (Taylor, 1995). Even the most critical and suspicious member of the NCF, the NTA Chairman, acknowledged the council and the CEI neighbourhood offices' openness and honesty:

> We have a very good relationship with the CEI! They have been very good, that is, in giving – mind you they have the money in the budget anyway – us an office and equipment to run in a proper fashion. They are APPROACHABLE! The whole atmosphere or relationship between the NCF and the CEI office is absolutely amicable and friendly. [...] It makes you suspicious doesn't it? But, it's a fact! I think they understand the problems. If they have any problems they explain them to us. If their hands are tied about a certain thing they will explain why their hands are tied.   (Interviewee 11)

NCF: A Force to be Reckoned With?

As a result of the aforementioned factors, the NCF evolved into a respected and influential partner within the regeneration process:

> I THINK when [the council] first came up with the idea of the NCF I DON'T think that they envisaged it being like it is! I think they're view of what the forum would be like would be a lot more limited than what it is now! I think the NCF has grown and flourished and become far more PRO-ACTIVE than what I think was envisaged in the first place! [...] MY impression IS that the NCF is a FAIRLY POWERFUL group! Behind the scenes it carries a lot of clout!   (Interviewee 22)

> The NCF is very very very powerful. There are only a few of us but it is very very powerful. Because, as I said, at first we used to come along to meetings and they – the architects, the council and the HAs to a lesser extent, would say this is what we're going to do and we'd all sit there like nodding dogs and say "OK! OK"! And then, a few of us started realizing that they were more or less saying – 'This is what you want' – and we'd be sitting there going "Yeah! Yeah! Yeah"! But after a while we started to realise that without the NCF they can't function. So, now they talk to us rather than talk at us!   (Interviewee 10)

CEI officers expressed similar, if somewhat more measured views, about the *extent* of power wielded by the NCF. It was acknowledged that the NCF had assumed a sense of control over its own destiny and approached its role within the regeneration process in a dedicated and professional manner:

> I think that [the NCF] have quite a lot [of influence]! They attend all the big CEI sub-committee meetings to make their OBJECTIONS! [...] They have quite a lot of say! Of course, not everything is as they see it or as simple as they see it! I think that they are quite ACTIVE in the influences and I think that they're not to be UNDERESTIMATED!   (Interviewee 13)

Despite this more measured assessment of the extent of community power, in the minds of NCF members they perceive themselves very much as a force to be reckoned with:

> I think that the NCF has been VERY VERY influential in a lot of changes and decisions that have been made on *Northside*. Cos' we've actually spoken to – how can I say... the big developers. We speak in the same language as them. We say to them – "You come here and make your money. What you do when you come to the community is not just come and develop something but develop in PARTNERSHIP with the community"! Cos' in the past people have just come and built and they've gone. [...] I think we've done a lot and it has gone from strength to strength and we've become a well-respected body even amongst the other forums on other estates. They're coming to us asking us for ideas about what we've been through and how can they get themselves on the same pedestal as us.   (Interviewee 12)

> I think why we get on so well with the Council is that we don't go barging in there and say – "we want this and we want that"! It's a two-way dialogue. The NCF

didn't have that before. The council used to come along and say – "this is what you're going to do, this is what you're going to do"! But, gradually we've got to the stage that we have a very good working relationship with one another.

(Interviewee 10)

Community Power in Action

As noted earlier, during the first 18-24 months of the regeneration process community participation was fraught with considerable problems. In particular, there were several policies within the regeneration programme that tenants (prior to the actual formation of the NCF) were not fully aware of due to the lack of consultation at the beginning of the programme. It was only after the NCF had been formally constituted and the tenants' advisor had been in place for some time that NCF members became more attuned to the nature and impact of policies contained within the programme. Furthermore, as the NCF slowly matured and became increasingly embedded within the process its members began to assert their 'right' to be more involved. The NCF reminded the council that the programme would only be a success if they directly participated in decision-making:

> [The council] were made to realise that it's part and parcel of their duty and part and parcel of the requirements of the DoE that tenants should be involved in discussions and decisions. They KNOW this and they know that IF this isn't carried out they will be in trouble as far as the NCF committee is concerned. Because the NCF is fully aware of this they KNOW that it has got to be a PARTNERSHIP between tenants and the CEI. [...] The Development Agreement says that tenants have to be consulted on everything, be involved in all consultations, decision-making and so forth. (Interviewee 11)

> The DoE said that the only way that the Council would get the money was if there was TENANT PARTICIPATION. So we looked at tenant participation and we went – TO WHAT LEVEL? [They said] – "You've got a say in how the [estate] is built". What do you mean? How much of a say? [They said] – "You can help us out on the design of your homes. You'll have things like Tenants' Choice, were, if your allocated a [new home], you will be able to say I want red walls with green lines going across it and it will be done for you! (Interviewee 12)

There were three key events during the early stages of the regeneration process where the NCF demonstrated astute policy nous and an ability to influence decision-making.

First, the NCF were not overly impressed by the size and housing density of properties built during the first phase of the housing redevelopment. The first phase of new houses, whilst conforming to a more traditional terraced design, were so small that they were colloquially referred to as 'the skinny houses'. The NCF approached the council to express their concerns and to lobby for the Development Agreement to be altered. The NCF convinced the council, who were also somewhat disappointed by the new homes, and the developers to increase space standards on all subsequent housing developments.

Secondly, the NCF managed to overturn the NHAC's housing allocation policy. This policy stated that families with at least two children of the same sex, irrespective of their age differences, had to share a bedroom. So, for example, a family with say two boys/girls, of primary and secondary school ages, would only be allocated a two-bed house or flat. Again, this policy sat very uncomfortably with the NCF. Their position was that a family of this type should be allocated a three-bed house/flat, so that both children, especially the elder one had their own room in order to do their homework and so on. After much negotiating the policy was altered to what the NCF demanded:

> The council's bedroom policy was that as long as there's no more than 16 years between the first child and second child they have got to share a bedroom. But, we said that can't work! We went backwards and forwards, backwards and forwards to the Council. They're telling us – "NO! IT HAS GOT TO HAPPEN! IT HAS GOT TO HAPPEN"! Well, we said – "NO IT CAN'T HAPPEN"! We sat down round the table with housing officers, decant officers and four of us [i.e. NFC members] and worked out a policy that is ONLY active on *Northside*. The policy is that if you've got two kids – one of 16 and one of 5 – you get the extra bedroom whether they are the same sex or different sexes. YOU GET THE EXTRA BEDROOM!
>
> (Interviewee 10)

As noted in the comment above, the change in policy only applied to *Northside*. Despite setting a precedent, the council had no intentions of introducing the new allocation policy in other estates across the borough

The most significant demonstration of the NCF ability to influence decision-making ability related to the '70/30 policy'. To reiterate, this policy was a prerequisite in order to secure central government funding. It stipulated that 70 percent of all new NHAC properties had to be allocated to homeless families on the council's homelessness waiting list. The NCF (and NTA) vehemently objected to the policy arguing that it was an unfair and contradictory. It was argued to be unfair on the grounds that established tenants, who had endured years of living in poor housing, were effectively being denied the right to a newly built home if they wished to remain on the estate. Furthermore, the NCF contended that it contradicted and negated the government's policy of creating sustainable communities. It was felt that allocating such a high proportion of new properties to the homeless, with no established or social attachment to the area, would obliterate whatever sense of community still existed within the neighbourhood. The following comment reinforces the sense of anger, as already highlighted towards the '70/30 policy' by tenant activists:

> When [the council] came about with the idea, at the beginning, about the 70/30 split we were afraid and we said – "Hang on! Hang on! What's happening here? If you're going to move 70 percent of homeless people back onto *Northside* then that means that the new *Northside* is going to turn back right around to what it was already". Cos' homeless people... the way *Northside* was, as I envisaged it in the past, everybody knew everybody and people kept the place clean and tidy. [...] So we thought and said to them – "You're breaking up a big community that has been

together for 20, 30, 40 years. How can you chuck away 70 percent and leave 30 percent?" Then that means that the 30 percent's job is going to be so hard. You're going to be swamped by 70 percent... you're going to find it very hard to encourage those people to participate in the community that was working before.

(Interviewee 12)

After approximately 4-6 months of lobbying the local council to change the '70/30 rule', then lobbying central government with the assistance of another community activist who had insider knowledge and contacts and finally gaining the support of the council, the policy was changed to 50/50. The NCF's ability to have a central government policy re-negotiated illustrated the reach of their community power.

Other areas where the NCF flexed its community power muscles included objecting to proposals contained within a self-build housing project. Specifically, the NCF objected to the proposed number of floors in the development and other design features that it considered incongruous with the rest of the neighbourhood. The self-build company was subsequently forced to reduce the number of floors on its proposed development after holding consultations with the NCF who in turn submitted their objections to the proposals to the local planning authority.

The establishment of the NCDT was a further indication of the nature of community power being accumulated within *Northside*.[4] The NCDT had evolved from one of the sub-groups (i.e. Community Facilities) on the NCF. It was an independent community-run organization, with charitable status, concerned with engendering social, economic and environmental sustainability within the neighbourhood for when the CEI programme ended. Its mission was to nurture grass-roots projects via applying for government – local, central and European – funding and forming partnerships with public and private organizations in order to realise its objectives. The NCDT was only in its embryonic stages of development, as fieldwork drew to a close, and was still formulating its aims and objectives. Nevertheless, the NCDT was clear about its strategic vision and had identified its primary client groups – the unemployed and children and young people. Additionally, the NCDT had just appointed a Director to develop a business plan and solidify its aims and objectives.

The NFC/NCDT was particularly clear about one thing – the new community and sports centre. In the run up to the completion of the new community and sports centre, which informally opened during the last few weeks of fieldwork, the NCF/NCDT expressed a keen interest in assuming control of it. They felt that the new centre should be a community-owned asset. The council, however, had some reservations about this. In order for the centre to sustain its existence it had to be run on a profit-making venture. It was felt that the NCDT lacked the appropriate business skills and knowledge to run the centre in this way.

---

[4] The NCDT was created towards the end of fieldwork in *Northside* and as a result no specific research was conducted on this community structure. Some data and information about the NCDT was however collected during interviews and observations of the NCF.

The council, however, did agree to the NCF/NCDT having input into the strategic management of the centre. Furthermore, it was tentatively agreed that the idea of transferring 'ownership' of the centre to the NCDT would be reviewed in the future. The NCF/NCDT, whilst disappointed, accepted this outcome but remained determined to realize their aspiration of owning the centre. It would not be difficult, given the NCF's track record, to imagine the NCDT eventually assuming some kind of 'ownership' of the new community and sports centre.

In concluding this section, the NCF's community power extended to securing changes to both local and central government policies. The NCF's ability to influence change was predicated on several key factors. These included (i) the development of a sophisticated understanding of the political nuances of the regeneration process; (ii) strong community leadership; (iii) presenting a united front; and (iv) forging mutually understanding and respectful relations with policy-makers, especially at the local level. In short, the NCF negotiated change by acting professionally and pragmatically.

The Politics of 'Race'

'Race' has been a highly contentious issue for LB Hackney. Paradoxically, this is despite the council being a leading proponent of anti-racism in the 1980s. The council's housing department, for example, was found guilty of racially discriminating against 'black' tenants (CRE, 1984). In the early 1990s, UNISON, a public sector trade union organization, and Hackney Race Equality Council accused the council of practising racist employment and disciplinary procedures. The issue of racist employment practices arose again in the late 1990s with the publication of the Crawford Report (1997). This report examined employment recruitment and promotion during the early-to-mid 1990s and concluded that BME employees had experienced significant levels of racial discrimination. Simultaneously, the report noted that the council was serious about tackling racism and the future in addressing this problem looked optimistic.

The longest running and arguably, the most damaging, racialized episode in Hackney's recent history relates to the 'Crofton-Yeboah Affair' (Gibson, 2002; Inside Housing, 2003; *The Guardian*, 2002; Weaver, 2001). In short, this event commenced in 1990 following the unearthing of corruption and fraud, mainly involving employees of West African origin, within the Housing Department by its then Director, Bernard Crofton. Crofton subsequently criticized the then head of Personnel, Sam Yeboah, who incidentally was African, for his role in failing to prevent the council from employing fraudulent employees. These criticisms sparked claims of racial harassment from Crofton and the council by Yeboah. The affair caused massive divisions amongst local councillors, many of whom supported Crofton. A long-running legal case ensued. At an employment tribunal in 1998 both the council and Crofton were found guilty of racial discrimination and ordered to pay a record £380,000 and £60,000 respectively in compensation to Yeboah. In 2001, the 1998 decision against Crofton was overturned on appeal; the council, however, did not appeal against the decision against it. In a retrial of the case in 2002 the original 1998 decision was reinstated. Crofton recently sought leave to appeal to the House of Lords against this decision only to be refused in August 2003 – he continues to protest that his actions were not racially motivated.

The problematization of 'race' within Hackney was, in part, due to the existence of historical racism, institutional and street-level bureaucrats. Simultaneously, it was also due to an over-politicization of 'race' by certain elements within the council consumed with the 'moralistic excesses of anti-racism' (Gilroy, 1992: 49). The politicization of 'race' combined with the general 'culture of mistrust and cynicism' (Jacobs, 1999:100) that permeated the council throughout the 1980s and early 1990s was used in an attempt to destabilize the leadership of the council.

Notably, highly charged racial politics was nowhere to be found within *Northside*. The neighbourhood had of course experienced some racialized problems but these were infrequent and minor in nature. Within the context of the NCF and NCDT and the regeneration process in general, 'race' was an unproblematic issue. In fact, it was essentially a 'non-issue'.

Northside and the Declining Significance of 'Race'

It would be naïve to claim that 'race' and racism had never been contentious issues within *Northside*. As noted earlier, the NTA was viewed as a racist community structure. Furthermore, as a socio-economically deprived and multi-ethnic area it would be impossible not to imagine some kind of 'soft' (i.e. verbal abuse) and/or 'hard' (i.e. physical harassment) forms of racism manifesting. For sure, as more and more 'black' families moved onto *Northside* during the late 1970s and 1980s relations between 'white' residents became strained. Furthermore, the British National Party (BNP), a far-right political party, sought to racialize and thus capitalize on community concerns about crime, anti-social behaviour and housing during local elections:

> Things started to get a little bit... WOUND-UP... with regards to the West Indians when all the muggings started and you had mobs of kids sitting out on the street corners. You had them shouting all through the night! People started to get very anti-West Indian because the young West Indians were, if you like, causing aggro to people! [...] People were frightened to walk down the road because of a bunch of youths sitting on the street corner thinking that they were going to get mugged! The chances are that that was TOTALLY wrong but that was the PERCEPTION that was CREATED in people's minds! And, that's why for a long time around here the National Front or the British National Party would stand in the elections and get quite a number of votes! (Interviewee 6)

It is tempting to conclude from the above comment that the implied stereotypical views of the 'black' community were the sole preserve of the wider 'white' community in *Northside*. Fieldwork, however, revealed that 'black' interviewees were equally critical about problems on the estate and implicitly apportioned blame on the 'problem families', who were largely 'black', that had moved to the area during the 1980s:

> I moved in in 1972 and the tower blocks had not long been finished. [The estate] was pretty good. [...] But! By the end of the 1980s you used to get people throwing things off their balconies. Fridges! Televisions! JUST ABOUT EVERYTHING! You took your life in your hand by going out on the balcony.
> (Interviewee 10)

> When we moved [here] everybody knew everybody. People kept the place clean [and] tidy. Then some people moved away – they managed to buy a house or whatever. But, the people that moved in and took their places threw rubbish, babies nappies and dust bags, out their windows. People didn't care anymore! You used to say to people: "Come on this is your community"! Then we found out that more and more people moved out but whoever took their place was five or ten times worse than the people who had lived there before.
> (Interviewee 12)

Personal experience whilst conducting fieldwork also revealed that there were racist individuals living within the wider neighbourhood. Whilst waiting in the reception of the CEI neighbourhood office to conduct an interview with a senior 'black' officer, an encounter with an elderly 'white' tenant, *Mr. Smith*[5], who had actually been encountered during the early phases of fieldwork[6], highlighted the existence of individualized prejudice and racism. *Mr. Smith* approached the reception and asked the officer, a 'black' male, on duty if he could speak to one of the senior officers, a 'black' female. As the officer left the reception to check if the other officer was available, *Mr. Smith* casually stated in a broad London accent and rather dismissive tone:

> For fucks' sake! I see they still 'ave the same old fucking shit workin' in 'ere! Half the one's in 'ere don't even speak English! You wouldn't see 'em doing anything to help the English – would ya?

As there was no one else in the waiting area his comment was clearly directed towards me. Moreover, they were said in such a way to provoke a confirmatory reply. No attempt was made to reply to *Mr. Smith's* comments. Instead, a bemused expression was offered to convey the message – are you speaking to me? The officer on reception duty returned before anything else could be said. He informed *Mr. Smith* that the other officer would be out to see him shortly. I was then led through the office for my appointment with another officer.

It latterly transpired during fieldwork that *Mr. Smith* had actually been involved in the regeneration process during the early stages of community consultation. He was quite well known for his bigoted views and antagonistic attitude towards the regeneration of *Northside*. For example, he considered the

---

[5]   Not his real name.

[6]   I happened to meet Mr Smith in the street and asked him directions to a street I was looking for during the early phases of fieldwork.

NCF Chairman to be a 'sell-out' on account of having good working and social relations with many 'black' tenants, especially those on the NCF. *Mr. Smith* was also somewhat aggrieved that BMEs would the main beneficiaries of the regeneration process. The negative attitude towards the regeneration of *Northside* was also partly fuelled by the fact that he did not stand to benefit directly from the regeneration programme. This was on account that he lived outside the boundary of the regeneration area.

Despite the existence of wider and individual racialized processes their influence on community relations, the regeneration process and community forums were virtually negligible. Research commissioned by the council (LB Hackney, 1998), for example, found that community relations were strong. In a survey of 201 households on the 'new' estate, with a 45 per cent response rate (N=91), the majority of respondents (76 per cent) agreed that the area was 'multi-cultural and the different [ethnic] groups got on well' (p.16). Only 5 per cent of respondents disagreed with this statement. A further indication of the generally unproblematic nature of 'race' within *Northside* was evident, as already noted, from the ethnically diverse profile of the NCF and NCDT and the positions of authority held by BME tenants.

Early observational research of community forum meetings revealed no obvious signs of racialized discourse or tensions within community structures or between the council and community structures. This was somewhat at odds with what had been expected based on a review of the academic literature (Brownill and Thomas, 1998; BTEG, 1995, 1997; Cooper and Hawtin, 1997a; Munt, 1991; Ouseley, 1997; Ratcliffe, 1992). But, as interviews and observations progressed doubts about the unproblematic nature of ' race' were increasingly dispelled.

Officer Perspectives on 'Race'

In overall terms CEI/NHAC officers and other professionals were of the view that 'race' and racism were generally and comparatively non-problematic issues within *Northside*:

> Funnily enough 'race' hasn't been an issue. IT HASN'T!   (Interviewee 19)

> I think 'race' relations are pretty good-natured! In some ways 'race' isn't an issue! I've been involved in groups as a committee member where there was real antagonism between 'blacks' and 'whites' on the committee!   (Interviewee 18)

> 'Race' has never been an issue. We've got a very mixed community there and it's very noticeable that the people represented on the NCF and the most active are elderly 'white' and younger 'black' females!   (Interviewee 3)

> I get the sense that ['race' and ethnicity] hasn't been a big PROBLEM. Completely unlike Central Stepney, for example, where it is DEFINITELY and issue between the Bengali community and the white community [...] Hackney has traditionally always been very much an ethnically diverse area of London for SO LONG now that in many ways people are more comfortable with ethnic diversity!   (Interviewee 20)

There was, however, an underlying expectation that 'race' and racism should have been problematic issues. This seemed to be grounded in officers' past experiences of regeneration schemes in multi-cultural locales where 'race' had been a *real* problematic issue:

> [Community relations] are actually quite good in *Northside*! They're very good because many people are in the same boat. Many of them have lived here for years so consequently they know each other and rely on each other for support. So, in that respect it's actually quite good! [...] There are certain estates where BME people wouldn't be wanted or wouldn't want to go because they would be scared to go! But on the whole I think [community relations] here are pretty good! In comparison to other estates I have worked, community relations on *Northside* are way way up! I think the reason for that is that the local community suffered cockroaches and various other things that have been quite significant on their lives. [All] that's brought people together!   (Interviewee 13)

> Personally, I have seen no racial tension AT ALL in nearly 5 years of working here! I'm familiar with racial tension and I'm familiar with racial harassment. [...] So, I was prepared to witness it here and I would have KNOWN if I had seen it! Surprisingly, I found in *Northside* a community that is LARGELY AT EASE with itself in terms of 'race' due to its diversity! [...] In *Northside* everyone is a MINORITY! So, colour, 'race' and religion aren't really issues!   (Interviewee 4)

Another officer, a 'black' female, recounted how 'race' was *falsely* constructed as a problematic issue in a neighbourhood, *Eastville*, that she had previously worked in by a leading 'black' community activist:

> I used to work on this estate, [*Eastville*] where there were HUGE ROWS [about 'race']! I used to spend half of my life dealing with all that and the personality problems – it was a NIGHTMARE! Whereas here on *Northside* I don't have to do that! We have some [personality] issues. But, by in large they're minimal and I can cope with it and I carry on! But, in Lambeth it was on a different scale! And, it actually held up progress! [...] As for 'race' being an issue there? The Chairman of one of the two community forums will tell you that it is! I have actually thought about it for so long and I think it's actually down to that Chairman and her needs to always be the person who is making decisions! She's got to have the power and she'll use 'race' in order to imply that the EMB and others are not representative. At first I was sucked into that actually! I thought that 'race' was an issue and I was led by that for a long while and went out of my way to try and come in with other structures. [...] But it was only after a period of time that I learnt my lesson!
>   (Interviewee 14)

Despite this officer's experiences of 'false' racism she, along with another 'black' officer (Interviewee 13) expressed disbelief that 'race' and racism were not problematic issues. At one stage during interviewing it seemed as if both of these interviewees almost wished that 'race' was a more problematic issue.

There were some concerns amongst officers about the under-representation of the Turkish/Kurdish community and other non-English speaking groups on community forums. But, the absence of such groups from community forums, as already discussed, had little or nothing to do with racial discrimination. Relatedly, the assertion by Interviewee 4 that all groups on *Northside* had some form of 'minority' status was reinforced in comments made by the NCF's original tenants' advisor. He noted that during the formative stages of the NCF when structures and priorities were finalized 'race' barely made it onto the agenda. Instead, a 'whole of community' feeling prevailed within the NCF:

> No, I don't remember 'race' ever raising its head to the point where you actually needed to have a sub-group looking at community relations! I think it's because – who were the minority on *Northside*? Was it the 'white' elderly? Was it the children? Was it the 'black' Afro-Caribbeans? I mean, it wasn't that clear really!
>
> (Interviewee 18)

A consortium of mainstream and BME housing associations, an ethnically diverse mix of staff working at the neighbourhood level and a fair housing allocations policy were also seen as contributing to the overall positive nature of community relations within the neighbourhood and the insignificance of 'race' within the regeneration process:

> Certainly from my experience [the local community] all work well together. I don't see any problems! I think its worked very well having a consortium made up of mainstream and BME housing associations.
>
> (Interviewee 19)

> It doesn't matter what your religion or what your ethnic background is, if you need rehoused then you get rehoused! And, all the different HA houses are intermingled on site! 'RACE', ETHNIC BACKGROUND, RELIGION HAS NEVER been a cause of contention! And, I'll tell you why it has not been a cause of contention. [...] Mrs. Smith from the West Indies has moved in next door to Mr. McLaughlin from Ireland who's moved in next door to Mrs. Begum from Pakistan who's moved in next door to Mrs. Kushlar from Turkey all at the same time! Consequently, no one has had time to take ownership of their territory!
>
> (Interviewee 16)

It was also clear from observations that officers' overall positive and open approach to community consultation/participation also contributed to 'race' being rendered a non-issue. Both 'black' and 'white' officers behaved professionally towards both 'black' and 'white' community activists in equal measure. There were no signs of a paternalistic relationship between officers and community activists, unlike in *Westside* (see Chapter 7).

In summary, there were some very minor concerns about 'race' amongst officers and other professional agents. On the whole, however, 'race' was seen as unproblematic. This view was also supported in the survey commissioned by the council which found that 'there was overwhelming support amongst officers that *Northside* was a multi-cultural neighbourhood and the different groups got on well together' (LB Hackney, 1998:18).

Community Activists' Perspectives on 'Race'

The generally positive views on 'race' expressed by officers are but one side of the story. The 'real' acid test of the significance of 'race' within the NCF (and NCDT) and the regeneration process in overall terms are the views and experiences of community activists.

One of the most striking features to emerge from the observational fieldwork of community forum meetings and related events plus numerous casual encounters with various individuals was the absence of any racialized conflict or antagonisms. There, of course, were individual and intra-group conflicts but these minor, infrequent and based more on personality clashes. The NCF Chairman, for example, was perceived by a 'white' female NCF member as something of a 'Yes Man' due to his close relationship with the CEI neighbourhood office. There was a hint of envy from several 'black' female activists towards the NCF Vice-Chairman (a 'black' male). And, vice versa, the NCF Vice-Chairman was critical of the leadership style exhibited by the 'black' females that headed up the NJMB. Such personality conflicts are inevitable within any formal organization.

Given the ethnic diversity and high levels of socio-economic deprivation within *Northside* and the wider geographical area and the occasional presence of the NF/BNP, it would be difficult to conceive that racism or racists *never* penetrated *Northside*. The NCFs Chairman, for example, acknowledged that there had been incidents of 'soft' racism within the neighbourhood but contended that it never manifested into anything more serious that this:

> I'm not going to say there was never any, what I call, 'racial abuse' which was mainly name-calling! There was never anything vicious or bad about most of our problems. We've never tended to have that sort of thing.   (Interviewee 7)

Similarly, the local ward councillor re-affirmed the existence of 'soft' racism within his ward constituency, noting that only a few people had come to him about this issue. Moreover, he was unsure if any of these incidents had actually taken place in *Northside*. He was of the view that when racially-tinted verbal abuse was used it formed part of ordinary neighbour disputes and was not an organized or systematic process:

> I think in the six years that I've been here I've had VERY FEW people come to me about [racism]. Those that have were all 'black', and, actually, one white tenant! [...]   I've had nobody come and complain about ORGANISED RACIST ATTACKS! I've had a few people come to me and say that their neighbours were racist and attacking their kids! But that may be a family or a neighbour dispute where they're probably referred to as "niggers" or "wogs get out" or something like. That is racist but it can be part of a neighbour dispute rather than any sort of organized racism! I think that if there were organized racism on the estate we would have known about it! But, I don't think there is because the 'black' community [in *Northside*] is bloody vociferous! They would certainly not keep quite about it! They're not the sort to shrink away or brow beaten by that!   (Interviewee 3)

It is important to stress that the issue of 'soft racism' (i.e. verbal abuse) is in no way being made light of herein and/or disregarded as having a serious impact on the quality of life of those that endure it. But, within the wider context of community processes and events within *Northside* such soft racism was not seen as a major or frequent problem. This can be seen in the following comments from BME community forum members:

> I haven't had any harassment problems here! I don't know of any other tenants who have and they haven't reported it to me or reported it to the estates' officer! [...] It's a cosmopolitan community! I find that everybody is friendly! [...] I haven't heard of any squabbles or whatever between different ethnic groups!   (Interviewee 17)

> Since I've been here I haven't had any problems anywhere! In England I didn't have any problem! The same in *Northside*! People here are friendly!   (Interviewee 21)

> To tell you the truth, I've heard people saying that there was racism going on in *Northside* and this and that but I have NEVER EVER EXPERIENCED IT! And, I don't know anyone, personally, who has said to me that they were racially harassed in any way.   (Interviewee 9)

Focus groups were conducted towards the end of fieldwork in an effort to verify the unproblematic nature of 'race' described in interview by community forum members and impressions developed from observational research. Three small focus groups with a total of 11 participants were conducted. These included three BME females; three elderly 'white' females; and three 'black' and two 'white' males. Participants were asked (i) to what extent did they agree/disagree that they had any problems in relation to becoming a member or participating in community forums? and (ii) had they ever experienced any prejudice or discrimination on community forums due to their age, gender or 'race'.

All 11 participants indicated that they had experienced no problems whatsoever in either joining and/or participating on the NCF, NJMB or NCDT. Similarly, none of the participants felt that they had been subjected to any discrimination within the NCF on account of their age, gender or ethnic identity.

Focus group participants were also asked to rank, on a scale of zero (i.e. 'very poor') to ten (i.e. 'very good'), past and current race relations within the neighbourhood. As can be seen from Table 5.5 race relations were seen to have improved over time within the neighbourhood. Almost 64 per cent of participants felt that current race relations were very good, giving it a score of 8-10. This compared to 45.5 per cent who gave similar scores for past race relations. None of the focus group participants felt that race relations had ever been 'very poor' (i.e. a score of 0-2).

Whilst the results from the focus groups are in no way statistically representative, the 11 community forum members that participated in them comprised a good mix of individuals in terms of age, gender, ethnicity and involvement in community politics. The focus groups provided an opportunity to triangulate participants' views expressed earlier in one-on-one interviews. The findings from the focus groups confirmed that 'race' and racism had become unproblematic and insignificant issues within *Northside*. Furthermore, the lack of ageism or sexism reinforced the over-riding pluralistic character and mindset within community forums.

Table 5.5 Attitudes to 'Race' Relations (*Northside*)

Score	How would you describe race relations in the past?		How would you describe race relations at present?	
	No.	%	No.	%
(High)				
10	3	27.3	4	36.4
8	2	18.2	3	27.3
(Medium)				
6	3	27.3	2	18.2
4	1	9.1	1	9.1
(Low)				
2	0	0	0	0
0	0	0	0	0
DK/NR	2	18.2	1	9.1
Total:	11	100.0	11	100.0

Of course, things were by no means perfect within the various community forums in *Northside*. Community forum members, like CEI/NHAC officers, were mindful of the passive involvement of newer and smaller non-English speaking ethnic minority groups such as the Turkish/Kurdish and Vietnamese. Both the NCF and NJMB sought to stimulate greater community involvement in local community politics by bringing the newly evolving community together through their Annual General Meetings (AGM) and social events such as fun days and street parties. The NCDTs AGM in 1998, held at the recently completed Community and Sports Centre, was a very pluralistic affair. It was relatively well attended with approximately 50-60 tenants, with over two-thirds of those in attendance non-community forum members and more than half were from BME backgrounds. At this event both the NCF and NCDT actively sought to recruit more people to participate in the regeneration process.

Conclusions

In conclusion, this chapter has sought to provide a 'thick description' of the evolving nature and extent of community consultation and participation practised within *Northside*. In overall terms, decision-making within *Northside* constituted what may be termed a model of *pragmatic pluralism*. This was achieved following a political transformation within the LB Hackney who expressed a strong, albeit gradual, commitment to community participation. In addition, residents' shared housing experiences were a primary factor in underpinning their determination to ensure that the regeneration programme bore their hallmark. Furthermore, this shared experience also explained why 'race' and racism were essentially unproblematic issues within the wider neighbourhood and, more specifically, within the confines of community structures. This was reflected in the lack of any racialized tension (or discourse) and the ethno-pluralistic profile of community structures. The regeneration of *Northside* has, of course, not been without its problems in relation to community power and consultation. Such problems however, were comparatively minor when contrasted with the experiences in *Southside* (see Chapter 6) and *Westside* (see Chapter 7) and resolved through negotiation and understanding between institutional and community partners.

Chapter 6

Southside:
Hyper-pluralism and the Fragmentation
of the Local Community

Lambeth became increasingly corrupt during the 1980s. [...] [This] ended at the elections of May 1994, following massive divisions in the Labour group and intervention from Walworth Road (Labour Party Headquarters). The new hung council has brought in a new partisan regime with a new, tough chief executive given sweeping powers to overcome the corruption and inefficiency.

(Dowding *et al*, 1999: 536, 538)

A strong and durable partnership will bring tenants and residents of *Southside* together with the business community, investors, transport providers and health professionals to participate in delivering the proposed outputs. The content of this bid is the result of a unique working arrangement involving the Council and the two housing associations who will be the main agencies for change.

(*Southside* Partnership Board, 1995: 3)

Introduction

The two preceding abstracts point to images of 'old' and 'new' Lambeth council respectively. This chapter, set within the context of the policy and organizational transformation suggested in both abstracts, considers proposals to set up an urban regeneration partnership (URP) in a neighbourhood known as *Southside*. As in *Northside*, the 'new' council in Lambeth expressed a policy commitment to community participation in *Southside*. Yet, as seen in the latter abstract, *Southside's* regeneration was the 'result of a unique working arrangement involving the Council and two housing associations'. Furthermore, these three institutional partners were to be the 'main agents of change'. The role of the local community, however, is unclear. For sure, the local community played virtually no role during the plan formulation stages of the regeneration process – just as in *Northside*. A set of proposals was eventually shown to the local community who perceived them as a *fait accompli*. The absence of any community input during the embryonic stages of the process, no clear community participation strategy and the council's lack of knowledge of who and/or what constituted the 'local community' were instrumental in explaining why *Southside* was beset with so many problems.

This chapter focuses on a number of issues. First, a brief descriptive of *Southside* is presented to provide some background information. Second, an overview of the evolution of the proposals to regenerate the area is presented. It is shown that this was a protracted process. Next, the decision-making structures associated with the regeneration programme are outlined. Then, the council's efforts to involve the local community are considered and are shown to lack any sense of strategy. Fifth, relations between the council and the local community are reviewed. This reveals that decision-making within *Southside* was essentially a battle between bureaucracy and community resistance. Penultimately, the nature of community power exerted within the regeneration partnership is outlined. Finally, the significance of 'race' and racism within the regeneration process and community forum(s) are considered.

Setting the Scene

Initial impressions of *Southside*, during early phases of fieldwork, were that it was a quiet and unassuming residential neighbourhood. Despite being quite a densely populated residential area, during most field visits to the area, there was little in the way of pedestrian activity. The neighbourhood only came to life during early morning and late afternoon as 'black' and 'white' children, many with their parents, made their way to and from school. Occasionally, elderly 'white' men and women, either alone or in small groups of no more than four people, were observed slowly making their way to and from the few remaining shops in the area.

In terms of the built environment, the area comprised an incongruous mix of housing and small commercial buildings. These included:

- 'the Mall', a 1970s pedestrianized shopping and residential development[1] comprising two brutalist five-storey blocks with retail units on the ground floor and flats/maisonettes on the upper floors;
- 'New' *Southside* Estate' (NSE), several blocks of low-rise post-war flats;
- 'Old' *Southside* Estate' (OSE), several blocks of low-rise inter-war flats;
- Old *Southside* Terrace (OST), a poorly maintained, largely abandoned, Victorian-built terrace comprising ground-floor retail units/workshops and upper floor flats;
- Lower *Southside* Estate' (LSE), a 1970s medium-rise block of flats and;
- *Southside* Housing Co-op' (SHC), a small 'hidden' complex of Victorian-era tenements and houses.

The architectural style, physical layout and varying state of repair of these various housing types gave the impression of a sense of territoriality within the area. This sense of separateness was reinforced by the fact that each of the

---

[1]   The shopping precinct formed the centrepiece of the regeneration programme and was earmarked for demolition and redevelopment in the initial set of proposals.

different areas listed above had their own tenant-based organization. Furthermore, as will be highlighted later, there were serious organizational and personal rifts within the local community that were exacerbated by the proposals to regenerate *Southside*.

Demographically, 'whites' (52 per cent) accounted for the majority of the local population (LRC, 1997). This was significantly less than the borough average of 70 per cent (OPCS, 1991). BMEs accounted for 48 per cent of the local population with Afro-Caribbeans (16 per cent) and 'black' Africans (16 per cent) constituting the largest groups Despite the high proportion of BMEs *Southside* tentatively clung onto its 'white' working-class 'cockney' identity. A number of weathered murals depicting images of the old music hall era and the once thriving local street market served as symbolic reminders of *Southside's* once vibrant, predominantly 'white' working-class, community. The empty shops along 'the Mall'; the dilapidated condition of the OST; the pitiful number of market stalls on market day and the general lack of pedestrian activity were testimony to the fact that the 'old' vibrancy of the neighbourhood was in a state of terminal decline.

High levels of unemployment and population restructuring (a high proportion (25 per cent) of senior citizens and BMEs (48 per cent) (LRC, 1997)) saw a reduction in local purchasing power which had a downward multiplier effect on the local economy. Furthermore, BME groups were argued to have greater socio-economic attachments to other neighbourhoods and shopping centres within the borough:

> I think that one of the things that was very apparent, and this came from residents, was that one of the reasons why the shopping centre had died was that with an increasingly 'black' population there weren't any shops catering for [their] particular ethnic requirements! So, 'black' people, who had probably been re-housed from somewhere like the Brixton area, were going back to Brixton to do their shopping! [...] The shops in the Precinct tend to be predominantly geared at the older 'white' population! [...] So, you've got declining purchasing power amongst the elderly [and a] new 'black' population coming in and NOT shopping locally. So, the two things together really militate against the sustainability of the shopping centre.
>
> (Interviewee 2)

It was clear from the first field visit, especially from the physical decay and economic abandonment within the area, that regeneration was sorely needed in *Southside*. There was universal support amongst local and central government representatives and, more importantly, the 'local community' that something had to be done. However, a complex mix of 'top-down' and 'bottom-up' factors conspired to ensure that the regeneration of *Southside* was a highly protracted process.

The Road to Regenerating *Southside*

Partnership-based regeneration activity within Lambeth has tended to be concentrated around Brixton, a neighbourhood renowned for its ethnic diversity and 'race' riots which occurred during the early 1980s (Scarman, 1981; Solomos, 1993; Solomos and Back, 1996). The socio-economic problems within and around Brixton have attracted significant regeneration funding. For example, the area was home to two of the council's highest profile schemes: the Brixton City Challenge (£37.5m) and the Estate Action-funded Angell Town Estate (£60m). As a result of the level of regeneration activity within the area it has been described as a laboratory for the testing of urban regeneration programmes (Spittles, undated).

Both the aforementioned regeneration schemes have been beset by problems in which the council *and* the local community have played a part. Gibson and Paice (1999) note that the council expressed only a 'luke-warm commitment' (p.12) to the Brixton City Challenge project. This lack of commitment and the overall slow pace of progress of the programme provoked the then DoE to intercede in order to stimulate momentum. The project proceeded but tensions prevailed between the council and Brixton City Challenge Company Ltd, the arms-length executive body of the programme, throughout its lifetime. Similarly, in Angell Town local community activists were frustrated at the council's bureaucratic approach to decision-making and community participation. Furthermore, intra-community organizational conflicts also contributed to the slow pace of progress (Hastings *et al*, 1996).

The analogy of a laboratory as used above is a pertinent one. It might rationally be assumed, given the council's history of experimenting with regeneration, that it would have become familiar with the socio-political nuances of community participation. Such things, however, are rarely that simple in Lambeth.

Inter-Departmental Conflict and Central Government Rejection

Initially, *Southside* formed only part of a much wider regeneration area. This wider area traversed a number of districts within the borough, following a major arterial route that had housing, commercial property and derelict land problems. The plans to regenerate this area emanated from within the council's Housing Department (HD) which was keen to secure additional regeneration funding to supplement its Housing Investment Programme funding for housing renewal. There, however, was inter-departmental opposition to the proposals from within the Environmental Services Department (ESD). The ESD felt that a more economically-orientated, as opposed to a housing-focus, regeneration programme was the more appropriate way forward. Moreover, the ESD was of the view that it was better qualified to manage regeneration projects. The HD proceeded with their plans and submitted them to the Government Office for London (GoL) for consideration.

The initial proposals were dismissed. The GoL, however, intimated that if the housing proposals were withdrawn any subsequent bid would be looked upon more favourably. The failure to have a housing-led bid did little to deter the HD from re-applying for funding. In the intervening period the HD initiated discussions with two teams of architects to look at the potential of developing proposals for housing *and* wider socio-economic renewal throughout the borough.

Bizarrely, both architect teams, unbeknownst to one another, approached the same regeneration consultant to conduct a viability analysis of two areas identified for possible regeneration. The consultant advised the council to focus on economic as opposed to housing-led regeneration. The former option offered greater development and investment leverage due to the location, accessibility and availability of a number of under-utilized sites in the proposed regeneration area.

A bid totaling £45m comprising a mix of SRB funding (£5m), other central and local government funding (£23m) and £17m from the housing association partners was re-submitted. It is important to note that there were no community signatories to this bid. The bid was 'signed off' by a number of institutional partners from the public, private and voluntary sectors. Ironically, however, the bid document stated that 'community empowerment' was a fundamental aim of the project.

The GoL were still unhappy with the new bid. It lacked confidence in the council's ability, due to ongoing issues surrounding political and bureaucratic corruption and personnel and organizational re-structuring, to deliver such a large-scale project. Informal discussions ensued in an effort to construct a more manageable project. The council was advised to narrow the geographical focus of its bid to the *Southside* neighbourhood with the redevelopment of the 'the Mall' being the centrepiece of the project. The following comment, by a GoL officer, reflects the complex machinations behind the project:

> I think, that we REALLY wanted to support the Bid and we were very clear that *Southside* was an area in NEED! But, we had to temper that with the knowledge that Lambeth was going through [a] huge re-organization at the time! There were STILL various people suspended from duty. And, there was an Acting Director of Housing. It was [also] around the time of the Appleby Report on the misdemeanours and corruption within the council, which we had to take into account! [...] A decision was taken at the final bid stage to downsize it by fifty per cent and there was [subsequently] an awful lot of internal discussion at that point! There was also a CLEAR line from us that we wanted Lambeth to focus on the housing problems within the area. [...] In the end, we just thought lets give them some money and get it up and running and give them a chance to prove they can deliver and take it onwards from there!   (Interviewee 3)

The council, primarily on the basis that funding would be lost if it failed to follow the advice of the GoL, reduced the geographical focus and financial scale of its bid. A revised bid, totalling approximately £30m, was submitted and provisionally approved.

By this stage, the number of institutional partners on the proposed *Southside* Partnership Board (SPB) fell to only three – the local authority and two housing associations – with the former assuming the role of 'accountable body'. These three partners then signed off the initial Delivery Plan that outlined in some detail the specific proposals for the regeneration of *Southside*. Even at this stage of the process, there had been no formal input from the local community. In fact, when the Delivery Plan was launched very few members of the local community were even aware of its existence never mind its contents.

Aims and Objectives

The overall aims and objectives of the regeneration programme were 'to transform *Southside* by creating a high quality, traditional street environment, offering new housing and diversity of tenure, increasing the accessibility and mobility of local people to new opportunities, supporting local business and employment opportunities' (*Southside* Partnership Board, 1996: 2). In short, the programme sought to meet all seven Strategic Objectives of the SRB (Government Office for the Regions, 1995). Key proposals for the area are listed below.

- *'The Mall'*: demolition and redevelopment of shops and flats and construction of a new community hall for the Upper *Southside* Estate Tenants and Residents Association (USETRA). The new redevelopment was to be owned/managed by one of the housing association partners on the SPB;
- *Environmental Schemes*: demolition and redevelopment of a new community hall and environmental improvements to the OSE and NSE;
- *Housing Improvements*: refurbishment and transfer of ownership/management of the housing stock managed by the SHC to one of the housing associations;
- *New Housing*: development of new housing on the OSE; demolition and redevelopment of the OST; and new housing on vacant land and land occupied by the Upper *Southside* Youth Club (USYC); and
- *New Housing and Commercial*: a retail strategy to help compensate for the loss of shops due to redevelopment of 'the Mall' and development of a small mixed-use site, outside the boundary of the regeneration area.

The total funding package for the programme was £28m. The SRB element accounted for £2.4m (9 per cent) of total programmed funding. This was in contrast to the £10m (36 per cent) contribution from the two housing associations. Most notably, however, was the fact that the majority (65 per cent) of the council's £4.8m (17 per cent of total funding) comprised housing and land 'in-kind' to the two housing association partners. Table 6.1 outlines the details of the funding package.

Table 6.1 Regeneration Funding Regime for *Southside*

Funding Source	£m	%
SRB	2.4	9
Housing Corporation	7.4	26
LB Lambeth	4.8	17
- Cash	(1.6)	(6)
- Housing/Land in Kind	(3.1)	(11)
- Other	(0.1)	(-)
Housing Association (HA)	9.9	36
- HA 1	(4.7)	(17)
- HA 2	(5.2)	(19)
Private Sector	3.4	12
Total	28	100

Source: SPB (1996)

Organizational Structure

After funding had been secured, the institutional partners set about formalizing the decision-making structures for the programme. A rather complex structure, comprising four levels of decision-making was designed (see Figure 6.1). Three of these are briefly outlined below.

Southside Partnership Board

The *Southside* Partnership Board (SPB) represented the strategic decision-making body in the regeneration process. Its membership comprised one representative from each of the three 'institutional partners' and two community representatives from the SCF, one with full partner status and the other with observer status. The GoL was also represented on the SPB and its role was primarily to provide strategic advice and to oversee that the programme was progressing as outlined in the Delivery Plan. Finally, the Programme Director also sat on the SPB and acted as its Chairman. In addition, as he worked closely with the three institutional partners and the 'local community', via the NO, he had knowledge of both sides needs, wants and concerns. He, therefore, also played the role of a mediator. Ultimately, the balance of formal power and agenda-setting within the SPB, rested with the institutional partners, especially the council:

> I think it's the old Animal Farm thing were each partner is equal, but, some are more equal than others are! I think it doesn't help if you come at this from the thinking that we're all equal! It's patently obvious, in terms of resources, understanding, history and POWER that tenants are not equal!   (Interviewee 4)

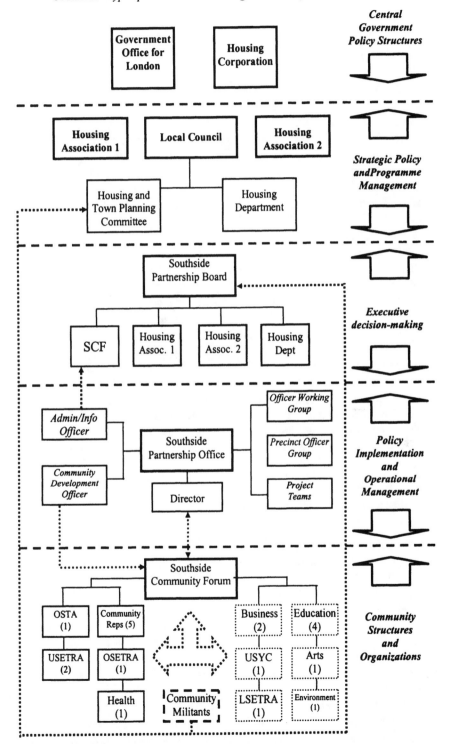

Figure 6.1 Organizational Structure of Regeneration Process (*Southside*)

This, however, should not be interpreted to suggest that the 'local community' were rendered completely powerless and unable to influence the regeneration process.

Southside Partnership Neighbourhood Office

In an effort to maximize effective management of the project a Neighbourhood Office (NO) was established. The NO was staffed by a small team that comprised a Programme Director, responsible for the overall management of the programme, an Information Officer to assist in the running of the NO and a Community Development Officer to facilitate community participation. The extent to which the SPB (i.e. the institutional partners) were committed to devolving management responsibility to the NO and community participation were brought into question by two key factors.

On the one hand, the Programme Director was only employed on a part-time basis, working 2-2.5 days per week. This cast an element of doubt as to the significance and purpose of the NO. Moreover, it gave the impression that the 'real' decisions about the regeneration programme were not being made by the SPB but within the structures of the individual institutional partners. On the other hand, and more significantly, the CDO was appointed several months after the programme had officially commenced. The CDO eventually appointed shortly resigned from the post however. After assuming the post the CDO learnt that her home and her neighbours homes, all of which were managed by the SHC, were earmarked for demolition and redevelopment. The fact that these proposals had been drawn up without any consultation with the SHC led the CDO to conclude that the regeneration of *Southside* was premised on a false partnership:

> So, I applied for the [CDO] job and I got it! [However] I became COMPLETELY disillusioned with the whole idea. [...] I found myself in a situation where I had to SELL to the people that I live next door to, plans that they might not agree with and they might see as intervening in their lives! That is why I could not really continue doing it as a paid worker! So, when I left the natural conclusion was that I would get involved with the SCF! [...] I do NOT disagree that the area needs regeneration – I DON'T have a problem with that! My PROBLEM is who is holding the purse strings? Who is determining the ins and outs, the structure of the regeneration? I NEED TO MAKE SOMETHING VERY CLEAR! I DON'T BELIEVE THAT THIS IS A REAL PARTNERSHIP!   (Interviewee 5)

The SPB was slow to re-appoint a new CDO. It was approximately 10 months before a new CDO was in post. During this period the SCF had to negotiate the regeneration process without any professional support. Invariably, this stifled the SCF's capacity to participate on a knowledgeable and equal basis within the SPB.

The SCF's status as a 'partner' was further undermined by their exclusion, a decision taken by the Programme Director, from the Officer Working Group (OWG). The OWG was where operational issues were discussed between architects, development officers and housing officers from the council and two housing associations.

Despite being professionally under-resourced and excluded from certain decision-making arenas, observational fieldwork revealed that particular members of the SCF made frequent 'social visits' to the NO. It became increasingly apparent over time that these visits were more than just social. They were an attempt to glean regular information about developments in the regeneration programme.

Southside Community Forum

Local residents could only be directly involved in decision-making through membership of a recognised community forum. There were already a number of council recognised tenant groups representing the various sub-areas within the neighbourhood. These included: the NSE, OSE, LSE and USE Tenants and Residents Associations, the OST Association and the SHC. It was decided, given the scale and geographical spread of the programme, to establish a new and representative community structure – the *Southside* Community Forum (SCF). The setting up of the SCF was a lengthy and difficult process.

The first real attempt to consult, or to be more precise, inform the local community about proposals to regenerate *Southside* occurred at an Open Day organized by the SPB in late 1996. It was at this event that a rather loose and provisional community forum was formed. This was unofficially, and subsequently officially, headed by the then Chairman of the largest tenant group, Upper *Southside* Tenants and Residents Association (USETRA), within the regeneration area. The Open Day, however, had a particularly low turnout:

> ... at the first Community Forum Open Day meeting which was held in a hotel, [although] it was very well done, there was more of THEM (i.e. 'the Partnership'), and the people who were advising the Partnership than there were of US (i.e. the community). First of all, it was held on a Saturday morning, which is not a good day for the people around here because they've got other things to do. Secondly, it was held in a hotel suite that you use for business management courses and things like that! And, although a wonderful setting it is NOT the typical setting for the average person around here – THEY ARE NOT COMFORTABLE WITH THAT!
> (Interviewee 7)

In an effort to garner more community involvement the SPB conducted a second Open Day, this time within the local area. At this Open Day an election was held to nominate and elect representatives to the SCF. Recognized community groups within the area were automatically entitled to appoint a representative to the SCF. In addition, there was a further five seats on the SCF open to 'ordinary' tenants. These 'community representative' places were subject to proposed nominees being elected by members from the wider community attending the Open Day. The election process was thrown into controversy following claims from certain individuals that their nominations had not been received or accepted. In addition, there were accusations that some of the nominees lived outside the boundary of the regeneration programme and, therefore, were not entitled to stand for election. The election of the community representative posts was declared null and void.

As a contingency, it was agreed that a postal ballot be conducted. This also ran into problems. Criticisms were laid that ballot papers were only sent out to those tenants who had attended the Open Day as opposed to all households within the regeneration area. The following comments reflect the stinging views on the process of setting up the SCF:

> [The election] was a disaster! It was a FARCE! The organization running the election declared that some of the nominations were not valid. The reason given was that one of the nominees didn't live or work in the area and that was one of the criteria. That person had also nominated others from outside the area. The vote was then called to a halt! Because people who had voted had actually left it was difficult to re-run the vote so it was decided on that day that there would be a postal ballot! A decision on whether or not to ballot the 2,000 people in the area, or to simply ballot the people who had turned up that day was needed. It was a difficult decision to make – personally I'm into openness, democracy and participation. But, at the same time, the ORIGINAL vote was restricted to the people who ACTUALLY ATTENDED! So we decided to try and stick to the spirit of the original and only sent papers out to people who had attended that day.   (Interviewee 7)

> [The election] was FARCICAL!   FARCICAL BEYOND BELIEF!   [...] Electioneers? ZERO! People facilitating it? THREE! As far as I was concerned, they couldn't facilitate their way out of a brown paper bag! They managed to ignore some nominations that should have or weren't delivered through the proper channels! My nomination was registered and effective within an hour! [...] There was also a certain amount of [community] politicking going on [that was] pretty amateurish, very fundamental, very basic... but extraordinary!   (Interviewee 8)

Throughout this whole period the SCF, as it sought to establish itself, was wrecked with internal conflicts. This conflict was grounded in the protestations of a small group of militant community activists who had representation on the SCF, but were vehemently opposed to the proposals to regenerate the area. In short, it appeared that the militants were out to sabotage the SCF and the regeneration process. Notably, the SPB did little to try and resolve the conflict within the SCF. Things began to settle down towards the end of 1997 with the gradual easing out of the militant representative and the election of a new pragmatic Chairman and Vice-Chairman. So, after 12-18 months into the regeneration programme the SCF was finally in a position to concentrate on defining its own internal management structures and participating in the regeneration process.

SCF: A Representative Community Forum?

A review of the membership of the SCF revealed that it was a socially pluralistic organization. Its 21 members came from a diverse range of organizational backgrounds and included: tenant associations; the health; educational and environmental sectors; the arts; and young people (see Figure 6.1).

In terms of the ethnic profile, BMEs accounted for just under one-third (29 per cent) of all members. In numerical terms, BMEs (and men) were significantly under-represented as can be seen from Table 6.2. Despite their numerical representation, BME members on the SCF were affiliated to some of the neighbourhoods' largest, and most influential, community organizations, the USTRA and the USYC. Both of these organizations, especially the USYC, were mindful of BME issues. In addition, the new Chairman was an advocate of anti-racism and was keen for the SCF to be sensitized to the needs of BME groups. Crucially, the under-representation of BMEs was not the product of racial exclusion operating within the SCF. BME under-representation and the lack of participation by SCF members in general were more the result of the intra-community conflict that had marred the SCF. A BME female left the SCF on account of the community militants' attempts to take control of it.

Table 6.2 Ethnic and Gender Profile of Community Forum (*Southside*)

Community Forum	Ethnic group		Gender	
	BME No. (%)	*'white'* No. (%)	*male* No. (%)	*female* No. (%)
SCF	6 (29)	15 (71)	6 (29)	15 (71)
Southside[1]	190 (48)	203 (52)	221 (56)	172 (44)

[1]*Southside* Survey (LRC, 1997) N= 393
Source: SCF Membership Lists (1996, 1997, 1998)

Despite having a total of 21 members, only a minority of SCF members actually attended the group's monthly meeting to decide upon its aims and objectives within the regeneration process. In fact, the SCF had immense difficulty in securing a quorum at committee meetings. Almost half (47 per cent) of SCF meetings during the fieldwork period (i.e. November 1997 to December 1998) lacked the necessary number of members (i.e. seven) in order for the SCF to conduct any business. The regeneration process, consequently, lacked any formal input from the 'local community'.

The lack of attendance at SCF meetings was largely due to members having lost faith in the purpose of the SCF. This was a function of the intra-community power struggle during the setting up of the SCF when militant tenant activists attempted to assume control of it. When this failed the militants resorted to disrupting SCF meetings and even 'intimidating' members in an effort to prevent it from inputting into the regeneration process. As a result of this many members simply stayed away from the SCF. Those that persevered, especially the new Chairman and Vice-Chairman were committed to the ideal that the SCF should seek to be representative of the wider community. They knew, however, that they faced an immense uphill struggle on this front.

Community Consultation and Participation

As mentioned earlier, the empowerment of the local community was a strategic objective of the regeneration of *Southside*. The council, as the lead body on the SPB, failed to initiate any meaningful community-wide consultation in the drawing up of the initial Delivery Plan. This effectively contravened the spirit of the SRB programme. Moreover, it set the tone for the disquiet that reigned throughout the regeneration process.

It would be wrong to assume that there had been no consultation whatsoever during the initial stages of the regeneration process. There had been some consultation but this was rather limited in nature. Consultation amounted to merely *informing* a small selective number of community representatives about broad proposals for the area and an implicit commitment to participation once funding had been secured. This approach, however, was the foundation as to why there was such a huge community backlash against the programme. The councils' lack of foresight regarding the significance of participation is reflected in the following comments:

> When we started the [consultation] process I have to say that the council was feeling VERY NERVOUS about it! The extent of detailed consultation was with the USTRA who we had a series of meetings with at their tenants hall. But, this was complicated by the fact that there were all sorts of ructions within the USTRA. [...] There was no estate-wide consultation. I think, there was one public meeting with people from the OSE. There was a walkabout at the very beginning with representatives from the two TAs. [...] In the period after the bid was submitted there was no sense of progress about where this consultation process was leading. I don't think that the council really appreciated quite how important it would be to have properly structured consultation. As a result they ended up with a series of very disjointed meetings. So, they weren't making any progress!   (Interviewee 2)

The SPB failed to devise a formal participation strategy after funding had been secured. Instead, it adopted an *ad hoc* approach. The SPB, consequently, was unable to allay concerns raised within the neighbourhood about the lack of participation and the ramifications of specific proposals on particular sub-communities. A period of intra-community resistance, of varying degrees of intensity, ensued for a period of 18-24 months. The various community organizations within the area asserted different strategies of resistance in order to protect their own sub-communities and influence decision-making. This resistance caused major disruptions to the regeneration process and resulted in several key proposals being abandoned or severely delayed.

Consultation and Participation: the Officer Perspective

The failure to initiate and sustain a structured programme of participation was acknowledged in interviews with representatives from the institutional partners on the SPB. A combination of factors explained the lack of consultation and why it was such a contentious issue throughout the first two years of the regeneration programme. These included:

- Structural constraints inherent to the SRB application process:

  > It wasn't full or informed consultation! The problem with SRB – and this was also partly our fault – was that you didn't receive your invitation to bid until quite late. In addition, we had to go through our committee system and there was an element of convincing the members that if we were going to get into SRB then the only area that we should be looking at was *Southside*. By this time we were within 6 weeks of having to submit our outline bid! Now, that doesn't allow you a lot of time to do full blown consultation particularly as the SRB guidelines, or the information we were getting, were stacked against us. So we had a series of dilemmas. How detailed should our bid be? How much time and effort do we put into the bid? How much money do we spend on the bid? How MUCH do we involve local people on what was looking like an immensely hazardous route for the Housing Department to take? So, I think, that combination of starting late, a bit of confusion about our aims and some reluctance meant we came in EXTREMELY light on consultation!
  >
  > (Interviewee 9)

- A pervading bureaucratic culture within the council which was a hangover from pre-1994 administrations:

  > One of the failings, I think, of the initial bid was that it appeared to have been drawn up without very much involvement from the local community and POSSIBLY with complete isolation from the local community! In terms of the council that's very bad! It tended to confirm people's views that LB Lambeth DOESN'T CONSULT and that it does its OWN THING! It has given rise to all sorts of tensions throughout the process! So, one of the things that the Board had to do was create its own local community partners if you like! Since it did that in the middle of the process it has brought all sorts of strains and tensions!   (Interviewee 10)

- Intra-community conflict emanating from a small, but extremely vociferous, group of militant activists:

  > Prior to putting in the outline bid, which was before our housing association and the other one became involved, as far as I am aware there was NO CONSULTATION WHATSOEVER! Prior to putting in the detailed bid there was AT LEAST one LARGE, and not very well controlled, public meeting to explain what we were trying to do! That meeting was deliberately disrupted by some elements within – I was going to say the *Southside* community – but some of those actors lived outside the area! Between the bid going in in September and Christmas there was at least one, probably two, further public meetings but similarly disorganized, difficult to control and deliberately disrupted by certain elements on the periphery of the community! I certainly don't think it's true to say that the community or community representatives had a GENUINE opportunity to change the direction of the regeneration bid at any time prior to GoL agreeing the final programme! It was very much handed down from on high, which was a mistake, and I wouldn't do it again!
  >
  > (Interviewee 11)

Despite acknowledging that community participation had been inadequate during the early stages of the regeneration process, the SPB continued to fail in its duty to construct and implement an effective participatory strategy. In fact, the institutional partners on the SPB seemed reluctant to engage with the 'local community'. One major reason for this was that they did not wish to become any more embroiled in the intra-community conflict, which their proposals had initiated, taking place within the neighbourhood.

Consultation and Participation: the Community Perspective

Invariably, the 'local community' felt that regeneration proposals were being imposed upon them and merely reflected a continuation of the council's old bureaucratic past.   Paradoxically, there was a general acceptance within the neighbourhood, even amongst the community militants, that regeneration was much needed. Retrospectively, the council thought it would encounter relatively few problems in implementing their proposals since these were to benefit the whole area.   As already noted, however, during the bid formulation stage consultation was rather superficial in nature and confined to only known or visible community groups.   Consequently, when the wider community became aware of proposals to demolish and redevelop particular parts of the neighbourhood this provoked widespread anger.

Despite this widespread anger, the local community were not united in their opposition to the regeneration programme. Instead, intra-community antagonisms were initially fragmented and processed in an internalized manner. In particular, two well-defined, but invisible, sub-communities – the SHC and OST – who felt that their existence and identity was under threat from proposals to demolish and redevelop their homes became highly self-protective. In addition, the USYC, a well respected and 'black'-led community facility, used mainly by local 'black' youths, also went on the offensive following proposals to relocate it by freeing up the land it occupied for housing development.

The following comments highlight how these particular groups became aware of the regeneration proposals; their anger at the lack of consultation; and disbelief at what the council proposed to do to their homes, premises and communities:

> We felt that there was NO CONSULTATION hardly at all!   There was no PROCESS of consultation up until the presentation of the plans.   We're going to knock down *Southside* and develop it!   They were going to knock down our homes and develop them!   Great!   Great?   [*said sarcastically*]   [...]   [Basically] we were presented with THE PLAN!   THE PLANS WERE TO KNOCK EVERYTHING DOWN!   [*said incredulously and angrily*]   To my mind consultation leads to the development of plans.   You sit down with people; you discuss the arrangement for them to return to the scheme; you discuss plans; and you ask what people ACTUALLY want!   (Interviewee 7)

> [We heard about the proposals] purely by accident!   What happened was that [one of the political parties] were introducing their new Parliamentary candidate to this

ward. They came here with their handouts and things [and] among other things they were saying great things about redeveloping the area! As it happened, amongst this bunch of press leaflets there was what we came to know as the Delivery Plan – this plan for DEVELOPING the area! There was a chapter that said that [the OST] was going to be demolished and that was the first that we knew of it! […] It dropped out of the sky!   (Interviewee 6)

There was talk that there was this funding available and then they were talking about some sort of development! Then I got a letter – A BLATANT LETTER – telling me that two HAs were in partnership with LB Lambeth to purchase the land the youth club sits on. At the beginning [the housing associations] were negotiating with the council making all these plans and doing all this crap before we [i.e. the youth club] were even aware of what was going on! [*said angrily*] The protracted situation that we are in now with the Partnership has been caused because of all that!
(Interviewee 12)

Notably, a small sub-group of militant activists expressed similar concerns about the lack of community-wide consultation. Their objections, however, were motivated more by their radical leftist agenda; an antipathetic attitude towards the council and a desire to assume control of the SCF as opposed to being directly affected by specific proposals.

When initially set up under the leadership of the then Chairman of the USTRA, described in interviews as being rather autocratic, the SCFs constitution only individuals and community groups residing within the boundary of regeneration area were entitled to become members. This policy effectively denied membership to several key militant protagonists. Moreover, it would appear that their exclusion was a deliberate ploy premised on a latent, yet rational, fear amongst other community activists *and* officers that the militants would sabotage the regeneration process. This fear was subsequently borne out during the first 12-18 months of the SCF. The militants 'invaded' SCF meetings, harassed members and used propaganda to discredit the regeneration programme. The following comment by one of the militants was indicative of this small group's intense opposition to the regeneration programme:

I really think that the ENTIRE thing – ALL OF IT – is CORRUPT! [*Said loudly and angrily*] I'm not talking about corrupt when people put brown envelopes stuffed with money into their pockets or go on holidays to Caribbean islands or whatever! It has been corrupt in the way that it has been set-up! In the way that it has been run! In the way that it has not REALLY involved the local community in its DELIVERY, service or plan or anything! I think that it has actually been designed that way. I really do! Because, when you consider that so many key players have actually [been] isolated, excluded and precluded! […] What they should have done from day one was [identify] the key players in this area and gone and [consulted] with them and, if they had said – "No! We don't want it"! Then they could have then said okay! At least then, one would have felt that there had been some sort of an ATTEMPT at involvement!   (Interviewee 13)

The above call for the council to identify and consult with the 'key players' needs to be treated with a degree of caution. The militants' perception of what constituted 'the local community' and the key agents within the neighbourhood was in itself biased and exclusionary. That is, not content with attacking the SPB or the regeneration process, the militants were also particularly scathing of the membership and role of the SCF. The militants, as the comments below imply, were totally dismissive of the existence and plight of those sub-communities (i.e. the OSE, SHC and the OST) directly affected by the regeneration proposals to which they categorically objected:

> I know someone who ACTUALLY worked for the SPB until quiet recently who has been EXTREMELY DISHONEST – and you can quote me on that! They're now elected onto the SCF as a voting member after having resigned their post at the SPB! [...] The previous SCF Chairman lives on the OST *[said dismissively]*. The OST is many many years old and is dilapidated, decrepit and falling apart! Now, apparently there's a proposal to spend £2m to refurbish it and they're going to set up a Trust to run it! *[said with disbelief]* [...] So, they're refurbishing what they should be knocking down. That part of the neighbourhood is an eyesore quite frankly! Regeneration, we thought, was to get rid of the eyesores in our community. Running sores such as the housing occupied by the SHC, which are virtually slums! And, they're knocking down what they SHOULD be refurbishing on what they actually gave a guarantee to refurbish or a commitment to refurbish which is the Mall! It actually smacks to me of corruption – it really does! [...] The OSE is simply interested because they want a new tenant's hall and a new communal garden! And they're getting them! The OSETRAs Secretary has sold the rest of this community down the river and stabbed it in the back! She's being doing it for years to get what SHE can for her own little patch! So what you've got is people like that who have got a vested interest!   (Interviewee 13)

It is worthwhile pointing out that the claim the OST was to receive £2m from the SPB was incorrect and part of the propaganda strategy deployed by the militants to disrupt the regeneration process. The aforementioned claim that the council was 'refurbishing what it should be demolishing' (i.e. the OST) and 'demolishing what it should be refurbishing' (i.e. 'the Mall') became a propaganda slogan aimed at discrediting the OST and the council. It was used on leaflets and posters distributed during a site visit by the council's Town Planning Committee in relation to the planning application for the demolition and redevelopment of 'the Mall'. Another poster and leaflet proclaiming '*Southside* Market RIP' was used to tap into the psyche of the local community, especially the elderly 'white' population, by flagging the areas' heritage as a former street market.

The 'reality' of the situation regarding the OSTA was that it had initiated its own successful counter-strategy to prevent proposals for one of the HA partners to demolish and redevelop its buildings. In short, the OST formed a 'micro-regime' by drawing on a network of contacts to garner support for their own proposals. These contacts included their local MP; an experienced community and housing advocacy group; and Regeneration Support Services (RSS)[2], a regeneration consultancy. The OSTA, with the aid of RSS, secured a small amount of funding (approximately £6,000) from the SPB to conduct a feasibility study into alternative proposals for the OST site. This was in the face of fierce opposition from one of the institutional partners on the SPB. The OSTA was keen to refurbish the OST for mixed residential and commercial use and, more importantly, assume ownership and raise its own funding via establishing a Community Development Trust (CDT).

Community Fragmentation and Factionalism

To reiterate, when proposals to regenerate *Southside* became general knowledge those sub-communities directly affected by proposals became highly internalized which in turn contributed to the fragmentation of the 'local community'. The militants proclaimed, in interview, the SPB was the sole cause of this fragmentation:

> THIS PARTNERSHIP HAS SET THIS COMMUNITY AGAINST EACH OTHER! IT HAS FACTIONALISED IT! IT HAS TORN IT APART WITH ITS DISHONESTY AND GAME PLAYING! I'VE NEVER SEEN ANYTHING LIKE IT – I REALLY HAVEN'T! [*stated loudly*]   (Interviewee 13)

This claim and others by the militants, however, were contradicted in interviews with SCF and SPB representatives. Basically, it was contended that the militants' (re)actions to the regeneration programme and attempts to assume control of the SCF were the root cause of community factionalism. It was claimed that militant activists 'invaded' SCF meetings and verbally abused members. Moreover, a campaign of intimidation was also waged against SCF members who were sent 'threatening' and 'slanderous' letters calling for them to resign. In particular, the experiences of two BME females illustrate the degree of harassment endured. Notably, one felt that there was racial undertone to the verbal abuse she experienced. The other felt that her experience had more to do with her diminutive stature and youthfulness in terms of her age, community activist experience and relatively short length of time she had lived in the area:

> One of the militants went to the then Chairman of the USTRA, who's now a local councillor, with complaints about my appalling and offensive behaviour! She wrote long letters to him and copied them to [central government] accusing me of being against the USTRA, the local community and that I was involved only for my own self-interest. The USTRA committee then had 6-7 letters from tenants saying that they wanted me out. One of them in particular said that the situation with me was so serious that they would arrange with one of the local community organizations to GET RID of me! Everyone who read it interpreted this as a physical threat. [...] It was all VERY VERY SCARY! [...] The militants also started to do background

---

[2]   The real name of the consultancy has been changed to provide anonymity.

research on me. They approached the SPB to get my address [but] they refused. But, [they] found it on the electoral list and they have now been putting letters through my letterbox. [...] She's also written to the SCF Chairman, saying he's corrupt. She's written to the former Vice Chairman, saying he threatened to assault her! She's written to the Secretary of LSTRA, calling her a liar!   (Interviewee 14)

The area was going to be improved and I thought that was a good idea! I was in favour of it! And, that's why I entered into the meetings and things like that. But, there was a certain group who was just AGAINST everything! They didn't even live in the area! That gang seems to create trouble everywhere! Not just here but in any other group! [...] [The militants] kept interrupting our meetings. Their view was that the SRB was just for the LSE and NSE! At a meeting I was about to Chair this gang came in and verbally abused me! [...] Those people were interrupting the meetings because they didn't want this regeneration happening! They didn't want 'the Mall' pulled down because there was a rumour that certain people were sub-letting their houses.   (Interviewee 15)

Such was the factionalism within the local community that another interviewee was so apprehensive about discussing the militants that he requested the tape recorder be switched off. He was concerned that what he had to say might be construed as libellous and used against him. The militants had already sought legal advice about obtaining a judicial review on the validity of the postal ballot to elect representatives to the SCF and the council's decision to overrule the outcome of the tenants' ballot on whether or not to demolish and redevelop 'the Mall'. This course of action was an effective scare and delaying tactic.

Ultimately, the whole débâcle that had emerged in *Southside* due to the lack of participation proved an invaluable lesson for the council as to the significance of involving the local community as early and thoroughly as possible. The council seemed to have at long last grasped the concept of trail and error. On a subsequent regeneration programme, in a neighbourhood close to *Southside*, the council devised a detailed participation strategy. In fact, community involvement on this project was so lengthy and intense that there were actually complaints of 'consultation fatigue' from community representatives. Ironically, despite the commendable participatory efforts of the council and its development partners, this project eventually came to a halt due to the (re)actions of the 'local community' *and* community militants.

The Declining Significance of Democracy

There was actually an element of truth behind the militants' claim that the SPB and the regeneration process were 'corrupt'. This 'corruption' had nothing to do with financial bribes nor was it an endemic aspect. Nonetheless, it lay at the centre of the most democratic event within the regeneration process – the ballot on whether or not to demolish and redevelop or refurbish 'the Mall'. This ballot represented the SPB's first genuine attempt at real and meaningful community participation.

An independent electoral voting agency was appointed to ensure that the ballot was conducted properly.

The ballot, in which only tenants from 'the Mall' were entitled to vote, comprised a single question. Tenants were asked to indicate if they were in favour of (i) demolition and redevelopment or (ii) refurbishment. The SPB, especially the council, sought a vote in favour of demolition and development. A preliminary survey conducted by the SPB some months earlier indicated that a majority (70 per cent) of tenants were in favour of the demolition-redevelopment option. Unfortunately, for the SPB, tenants voted narrowly in favour of refurbishment.

Needless to say this outcome upset the council. So much, in fact, it took the rather unprecedented and, ultimately, undemocratic step of interrogating the voting pattern of the ballot. This revealed that a slight majority of tenants on one side of 'the Mall' were in favour of demolition and redevelopment. The council decided to split the vote and declared its intention to redevelop one side of 'the Mall'.

This decision was adopted for two key factors. On the one hand, there was a bureaucratic necessity and expediency to do so. The SPB risked losing SRB funding if it failed to deliver stated outputs as outlined in the Delivery Plan. In addition, the housing association earmarked to assume responsibility of the site was considering withdrawing from the process. On the other hand, and, more contentiously, there were claims that community militants had orchestrated a propaganda-fuelled and intimidatory anti-demolition campaign a few days prior to the ballot resulting in a reversal of earlier support for demolition:

> Well, the democratic process – and I use the term very LOOSELY – said that a majority of people living in 'the Mall'… didn't want their homes to be demolished! For research purposes, as much as anything else, we ran the ballot in such a way so that we could split up areas of 'the Mall' to see who was MOST IN FAVOUR of demolition and who was least in favour of demolition! This clearly showed a clear majority in FAVOUR of demolition on one side of the precinct! The reason why I say I use the term 'democratic process' loosely is that there WAS a great deal of very misleading propaganda put around about what was entailed in the process of demolition by people from outside the area and some from within the area! […] For instance, literature came out a day or so before the ballot claiming that we were just demolishing people's homes so that we could sell to private developers and put yuppies in there! We just couldn't get literature out countering that and giving people a guarantee otherwise! So, people across the WHOLE of 'the Mall' voted against demolition on the basis of incomplete information! But, even given that misinformation, tenants on one side of 'the Mall' clearly said that they wanted their block to come down and for them to be rehoused in one way or another! [They] expressed to SPB officers their concerns that the ballot had gone against them as it were and they were going to be stuck in living circumstances with which they were unhappy!
> (Interviewee 11)

Interviews with SCF members confirmed that the militants had indeed initiated a vociferous anti-demolition campaign. In particular, one interviewee, who had been the subject of personal attacks and criticisms from the militants,

admired the effectiveness of their campaign whilst simultaneously expressing
reservations about the decision to split the vote on the ballot:

> Three days before the ballot took place the militant group SUDDENLY mobilized!
> They did a great job, in that, they fly-posted the whole area about the vote and they
> visited as many flats as they could! The SPB would say – and they would be quite
> right in a way – that it was a campaign of disinformation and misinformation and
> frightened the life out of a lot of people about what was going to happen. But, they
> did a THOROUGH campaign! They did a good militant campaign! […] They held
> the ballot and it came up with a small majority against demolition! Now, as far as
> we were concerned that was it! I mean, we've got nothing to do with that part of the
> neighbourhood. That was the end of the SRB because that's the centrepiece! But,
> do you know what they did? [said incredulously] They actually looked at the ballot
> and were able to say a majority of people in one block had voted 'YES' and they
> SPLIT the ballot! You can't play a democratic card one-minute and then play an
> autocratic card the next! But, that is what the council did!   (Interviewee 6)

Even more interestingly, although the decision to split the vote was
described as 'dangerous' and undemocratic, it was tacitly supported from within
GoL further signalling the bureaucratic necessity underpinning this proposal:

> The ballot they did on the Precinct, which they then broke down between the two
> blocks, was a DANGEROUS thing to do in some senses because there was no
> overall majority vote for demolition! But, I can see that the council was still trying
> to give power to the community. They weren't trying to just dictate and say that
> they were going to demolish *Southside* Precinct and you've got to move out! I
> think, at least they took into account people's views and are only going ahead with
> demolishing one side of the precinct!   (Interviewee 3)

The decision to proceed with the demolition of one side of 'the Mall'
illustrated the council's contempt for the rule of democracy and did nothing but
galvanize the efforts of the various sub-communities, including the militants,
within *Southside* to influence decision-making.

Community Power and Influence

It is difficult to imagine, given the inability to make any decisions of its own due to
intra-community conflict, a lack of professional support and being excluded from
certain decision-making arenas, that the SCF could have exercised any influence
over the regeneration process. The SCF may well have been the fourth partner
within the SPB but it was a powerless one. This was due to a combination of
factors.

First, the initial bid and Delivery Plan had been prepared and signed off by
the institutional partners with no 'real' community participation. Consequently,
the programme had a pro-demolition and development agenda:

In terms of being a partner in the decision making process, if we go back to when the Bid was being drawn up, the discussion around the Delivery Plan and how they were going to deliver the outputs that they were signing up to this was very poorly done! There wasn't a community forum! There wasn't an SCF! I THINK that has obviously caused a lot of problems for the council! People in the community just had this Delivery Plan SHOVED at them and the various plans about what was going to be done and they weren't involved at the start! I think they feel that they've always been presented with a *fait accompli*! (Interviewee 3)

Second, the absence of any community representation on the SPB during its first six months inhibited the SCF from becoming familiarized with the procedures and nuances of the regeneration process. The late arrival of the SCF meant that it was effectively accorded the status of 'junior partner':

[The SCF have had no influence!] NONE! NONE WHATSOEVER! None whatsoever! 'The Mall' has been very much CONTROLLED by the SPB! [...] The SCF has had very very little input into that! [...] This regeneration just seems like a *fait accompli*. The SCF does not feel that it can do anything! [...] In terms of how much power or influence the SCF has in this process? BOLLOCKS! It has got none! It has got none! This is a partnership between three adults and a child! So, NO! There is NO power! [...] They tell us that they want to give power to us but they are the ones that make the decisions! (Interviewee 5)

Third, as a consequence of only having one vote on the SPB the SCF stood little to no chance of influencing decision-making whenever the institutional partners all had a shared mutual interest (i.e. demolition and redevelopment) in the regeneration programme:

I don't know what the SCF's primary aims and functions are! I think its there for the sake of it. I don't know what it can achieve. We can say a few things: that we want this or we don't want this but what happens or not is not dependent on us! The decision-making power does not lie with the tenants. [...] Participation means that you take part in making decisions. But, there's only one tenant sitting on the SPB. Only one tenant rep! [...] I wrote several letters to the Chief Executive and the Deputy Chief Executive asking for a minimum of three tenants eligible to vote on the SPB. That's a fair balance! If we didn't like something then we could turn it down! One person on the SPB does not make any difference there! It's got to be three tenants or it just wouldn't work! Because those three – the [institutional partners] – all stick together in whatever it is! (Interviewee 15)

Next, the institutional partners came to the SPB with considerable resources in financial, human and expertise terms, placing them in a much stronger position to operate within the regeneration process. This was in stark contrast to the SCF who entered the regeneration process with virtually no resources other than members' own determination to counter those proposals directly impacting on their own communities. Moreover, the SPB failed to provide the SCF with sufficient resources and sustained support to enable it to develop an autonomous identity, strategic purpose and necessary skills to participate effectively in decision-making:

I left my post as community development worker in November 1997, about 5-6 months ago, and there has been no one there [since] to support the SCF! The SCF cannot say that they are going to employ someone – it cannot! So, as far as I am concerned, if you don't have money you do not have the POWER behind you of being able to say that you can pay for something and then have it!   (Interviewee 5)

Finally, the SCF was inhibited from developing organizationally due to community factionalism that was generated initially by individual regeneration proposals and entrenched by the actions of militant activists respectively.

I don't think that it has had very much power! [...] I think that the SCF, up until fairly recently, have been quite weak – it has been in its formative stages! It has also been under immense pressure and attack from outside [i.e. militant activists]! I think that it is still feeling its way! So, I think that neither its power nor its influence has been very strong! I don't think that it has had a great influence on what has happened!   (Interviewee 9)

From Insignificance to Influence

The SCF was effectively an insignificant structure within the formal decision-making structures of the SPB. The 'Animal Farm' metaphor, used earlier by the SPB's Programme Director, to suggest that the SCF were 'less equal' partners simultaneously implies a potential for revolution. For sure, individual sub-communities represented on the SCF and the community militants 'revolted' against the regeneration programme by stepping outside the confines of the SPB. By adopting an individualist approach and agitating the SPB from outside SCF members were able to exercise quite considerable influence over the regeneration process:

I think that the SCFs been negligible in terms of its influence as a body! I think the various individuals on the committee have been very active and have brought about quite considerable changes in the original plans of the developers! [...] They were going to knock down our houses but now they're not going to do that anymore! They were going to knock down the OST: They're not going to do it anymore! [...] People have said that they have been openly lied to by the SPB, that it was trying to PUSH an agenda! Of course, this meant that the community pushed back!
                                                                                                (Interviewee 7)

The housing association partners were also of the view that individual SCF members exercised considerable influence:

If there was a league table in terms of power and influence, the council is first. The community is second. Our HA is third and the other HA is fourth! [...] In terms of why the HAs have got such a low capacity to influence decision-making, it's not that the community is being PARTICULARLY empowered! It's that the HAs are being particularly disenfranchised! This is because of the CONTEMPT in which HAs are held at senior levels within the council! The community DOES HAVE POWER! IT'S LARGELY A POWER OF VETO! There are particular schemes where they've said that they didn't want it a certain way, it's only if we get it like this that we will allow it to go forward.   (Interviewee 11)

In overall terms, the 'revolt' against the SPB points to decision-making within *Southside* as being *hyper-pluralistic* in nature (Waste, 1986; also see Chapter 3). More specifically, the different strategies adopted by individual SCF members gave rise to a three-fold typology of localized hyper-pluralism.

Typology of Localized Hyper-pluralism

The first signs that decision-making had entered into the realm of *hyper-pluralism* emerged immediately following the official launch of the Delivery Plan. The sudden announcement that (certain parts of) *Southside* was to be regenerated provoked neighbourhood-wide anger amongst the various 'visible' (i.e. LSETRA, OSETRA, and NSETRA) and 'invisible' (i.e. the OSTA and SHC) sub-communities in the area. By the time the SCF had been set up and eventually incorporated as a partner on the SPB, the different sub-communities, including the militants, were effectively boycotting the regeneration proposals. Furthermore, they had turned their attentions to devising ways of altering and/or stopping proposals outlined in the Delivery Plan. The approaches adopted by the different sub-communities may be classified into three broad types of hyper-pluralistic action: *Passive*; *Rationalized* and *Traditional*.

Passive Hyper-pluralism

In essence, this approach entailed forging positive, yet critical, dialogue and relations with the SPB. This strategy was adopted by the OSETRA, or, to be more precise, its Secretary – an elderly 'white' female. The Secretary was *the* OSETRA. She was revered as something of an institution within the neighbourhood. For these reasons, she commanded considerable respect from senior SPB officers. The same was also true of other community activists, excluding the community militants, who admired her diligence, knowledge and ability to raise difficult questions within the SPB.

The OSETRA Secretary's strategy involved paying frequent, generally once a day, and often quite lengthy (1-1.5 hours on average) 'social visits' to the Neighbourhood Office where she would engage in 'friendly' conversation with the Programme Director, Information Officer and whoever else associated with the programme who happened to be there. The Secretary's affable manner (and her senior citizen status) combined with the regularity of visits to the NO enabled her to develop a positive, if at sometimes pestering, relationship with SPB/NO staff.

These visits, however, were not merely 'social'. They were, in fact, part of rather ingenuous strategy to influence decision-making. Put simply, the OSETRA Secretary was covertly gathering information as to the machinations, direction and condition of the SPB and the regeneration process. The information she gleaned helped to increase her knowledge base that in turn increased her power base both within her own local community and the regeneration process. On subsequent visits the OSETRA Secretary would subtly remind SPB officers of problems within the regeneration process by asking delicate but provocative questions. In addition, she emphasized her and the wider OSE community's disquiet about certain aspects of proposals and/or the lack of progress being made:

> Did the local community have power or influence? Yeah! Oh yeah! Yes! I mean, they have power of support or the denial of support, which can make things happen or can obstruct things! So, they do have very REAL power! For example, some of the sites were excluded because tenants on the [OSE and NSE] said – "Don't be so bloody silly"! They also have significant influence in terms of whether sites get planning permission for example; Or, whether the form of building that is going up on a site is the right one! So, for example, the OSETRAs feisty representative who knows exactly what she wants will fight tooth and nail to get what she wants and usually does get it!   (Interviewee 17)

> A good example of the local community [flexing its muscles] was the housing and community hall development on the OSE where [its] SCF representative... have been TERRIBLY EFFECTIVE! At various stages during the design process they have exercised a very effective veto over design proposals! So, the scheme now looks quite significantly different from how it would have looked had that consultation not taken place! It's also a great deal more COSTLY for the other HA to implement than it would have been!   (Interviewee 11)

In conclusion, the roots of the OSETRA Secretary's ability to influence decision-making lay in her reputation as a venerable, knowledgeable and no-nonsense individual when it came to getting things done for her part of the neighbourhood.

Rationalized Hyper-pluralism

Those sub-communities that adopted a 'rationalized hyper-pluralistic' approach to influencing decision-making also developed alliances with external agents to garner support and assistance in the construction of their own proposals. This approach was adopted by the SHC and OSHA, two sub-communities initially unknown to the SPB (and the council).

In terms of developing alliances with other agents, both groups lobbied their local political representatives. The SHC embarked on an intense round of informal discussions with local councillors from across the political spectrum and met with their local MP. These discussions focused on several key issues. First, the lack of community consultation by the SPB. Second, the SHC's initial denial of representation on the SCF as a result of it not being recognized as a legitimate community organization. And, finally, the threat to the SHCs sense of community and function as a localized social housing provider by proposals to demolish, redevelop and transfer of ownership of 'their' homes to one of the housing association partners:

We were going to all the Councillor's surgeries. Labour! Tory! Liberal Democrat! The local MPs surgeries! We've met all of these people! We met the Lib-Dem councillor and sat for four hours talking to him over wider issues as well as this local stuff! [...] I think that we all went to see the local MP regularly. [...] We were arguing and arguing and arguing! But, this has clearly had an effect! There has been a sea change, I would say, in the way that the community has been treated!

(Interviewee 7)

The OSTA also approached its local MP, with whom some members already had a fairly well developed relationship, for support following the discovery of a planning application to demolish and redevelop the OST. The local MP even attended a Town Planning Committee (TPC) meeting calling for the OST to be preserved and refurbished because of its historical significance to the neighbourhood. The various tenants who lived in and/or had workspace units within the OST also put forward their objections at the TPC meeting. Bizarrely, the Housing Department was completely unaware that a community of people lived and worked in the OST. This unawareness was a product of the failure to conduct a thorough consultation exercise during the initial stages of the regeneration process.

The revelation of a vibrant sub-community residing within the OST perturbed the TPC. It had been led to believe, by council officers, that the OST was an abandoned building. The same was also true for the housing association that had submitted the planning application for the redevelopment of the OST. This incident reinforced the local community's view of the council's bureaucratic ineptitude:

The [TPC] came down to do a site visit and much to their surprise when they arrived there were all these people who came out of the OST to talk to the councillors! So, what the councillors had been told was there was quite clearly not there! There was a lot more – not just on the residential bit – but behind we've got commercial workshops and that block was really very active! That didn't match [with what they had been told] at all! The TPC was really quite angry! [...] Literally before the start of the TPC meeting the housing association tried to withdraw their application saying that they wanted to defer it because they suddenly realized that they were going to have this big objection. [...] Our MP turned up on our behalf and asked if she could talk about the [application]. She's the real reason why we've got were we've got on this – she supported us on this all the way along! She objected and said that there was a lack of consultation and she really gave the case for RETAINING this building! (Interviewee 6)

The actions taken by the SHC and OSTA resulted in positive outcomes for both groups. The OST, arguably, made the most significant gain. Following the deferral of the planning application for the OST by the TPC, the housing association withdrew its proposal altogether. This provided the necessary window of opportunity for the OSTA to devise its own proposals. These comprised refurbishing, as opposed to demolishing and redeveloping, the OST for residential and commercial workspace use and the setting up of a CDT to assume ownership and management control of the building. The OSTA presented an opportunities report to the SPB, which was also reviewed by representatives from the GoL and Housing Corporation, outlining that their proposal fitted into national urban policy objectives. The SPB agreed to pay for a survey of the OST.

> We started to talk amongst ourselves and said that the alternative, instead of having a totally housing driven [scheme], was to have a commercially driven scheme! [...] We produced an Opportunities Report that was presented to a meeting that was attended by GoL and the Housing Corporation. [...] Our proposals fitted with current brownfield site policy! So, when we actually put it forward the SPB agreed to pay for an architectural survey. [...] So, we're in the process of forming a [CDT] and the basis that it needs an asset and the asset is precisely the asset that the housing association was going for and that's the land! [...] The stage that we've got to is forming the CDT and formulating a business plan that gives our proposal credibility with officers in the Housing Department to recommend to the Housing Committee and work out some terms under which they would agree to let us have the land! Then we have to find partners! We're looking to people like English Partnerships, funding partners who are also in the regeneration game and partners like a housing association for the residential premises.   (Interviewee 6)

The OSTA's proposals progressed towards becoming reality as it drew upon support from a network of contacts, including a highly experienced community housing advocacy group and a regeneration consultancy. In a bizarre turn of fate, the OST was guaranteed protection from demolition when it was designated as part of a local conservation area. The OSTA had also managed to identify a new development partner, another housing association.

In comparison, the SHC's approach was much more individualistic and protracted in nature. Put simply, they had to lobby hard in order to, firstly, get recognized as a legitimate community group with a right to representation on the SCF. Secondly, political support for their cause was not as explicit as that secured by the OSTA. Finally, their challenge to proposals to demolish and redevelop their homes was constructed almost entirely in-house. SCH members drew upon their 20 years of experience in social housing management and maintenance to demonstrate their ability and 'right' to be fully involved in any decision-making process impacting on their homes and community. Although the initial proposals were not withdrawn, during the time of fieldwork, there was a radical overhaul in the SPBs attitude towards SHC:

> I think what has happened is that there's been a very clear change in the way that we're being treated now! For example, we've been ASKED to come up with a joint development scheme! We ARE now meeting DIRECTLY with the Council! We are attempting to raise money and find out what social housing grant money is available! We've had the senior officers from the Partnership meet us to discuss what is possible! We've had to fight to get back to the beginning! We are NOW back at the beginning! The development is going ahead but its development from the bottom-up! It's not imposed development!   (Interviewee 7)

The ability of the local community to exercise influence outside the realms of the SPB was acknowledged by senior officers who highlighted the difficulties in getting proposals through the TPC and the resistance and initiative shown by the OSTA:

> That doesn't always mean that they [i.e. 'the local community'] are less powerful! The TPC is a good case in point! It will give much more credence to the SCFs view on a planning issue than they will to a developer! If it came to making a decision on an issue supported strongly by the community, a new community hall for example, there is a much better chance of that going ahead than if I went to the TPC and said the community hall was a good idea. They can exercise their power through a number of ways and have done so. (Interviewee 4)

> [The local community] do HAVE very REAL power! At the moment we are going through ANGST because one of the sites that's been approved by [the TPC] – I think, by about five [TPCs] – has taken OVER A YEAR! […] The residents there don't want it to happen and the politicians are unable to make a decision as to whether it should happen or not! Now that it's down to the detail of implementation the power of a local lobby is enough to encourage the Council members to not make a decision! […] The [OST] was another case. There were proposals to demolish and rebuild it. But, that encountered PHENOMENALLY FIERCE OPPOSITION to the extent that the housing association withdrew from the scheme! (Interviewee 17)

The end game of the rational hyper-pluralists was to win over the co-operation of the SPB through the construction of visionary and workable community-centred alternatives. This contrasted with the approach adopted by the community militants who shared the same concerns as the OSETRA, OSTA and SCH about the imposition of proposals from above with no meaningful community consultation/participation. The militants, however, opted to follow a traditional hyper-pluralist approach to influence decision-making. In short, their objective was to subvert and bring the regeneration process to a halt via assume control of the SCF.

Traditional Hyper-pluralism

In simple terms, this approach entailed militant community activists literally taking to the streets to express their objections to the regeneration process. Their strategy may be described as 'street-fighting pluralism' (Waste, 1986; Yates, 1977). As already outlined, their tactics entailed invading and subverting SCF meetings, intimidating SCF members and mobilizing propaganda campaigns within the neighbourhood. This form of hyper-pluralism manifested itself most explicitly during two key inter-connected events related to 'the Mall'.

First, as discussed earlier, the militants orchestrated a successful fly poster and door-to-door anti-demolition campaign in the run-up to the tenants' ballot on the Precinct. Whilst their campaign contained elements of truth, truth and reality faded into obscurity under the rhetoric and propaganda they used to realize their objective. The community militants failed to offer any alternatives to those proposals obtained within the Delivery Plan and refused to recognize the existence and plight of the OSTA and SCH.

The militants presented proposals to demolish and redevelop 'the Mall' as amounting to the 'privatization' of council housing. They, subsequently, called upon tenants to reject this and vote for the housing stock to be retained within council ownership. This stance was somewhat contradictory in that the militants did not trust the council and wanted to see it fail. Notably, the militants failed to offer any real alternative proposals as to how 'the Mall' could be rejuvenated. Instead, their strategy appeared to be to prolong its inimitable death in an effort to discredit the council yet further:

> The idea was that 'the Mall' would be demolished, tenants would be decanted and they would all get a right to return to a HA property! But, it was difficult for us to get that message across! Basically, local activists who have a particular gripe against the local authority quite often hijacked the big public meetings! They were causing hysteria basically amongst *Mr.* and *Mrs. Average*. The council decided to have a ballot! We announced that we were going to have a ballot but we didn't really go hammers and tongs at trying to sway people into voting pro-demolition! It was just a case of: Are you in favour of the demolition of *The Mall?* In fact, we didn't really mention to tenants that they would be entitled to a £1500 home loss payment. We didn't feel that was appropriate! But, at the same time there was a FAIRLY WELL organized, fairly high pressured ANTI-DEMOLITION CAMPAIGN put together by these local activists! [...] These people were just ANTI-, ANTI-, ANTI- everything! They didn't even come up with alternatives!
>
> (Interviewee 18)

This 'anti-everything' perception of the militants was also held amongst SCF members:

> There is a real militant tendency here. There's a local person who attracts a certain group around him and he is very articulate but he's just so left wing! It's very difficult to know WHAT motivates and drives a man like him. He's a destroyer! He's a wrecker! That's one of my definitions of militants! They're wreckers! They're not constructive! They've NEVER come up with a constructive idea! But what they are always doing is opposing and saying "don't do this and don't pull that down! Don't do this! Don't do that"! They're out to wreck any constructive ideas!
>
> (Interviewee 6)

Following the council's decision to split the vote of the tenants' ballot, attempts to secure planning permission for the pro-redevelopment side of 'the Mall' were fraught with a series of setbacks. These included, a small number of tenants who steadfastly refused offers of rehousing for several months until they were offered accommodation that matched their wants and in a location of their preference. In addition, a retailer refused to vacate his premises until he was suitably compensated for loss of business and earnings. This latter situation became extremely protracted as the SPB rejected the amount of compensation being claimed. The retailer, consequently, sought legal redress to resolve the situation. This situation prevailed for almost 12 months and was still ongoing by the time fieldwork had been completed with no sign of a resolution in sight.

The biggest delay to proceedings on 'the Mall', however, was due to the planning application being constantly deferred by the TPC. This was grounded in two key inter-related factors. Firstly, there was persistent opposition, mainly from militant activists, to the planning application at TPC meetings. Secondly, and more notably, as there were local elections looming councillors were ambivalent about taking any decisions or indeed any explicit interest in controversial issues affecting the local community until after the elections.

After the elections, however, it became necessary to make a decision on 'the Mall' as it was increasingly blighting the local area and there were reports that squatters had moved into some of the empty flats. If this latter issue proved to be true then the council faced the prospect of even more delays. Moreover, the GoL had become increasingly impatient at the lack of progress on this proposal.

A site visit by the TPC to assess the state of 'the Mall' and to determine local attitudes was eventually scheduled – this was approximately 20 months after the controversial splitting of the ballot – with the view to making an absolute decision. Events at the TPC site visit represented the second example of explicit street fighting pluralism involving militant and other tenant activists.

The TPC Site Visit: Street Fighting Pluralism in Action

Advance notification of the TPC site visit by the SPB to the local community provided militant activists with the opportunity to prepare their anti-demolition campaign. On the day of the site visit 'the Mall' was a hive of activity. A large number of people (approximately 50-70 people), young and old, 'black' and 'white', men and women and locals and non-locals were littered along 'the Mall' patiently waiting for the TPC members to arrive. At the centre of this activity the two key militant protagonists were busily distributing anti-demolition fly-posters to passers-by and keeping a watchful lookout for the arrival of the TPC. Posters were also pasted on walls and shop fronts along 'the Mall'. Notably, none of the posters were attributable to any organization or group. They had merely been printed off on plain A4-sized paper. They stated:

"SAY NO TO DEMOLITION"

"SOUTHSIDE MARKET – RIP"

"THE COUNCIL ARE REFURBISHING WHAT THEY SHOULD BE KNOCKING DOWN & KNOCKING DOWN WHAT THEY SHOULD BE REFUBISHING"

In what was seen as typical Lambeth council fashion, the TPC members arrived late. Their late arrival had provoked whispers that they were not going to show up because of local opposition to proposals for the area. By the time of their arrival the atmosphere had become very impatient and anxious. As the TPC members assembled at one end of 'the Mall', those that had turned out to meet them quickly came together, headed by two key militant activists, and marched towards the councillors. The entire scene had a distinctly confrontational air to it, especially when both sides came face-to-face.

The councillors introduced themselves to the assembled crowd and briefly outlined the purpose of the site visit. They asked for community activists to represent and outline the views of the local community. This was difficult to achieve, however, as numerous people vied to convey their concerns and views. In particular, several elderly women persisted in repeating their concerns about the lack of shopping facilities. A few other people complained about their offers of re-housing. Others raised concerns about the demolition process.

Trying to elicit the community's concerns proved too chaotic however. The Chairman of the TPC called proceedings to order and requested that two people should be 'nominated' to act as a conduit for the rest of the community. The two key militant protagonists, who had strategically (and deliberately) positioned themselves at the front of the crowd, automatically assumed this mantle. The first militant laid claim that he spoke for the whole community on the basis that he was actively involved at the cutting edge of community action within the local area. The other militant activist, although only having recent and peripheral involvement with the regeneration programme, as an observer on the SCF, explained that he too spoke for the whole community on account that her was Vice Chairman of the local neighbourhood housing forum.

The latter militant activist took the lead in outlining the community's perspective on proposals to regenerate 'the Mall' and immediately tapped into their key concerns. He highlighted the need for shopping facilities for the elderly and the historical significance of the area as one of London's oldest street markets. Moreover, he highlighted that the council had a policy, as outlined in the borough development plan, to preserve and facilitate the development of street markets within the borough before posing the question why were the council failing to do this in *Southside*. The loud cheer and clapping from the crowd signalled their approval of these comments.

When the first militant resumed control of proceedings he was interrupted on several occasions. In particular, two females, one 'black' and the other, 'white', who had earlier been observed conversing with the militants and distributing anti-demolition flyers, interjected in an attempt to highlight their specific concerns. More crucially, however, they also objected to the militants' claim that he represented the whole community. The militant retorted to these comments in a forceful tone, stepping forward and shouting at both women that he had never seen them at any meetings related to 'the Mall'. In other words, since they had not been actively involved in the long running anti-demolition campaign they had no right to be speaking out now.

Whilst the two militants may have confidently and clearly conveyed the general concerns of the 'local community', many of those in attendance were clearly frustrated at being denied the opportunity to have their say. Additionally, there were reservations as to whom the militants actually represented and their motives. Interestingly, none of the representatives from the SCF participated in the TPC site visit. The SCF's absence was peculiar especially in view of the fact that it was supposed to represent the wider local community. In fact, only one member, the OSETRA Secretary was present. She played an extremely passive role throughout the site visit. She deliberately positioned herself on the periphery of the crowd in an apparently determined effort to avoid contact with the militant activists. Subsequent informal discussions with several SCF members revealed that they had avoided the site visit because their relationship with the militants had become increasingly fragile and they had no desire to become embroiled in any conflict with them in public.

This fragility was premised on a letter written to the council by the Vice-Chairman of the NHF, in its name, criticizing the aims, objectives and structure of the SCF. This letter had come as something of a shock to SCF members as they had been attempting to reconcile their relationship with the NHF by permitting its militant Vice-Chair to sit in on meetings. Admittedly, the SCF had been having difficulties in obtaining a quorum at monthly meetings and thus preventing it from moving forward as a body. The accusations within the NHF's letter, however, were very much misplaced. The SCF, as observed by the Chair and Vice-Chairman of the NHF, had been working extremely hard to resolve the lack of attendance at meetings and defining and strengthening its role within the SPB.

It, subsequently, transpired that the letter which purported to be from the NHF had not been ratified by its committee. In fact, they were not even aware that it had been written and sent to the council. Naturally, the SCF were particularly aggrieved by the letter and perceived it as a further attempt by the militants to undermine both it and the overall regeneration process. Notably, the NHF Vice-Chairman was absent from subsequent SCF meetings after it became aware of the letter.

For the remainder of the site visit, the TPC and local people toured the part of 'the Mall' scheduled for demolition. Throughout the tour the two key militant agents were constantly engaged in intense discussion with local councillors about what would happen to 'the Mall'. At the conclusion of the site visit, the TPC thanked everyone for attending and informed them that a decision would be made at the next TPC meeting. There was an air of optimism amongst the militants that they had won over the TPC, mainly as a result of the turnout of tenants. Several months later, however, planning permission for demolition and redevelopment was granted thereby ending the fate of the most contentious proposal within the regeneration *Southside*.

In light of all the difficulties surrounding 'the Mall', the SPB committed itself to fully consulting with the SCF and USETRA on the demolition process. This was to commence with a full presentation on the demolition method statement that covered issues such as health and safety, hours of work and access for goods vehicles to the site.

By stepping outside the realm of the official structures of the SPB, tenants were more than capable of asserting community power over the pace and direction of the regeneration process within *Southside*. Despite regeneration proposals initially being imposed upon the local community, the diverse and complex mix of sub-communities and intra-community relations within *Southside* gave rise to various forms of hyper-pluralistic reactions. Interestingly, the sense of identity, resistance to the regeneration process, and intra-community conflict within the

SCF asserted by the various sub-communities within *Southside* was structured more around 'territory' than other interests such as gender, age or, more importantly, 'race'.

The Contested Significance of 'Race'

Ambiguity surrounded the significance and problematic nature of 'race' within *Southside*. For a small minority of SCF members interviewed 'race' and racism were seen as problematic issues within the SCF, the overall regeneration process and/or the wider *Southside* neighbourhood. Other interviewees acknowledged that 'race' had in the past been a contentious issue within the wider community but this had largely subsided. In overall terms, data gathered from interviews and observations pointed to 'race' being a fairly insignificant issue within the SCF and the regeneration process, during the course of the fieldwork period at least.

Community and Race Relations

A survey conducted for the SPB revealed a generally optimistic attitude about race relations (LRC, 1997). A slight majority (51 per cent) of total respondents felt that race relations in the area were either 'very good' (6 per cent) and/or 'quite good' (45 per cent). This contrasted with only 19 per cent who considered relations to be either 'quite poor' (13 per cent) and/or 'very poor' (6 per cent). This attitude was generally consistent across different ethnic groupings. 'Black' Caribbeans, however, exhibited a higher degree of ambivalence as indicated by 25 per cent who considered relations to be 'neither good/poor' (see Table 6.3).

Table 6.3 Attitudes to 'Race' Relations (*Southside*)

	Response by Ethnic Group (per cent)				
	'Black' Caribbean (N=64)	'Black' African (N=61)	BME Other (N=63)	'White' (N=203)	Total (N=391)
Very good	5	7	5	7	6
Quite good	44	48	48	44	45
Neither good/poor	25	15	14	17	18
Quite poor	11	16	18	12	13
Very poor	5	3	8	5	5
Don't know	11	12	8	14	12
Total (%)	100	100	100	100	100

Source: LRC (1997) *Southside* Partnership Baseline Survey

The view that race relations were generally positive in the area and thus a contributory factor in explaining the relative insignificance of 'race' within the regeneration process was posited by a number officers and other professional agents associated to the SPB and/or SCF in interviews:

> I can't say that we've ever had a discussion about 'race' or ethnic minority issues! The residents of the area are seen as the residents of the area! [...] I don't think that it's ever been raised as an issue for the SPB to consider! It's probably a product of the fact that 'race' is NOT seen to be a significant issue down there [on *Southside*]! I would say that Lambeth is much more MIXED UP ethnically than other places that I have worked! Paradoxically, 'race' is much less an issue. In Bermondsey (Southwark), for example, racial harassment was and IS an enormous problem. In Lambeth it doesn't appear to be a problem at all because it is more heterogeneous. I would think that because it is so mixed-up probably means that there are less tensions of that sort! What I think is significant is its absence! It's not an issue! It's not an issue for the SPB! It's not an issue for the local housing management office either! (Interviewee 4)

> I don't think that there's much racial tension in this area! I mean the largest group is Afro-Caribbean and the next largest group is Asians! It's one of the things that I really like about this area is the diversity and the fact that everybody does seem to get on okay together! There's quite a different feeling to when I lived in Essex. You felt very MUCH that there was an issue about 'race'! The National Front is very strong and very OBVIOUS in those kinds of areas! You don't have that kind of thing here! (Interviewee 19)

> TO BE QUITE HONEST 'race' has NOT RAISED itself as an issue in the whole process during the time that I've been there! Bear in mind that this was one of those traditionally 'white' working-class areas up to about 20 years ago and has become ethnically diverse since then! I do remember a stage in the 1980s when there was TAs and shadow TAs – one was 'white' and the other 'black'! It has gone past that! (Interview 7)

The preceding comments point to officers having a mainly bureaucratic perception and understanding of 'race' issues. That is, their policy approach to 'race' was essentially a 'colour-blind' and reactive one. Indeed, a small number of SCF members challenged the assertion that 'race' and racism were unproblematic issues contending that the regeneration process was structurally and institutionally discriminatory.

Structural and Institutional Discrimination

One SCF member, in particular, contended that 'race' issues were automatically precluded from getting onto the agenda of the regeneration process on the basis of who had constructed it. That was: 'white', middle-class heterosexual men with no comprehension of the needs of BME communities:

> I think we also have to look at the people who are answering the demands of this area. These have been constructed by white middle-class men! And, it's not just the 'white'! It's the class! And, it's the gender! Which means what would a plan

drawn up by three white, middle-class straight men, for that matter, have to do with a 'black' family of a single mother?   (Interviewee 5)

In addition, this interviewee contended that 'black' tenants were denied representation within the SCF due to latent and explicit racism operating within the wider community and one of the TRAs, both of which were dominated by 'white' English working-class tenants:

> 'Black' representation on the SCF is VERY Very Bad! Very Bad! There is explicit racism! There is a very clear 'white' working class history behind old *Southside*! It's very funny from where I'm sitting from because there is also a VERY LONG 'black' history in *Southside*. But it's a very uneasy alliance! For example, when I started working there we had clear issues of people not wanting some representatives to sit on the group! The representatives who were not wanted would very clearly say that this was a 'race' issue and they were doing that because they were 'black'! So, there is a RESISTANCE! There is a resistance about 'black' people! I DO NOT think that they LIKE 'black' people! It's as simple as that! I don't think that they see 'black' people as part of the history of *Southside*! And, by 'black' I mean everyone who is not 'white' English! [...] But I'll tell you the REAL difficulty! The real difficulty is that the people who ARE reluctant to take on the 'black' issue are the ones within the SCF. [...] Mainly, it comes from the [OSETRA] as opposed to [USETRA]. Funnily enough, both of the reps from the USETRA are 'black'! But there is a VERY BIG resistance from the OSETRA! VERY VERY BIG RESISTANCE!   (Interviewee 5)

A similarly negative viewpoint was expressed by the USYCs representative in relation to the SPBs approach to involving BMEs in the regeneration process, which he described as coming from a very 'British' (i.e. 'white' English) perspective:

> Well, at the end of the day, you know, you have to look at it from a BRITISH point of view! At the end of the day, like I said, when your dealing with a community as diverse as ours you have to make sure that the information you send out is appropriate and adequate! So, you can't send out everything in English when there's a large section of ethnic minorities who don't have English as their first language! [...] Well I haven't seen their information going out in other tongues! All of it is in English! That's discrimination right a way, in my view!   (Interviewee 12)

More fundamentally, the USYC representative was of the view that his organization had deliberately *and* exclusively been discriminated against by the SPB. This viewpoint was premised on the fact that despite being the key 'black'-led community group within the neighbourhood, the SPB had failed to consult the USYC over proposals to develop new housing on the land it occupied. Furthermore, it was claimed that the SPB had taken soil samples from the grounds of the USYC without having asked it for permission to do so. This act reinforced the USYC representatives' view that the SPB had no respect for his organization and the 'black' community in general:

Up until now the ONLY thing that we have had from the Council is a notice to quit the premises! I think that was given on malicious forethought! So, I think that if they pursue their line of action then they are going to encounter opposition! PEOPLE ARE GOING TO HEAR ABOUT THIS - The Newspapers! The media will take this up! [...] For me, as a 'black' man, it reminds me of when they went to Africa to take slaves: With the bible in one hand and a gun in the other! My place is located on prime land on the main road! So, the interest is very high here! Not considering that 95 per cent of the users ARE 'black'! So when you dismantle us what's going to happen? Where are we going to go?   (Interviewee 12)

In response to the way it had been treated, the USYC sought to influence the regeneration process from outside the confines of the SPB and SCF. A two-pronged strategy was used.

On the one hand, the USYC 'boycotted' the SCF by refusing to attend committee meetings. If the USYC had attended meetings the SCF would have had the requisite number of members to make executive decisions and thus been in a potentially stronger position to influence decision-making within the SPB. This boycott was premised on a misguided perception that the SCF was colluding with the SPB and that it did not support the USYC's plight against the SPB. On the other hand, legal redress was sought against the council, who actually owned the land occupied by the USYC, for its failure to inform and consult the USYC about proposals to redevelop the land it occupied. The services of a prestigious law firm were secured on a *pro bono* basis. A protracted and prolonged legal process ensued that eventually resulted in the proposals for the USYC site being withdrawn from the following years Delivery Plan. This decision reflected yet another successful example of how the local community was able to exercise influence over decision-making from outside the formal structures of the SPB.

The USYC representative's perception that his organization was the subject of institutional racism was myopic and, more importantly, misplaced. In short, the USYC had failed to recognize, and acknowledge, that the SPB had systematically failed to inform, consult and involve the various sub-communities that made up the SCF. This was due to two inter-related factors. First, the USYC representative had too readily accepted the (mis)information propagated by militant activists about the SPB, the SCF and its individual members. Second, as a consequence of having boycotted SCF meetings, the USYC representative was unable to witness first hand the other members' struggles against the SPB and the community militants. Furthermore, by boycotting the SCF this inadvertently contributed to the exclusion of 'race' being articulated as a matter of concern within the regeneration process. This was acknowledged within the SCF and the SPB who were both very keen for the USYC to become more involved in the programme:

If the USYC came to the SCF regularly the agenda would change because they would be banging on about 'race' issues. Unfortunately, because of this rather torturous process we've had regarding the USYC and its redevelopment they have become disengaged! That's unfortunate because their representative is not just "Mr. Youth Club". He's also very well respected in his particular community! He

KNOWS an awful lot about the community and has lived in the same area for 30 years. He knows the issues and would be a REAL resource for us.   (Interviewee 4)

Other interviewees disputed the existence of structural and institutional discrimination within the regeneration process. In fact, even those who felt that such discrimination underpinned the under-representation of 'black' tenants and 'race' issues were of the view that it was largely an historical problem with diminishing significance. It was highlighted that there had been a much more explicitly racialized atmosphere within the neighbourhood, and the borough in general, during the 1980s. It was accepted that the neighbourhood probably contained some people who held racist attitudes. Such individuals, however, individuals would be excluded from the SCF.

Optimism about 'race' relations were also expressed during an informal conversation with the USYC representative and the SCF's new CDO, both of whom were 'black', where the issues of race relations and sectarianism arose. The USYC representative made it quite plain that he thought race relations in Britain were generally positive and more progressive than they were in the USA. Indeed, he had previously expressed similar views in other contexts. The SCF Chairman noted:

The USYC rep actually made a very interesting statement at one of the meetings. He talked about how he lived in the area for many many years and when he came here he was actually OVERWHELMED by the warmth of the reception that he received in the local community! He hasn't experienced racism to the extent that he's experienced in other parts of the world or the country!   (Interviewee 7)

One of the USETRA representatives, a 'black' female, on the SCF noted that she had not experienced any racism or exclusion within her own TRA and/or the SCF because of her ethnic identity. The only difficult that she had encountered was intimidation from one of the community militants. This intimidation was not thought to be racially motivated. It, however, was acknowledged that within the wider community some people did hold racist attitudes:

I haven't witnessed or experienced exclusion in terms of 'race' or gender! [...] I haven't felt excluded for being a West Indian female but more for being a small female and looking young. In fact, actually, I think a lot of young people, male or female, would have that feeling regardless of their background and 'race' or whatever! It's because the older people here have quite a long history of community involvement. You would get a sense of exclusion in some of the shops where conversation would stop. It was like that in the old greengrocers'. But, I have to be honest and say that so far of the people that I have met I've never had that problem!   (Interviewee 14)

Observational fieldwork of the SCF meetings revealed no racialized atmosphere. On the contrary, an increasingly inclusive atmosphere emerged within the SCF over the course of the fieldwork period. This was due to a combination of factors. These included: the appointment of a new Chairman and Vice-Chairman who both held progressive liberal attitudes; the 'suspension' of the community militant from the SCF; and the appointment of a new CDO, who happened to be of Afro-Caribbean origin.

Bureaucratic Expediency

As noted earlier, the SPB's perspective on 'race' was quintessentially bureaucratic. In other words, it was colour-blind. As far as the institutional partners on the SPB were concerned, they saw their role as primarily developing (and subsequently managing) new social housing for *all* members of the local community in housing need. It was contended that if there had been specific ethnic housing demands and needs then these would have been duly taken into consideration within the development process. Since no such demands were made from within the local community, 'race' was automatically assumed to be an unproblematic and insignificant issue:

> I don't think that 'race' has had a very SUBSTANTIAL effect because we've been concentrating on HOUSING! Now, had there been a large Islamic community within the area – which there isn't – THEN one would have VERY DELIBERATELY separately consulted with that Islamic community over design issues because they have different design criteria! But that wasn't the case here! [...] So, I have to say that I don't think issues of ethnicity have been PARTICULARLY salient! Why? Because issues of cultural diversity and so on have NOT R-E-A-L-L-Y raised their heads! And they haven't been PARTICULARLY relevant to the process of providing new housing!
> (Interviewee 11)

> 'Race' and ethnicity have not had an input into *Southside* particularly [...] because at the end of the day it's viewed, within GoL, as a housing project that will benefit the community as a whole – we trust! [...] There was certainly a 'race' element in Brixton! But with *Southside* I've never got that feeling!   (Interviewee 3)

As the regeneration process was thrown into disarray by the hyper-pluralistic actions of individual SCF members, the institutional partners became increasingly bureaucratic. That is, the SPB turned all of its energies towards preventing further slippage in programmed outputs. In other words, it became bureaucratically expedient that programmed outputs, especially planned housing developments, were completed to ensure that central government funding was not withdrawn for failing to do so. This bureaucratic expediency was another contributing factor in explaining why 'race' was such an insignificant issue within the SPB.

Conclusions

In conclusion, regeneration and decision-making were extremely protracted processes within *Southside*. The SCF, as an organizational partner of the SPB, was unable to exert any influence over decision-making. This was due to two primary factors. On the one hand, community factionalism, initiated and sustained by a small group of community militants, prevented the SCF from functioning as a coherent organization. On the other hand, the way in which the SCF was treated by the SPB – lack of consultation, resources, assistance and *de facto* exclusion from the decision-making arenas of the institutional partner – meant that it was ill-equipped to influence decision-making.

Nevertheless, by 'boycotting' the regeneration process, stepping outside the realms of the SPB and pursuing their own strategies, individual SCF members and the community militants were able to exercise quite considerable influence over decision-making – initial proposals were either modified and/or completely abandoned. In short, the SPB effectively lost control over the pace and direction of the regeneration process as a result of this community backlash. The overall pattern of community power within *Southside*, therefore, may be best described as *hyper-pluralistic* in nature.

The significance and problematic nature of 'race' within *Southside* was a contested issue. A small minority of community interviewees contended that structural and institutional racism pervaded the regeneration process. Other community members acknowledged that the neighbourhood had suffered from racism but this was largely consigned to the past. There was no evidence, from observational research, to suggest the existence of racially motivated exclusion within the SCF and/or the SPB. It was contended that the SPB was institutionally racist. The 'reality' of the situation was that the SPB had *discriminated* against all the sub-communities within *Southside* through its failure to consult the local community at the outset of the programme. It would be more accurate to say that the SPB had shown itself to be institutionally naïve and incompetent in relation to the concept of community participation.

Chapter 7

Westside:
Paternalistic Pluralism and the
(Over-)Significance of 'Race'

Involvement of the local community lies at the heart of this initiative; from the management of the overall initiative and individual projects through to participation in the design, organisation and implementation of the projects arising out of the first two stages. The success of this approach will provide a model for community-led regeneration elsewhere. This vision has been developed by local people, with the support of professional agencies in the Partnership that will now drive it forward.

(*Westside* Community Forum, 1997)

Introduction

As with *Northside* (Chapter 5) and *Southside* (Chapter 6), community participation was a, if not, *the* central objective of the regeneration of *Westside*. In short, the 'local community' was to become empowered through their involvement in decision-making. The proclamation in the preceding abstract that community involvement lay at the heart of the regeneration of *Westside* and that success depended on this was an aspiration as opposed to reality. The *Westside* Community Regeneration Project (WCRP) was conceive, nurtured and controlled by a core group of professional voluntary sector agents who had varying degrees of contact with particular (ethnic) groups within the neighbourhood. There could be no denying the commitment of these professional agents to the ideals of community participation and empowerment. Their paternalism, unfortunately, precluded the WCRP from becoming a model for community-led regeneration.

This chapter focuses on a number of key issues. First, a brief descriptive overview of the *Westside* neighbourhood is outlined in order to provide some background about the area. Second, the local authority's regeneration agenda is set out. Next, the conception and evolution of the *Westside* Community Regeneration Project (WCRP) scheme are outlined. Fourth, the primary decision-making structures of the WCR programme are discussed. Fifth, the community consultation and participation strategy adopted is highlighted. Then, some concluding comments as to the significance of 'race', which is interwoven throughout the discussion in the aforementioned sections, are made. Finally, some overall conclusions are drawn.

Westside: **Setting the Scene**

In comparison to *Northside* and *Southside* which were people vibrant and architecturally eclectic localities respectively, *Westside* lacked a strong sense of atmosphere on both of these fronts. *Westside* was similar to *Southside* however in that it was a very quiet area in terms of pedestrian traffic. This was despite being a densely populated neighbourhood. The area only seemed to really come to life during the early morning and late afternoon rush hours as people made their way to and from school and work.

On numerous visits to and through the area, to attend meetings and conduct interviews, the small numbers of people observed were mainly women and children. Furthermore, they were largely of 'Asian' and 'black' origin. On a small, but regular, number of occasions small groups of young and elderly 'Asian' males were also observed. It subsequently transpired that they were making their way to and from the local mosque. Interestingly, despite being the largest ethnic group within the neighbourhood, the 'white' population was a relatively 'invisible' group. In many ways *Westside* resembled something of an ethnic enclave. This impression was structured and reinforced by the people observed within the neighbourhood; the geographical isolation of the area – a result of it being bounded on all sides by several main roads; and. the racialized discourse amongst those agents responsible for managing the WCR programme.

In architectural terms, the built environment in *Westside* was uniform and monotonous in nature. The neighbourhood was predominantly residential and comprised largely of 4-5 storey purpose-built blocks of deck access flats. Besides mainly residential buildings, the only other building of any major significance within the neighbourhood was the Community Centre. This was a rather large two-storey modernist building, built in the 1970s, situated at the geographical heart of the neighbourhood and run by the Central *Westside* Community Group (CWCG). The Community Centre was showing signs of age and in need of refurbishment.

As a consequence of its function and location the Community Centre was the epicentre of community activity. It provided a wide range of services for the local community. These included: advice on welfare benefits, a small nursery, a meeting place for the elderly, English language classes, activities for young children, a disco for young teenagers and regular surgeries with the local councillor and MP. The Community Centre was also the 'headquarters' of the local tenants' association, and other community groups within the neighbourhood. In short, the Community Centre acted as the social glue within *Westside* bringing different groups and communities into contact with one another. As the key community node within the neighbourhood the Community Centre was used to launch the consultation process of the WCR programme.

Westside was a typical 'inner city' neighbourhood. The ward within which the neighbourhood was situated lagged behind the rest of the borough on a number of socio-economic indicators (see Table 7.1). In terms of housing tenure, for example, two-thirds of households lived in council-rented accommodation as opposed to just over half (51 per cent) in the borough as a whole.

Table 7.1 Socio-economic Profile of *Westside* (per cent)

	Westside 1981	*Westside* 1991	LB Southwark 1991
Housing Tenure:			
Owner Occupied	4	14	27
Council	81	66	51
Other Rented	13	11	11
Housing Association	3	11	10
Housing Type:			
Detached	-	1	1
Semi-detached	-	1	4
Terraced	-	9	19
Purpose built flat	-	81	63
Converted flat	-	8	13
Shared flat	-	0	1
Employment Status:			
Full-time	69	59	61
Part-time	14	11	12
Self-employed	5	8	9
Unemployed	13	21	18
Other:			
Economically Active	66	61	63
Economically Inactive	34	39	37
Long-term illness	-	13	13
BME population	-	31	24
No Car Households	-	66	58
No Central Heating	-	16	17

Source: LB Southwark (1993)

Furthermore, although there had been a marked increase in the level of owner occupation from four to 14 per cent between 1981-1991 there were still almost twice as many owner-occupiers (27 per cent) in Southwark generally. There was also a striking difference in the type of housing within the area. A staggering 81 per cent of households lived in 'purpose-built flats', most of which were constructed pre-1945. This compared with 63 per cent for the borough overall. And, whereas almost one-fifth (19 per cent) of LB Southwark's residents lived in traditional terraced housing, less than half (9 per cent) of this lived in the same type of housing within *Westside*.

Unemployment was also a particularly acute problem within *Westside*. Census data for 1991, for example, showed that unemployment in the area (30 per cent) was twice that of the borough (15 per cent) (LB Southwark, 1993). This had fallen to 20 per cent, just three per cent points above the borough average by March 1996 (*Westside* Community Forum, 1996a). A community audit survey

(N=426), conducted in late 1997, of the greater *Westside* neighbourhood[1] found that unemployment had increased to around 25 per cent. This was more than three times the then rate for London (SBU, 1998). Interestingly, the community audit also found that overall 'white' and BME unemployment rates were broadly similar to one another. Closer analysis, however, revealed that 'Asians' had the lowest unemployment rate at 13 per cent (N=31), followed by 'whites' (23 per cent; N=90) and then 'blacks' with 26 per cent (N=54).

   Westside also had a high proportion of ethnic minority groups. Data from the 1991 Census showed that BMEs accounted for almost one-third (31 per cent) of the population. This contrasted with 24 per cent for the borough in general. The community audit (SBU, 1998), conducted mainly on the Central *Westside* Estate[2], found that 'whites' constituted the 'minority' (39 per cent) whilst BMEs accounted for the 'majority' (61 per cent) population (see Table 7.2). This differs significantly from 1991 Census data that showed 'whites' accounted for almost 70 per cent of the ward population.

Table 7.2 Ethnic Population Profile of *Westside* (per cent)

Ethnic Group	Community Profile[1] (1997)	Westside Ward (1991)	LB Southwark (1991)
All groups (No.)	426	9285	244,834
'White'	39	69	76
'Black'	27	17	17
(Black Caribbean)	(3)	(5)	(8)
(Black African)	(18)	(10)	(7)
(Black Other)	(6)	(1)	(2)
'Asian'	16	10	3
(Indian)	-	(1)	(1)
(Pakistani)	(1)	(1)	(1)
(Bangladeshi)	(15)	(8)	(1)
Chinese/Other	17	11	5
(Chinese)	(2)	(2)	(1)
(Other Asian)	(2)	(1)	(1)
(Other, incl. Irish)	(13)	(8)	(3)
TOTAL	100	100	100

[1]Data refers to sample survey (N=426) in Central *Westside* Estate; Northern Estate; Southern Estate and Eastern Estate within the *Westside* ward.
Source: OPCS (1991); SBU (1998)

---

[1]   The greater *Westside* area comprised 4 estates: 'Central', 'Northern', 'Southern' and 'Eastern'.

[2]   The Central *Westside* Estate actually forms the focus of the WCR programme despite the claims in the initial bid document that programmes would be developed for the Greater *Westside* area.

The significant ethnic population restructuring suggested by the community audit should be read with a degree of caution due to the random sampling technique used combined with the fact that the survey was mainly conducted on the Central *Westside* Estate. Nevertheless, anecdotal evidence based on observations from visits to the estate clearly suggested that BMEs, in particular, West Africans, Somalis and Bangladeshis, constituted a significant and growing proportion of the local population. The opening of two 'Black' African-owned stores on the boundary of the neighbourhood was a further indication of the growing prevalence of the BME community within the area.

Closer analysis of the BME community in *Westside* showed that three groups, 'Black' Africans (26 per cent), Bangladeshis (22 per cent) and the Irish (17 per cent), accounted for almost two-thirds (65 per cent) of the BME population (see Table 7.3). The Bangladeshi community was significantly over-represented (22 per cent) within the ward in comparison to figures for the council (3 per cent) in overall terms. Furthermore, it was estimated that 80 per cent of first generation Bangladeshis on the estate could not read, write or speak English.

Table 7.3 BMEs in *Westside* and LB Southwark (per cent)

Ethnic Group	Westside	LB Southwark	Difference
'Black'	45	62	-17
Black African	26	25	1
Black Caribbean	14	29	-15
Black Other	5	8	-3
'Asian'	30	12	18
Indian	3	4	-1
Pakistani	1	1	0
Bangladeshi	22	3	19
Asian Other	4	4	0
'Other'	26	26	0
Chinese	4	4	0
Irish	17	16	1
Other BMEs	5	6	-1
Total	100	100	0

Source: LB Southwark (1993)

As will be seen later, the Bangladeshi community was a priority concern amongst *Westside* Community Forum (WCF) members. This was due to a combination of the Bangladeshi community's low socio-economic status and close links key members of the WCF had with this ethnic group. The interest shown in the Bangladeshi community was often at the expense of other ethnic groups within the area, chiefly Black Africans and 'whites' who were the largest BME and single ethnic groups respectively. This (over-)interest in the Bangladeshi community created an underlying tension within the WCF. Ironically, a member of the WCF, a local resident of Black African origin and representative of the Black and Ethnic

Minority Tenants Associations, a BME umbrella organization, was of the view that the WCF was 'biased' towards Bangladeshis. Furthermore, observational and interview data revealed that the WCF displayed no particular interest in the plight of the 'white' community.

Looking forward slightly, one of the key aims of the WCRP was to tackle youth racism within the neighbourhood. The WCFs concerns with this issue transpired to be over-zealous and misplaced. In short, this was grounded key WCF members having a narrow or traditional perspective of anti-racism and multiculturalism (Gilroy, 1992) and a lack of understanding as to the meaning and relevance of 'whiteness' (Bonnett, 1996a, b, 1997; Jackson, 1998).

Rebranding Southwark through Regeneration

Interestingly, LB Southwark's Regeneration, Housing and Planning Departments played virtually no role in the plans to regenerate *Westside*. Their lack of involvement stemmed from a general disinterest in social regeneration. These departments and the council in general, seemed more interested in large-scale physical and economic regeneration-type projects.

The council's regeneration agenda throughout the 1990s appears to have been primarily about re-branding itself politically, physically, economically, socially and culturally. The basis for this approach lay in the rather simple fact that Southwark was suffering from a major image problem and was in need of a serious makeover. Southwark had entered into a spiral of decline following the demise of the docks, food processing and warehousing industries in neighbourhoods such as Borough, Bermondsey and Rotherhithe during the early 1970s. Industrial decline led to the abandonment and demise of large parts of the built environment along the river. Elsewhere in the borough, housing neighbourhoods such as the Aylesbury, Heygate and Peckham Estates and the infamous Elephant and Castle shopping centre and road system, began to display signs of growing socio-economic, physical and environmental problems by the early 1980s.

In the face of this myriad of problems, LB Southwark adopted quickly to the competitive bidding funding regime set in place by the Conservative government. The level of public and private funding secured provides an indication of how successful the council has been in playing the regeneration game (see Table 7.4). In 1994, for example, the council secured the largest ever amount of SRB funding (£60m) to regenerate the five estates that made up the Peckham neighbourhood (Government Office for London, 1994; LB Southwark, 1994). LB Southwark has performed well within the SRB in overall terms, securing between £104m (GLA, 2002) and £163m (North *et al*, 2002) of funding.

When the Government announced its New Deal for Communities (NDC) programme in 1998, the Aylesbury Estate was selected as one the 17 pathfinder partnerships and allocated a total of £56m. Symbolically, the Prime Minister, Tony Blair, launched the NDC programme from the Aylesbury Estate declaring that its aim was to eradicate social exclusion via empowering local tenants.

Table 7.4 Key Urban Regeneration Projects in LB Southwark

Project	Public (£m)	Private (£m)	Total (£m)
Peckham Partnership	60	210	270
Cross River Partnership[1]	59	61	120
London's Larder	2	18	20
Pool of London	14	52	46
Aylesbury Plus	56	94	150
Elephant and Castle[2]	350	650	1000
Total	541	1085	1606

[1]Includes LB Southwark, LB Lambeth, City of Westminster and Corporation of London.
[2]Includes £25m SRB V funding plus projected £325m of other public expenditure on transport infrastructure, housing and community facilities.

Sources: Government Office for London (1994; 1995; 1996); Southwark LBC (1994; 1999, 2000); *WCF* (1996); Cross River Partnership (2000).

Despite winning significant amounts of regeneration funding and expressing a commitment to partnership-based regeneration *and* community participation, the council has encountered a number of serious setbacks within several of its key regeneration projects.

On the Aylesbury Estate, for example, the local community rejected proposals involving the transfer of council housing stock to a housing association (Triggle, 2001, 2002). The council faced similar community resistance on another SRB-funded project, Elephant Links. In this instance community activists successfully fought to have a much greater input into decision-making and over-turned proposals to re-build fewer council houses. Relations within and between the community forum and the council began to fracture primarily on the basis that the forum was perceived to have been hijacked by an unrepresentative and unruly groups of activists (North, 2003). Eventually, the council decided to shut down the community forum. The council also terminated its relationship with it developer partner who had designed a master plan for the area and engaged in quite extensive consultation with the local community (Wehner, 2002). As a result of these actions by the council the regeneration of the Elephant and Castle came to a temporary standstill and its future looked uncertain. It transpired, however, that the council had been working on other, smaller, plans for the area and had also been negotiating with housing associations on alternative redevelopment proposals for the Heygate Estate (North, 2002).

Regeneration for Who?

During the last 5-10 years there has been a proliferation of physical regeneration activity, both public and private, within Southwark. This has been particularly pronounced along 'Bankside', an area that extends east to west from Tower Bridge to Blackfriars Bridge along the River Thames, in the north of the borough. The council has claimed a hand, directly and indirectly, in bringing to fruition a number of prestigious developments, including the Tate Gallery of Modern Art, Shakespeare's Globe Theatre, the Millennium Bridge and the new headquarters for the Greater London Authority. These developments, and others of a commercial and residential nature, have added to the rejuvenation and extension of the entire South Bank – the 'new' cultural and arts capital within London. The South Bank now effectively commences at Tower Bridge and extends to Westminster Bridge (LB Lambeth) and incorporates other notable 'regeneration' projects. These include: County Hall, the former Greater London Council's headquarters, which has been converted into a luxury hotel, museum, art gallery and aquarium; the *London Eye*, the world's largest ferris wheel; Coin Street and the Oxo Tower (Brindley, 1995, 2001).

The £1.6bn of projected regeneration funding for Southwark as suggested in Table 7.4 is a conservative estimate. The area is set to benefit from a further £1-2 billion worth of 'regeneration' activity from recently completed and on-going projects that will enhance the overall economic, physical and social character of Southwark. These developments include:

- two new underground stations, *Southwark* and *Bermondsey*, on the Jubilee Line providing direct access to Central London and London Docklands;
- the *Millennium Bridge*, linking St Paul's Cathedral and the Tate Modern on the north and south sides of the River Thames respectively;
- the on-going rejuvenation of Borough High Street and Markets which forms part of *Historic Southwark*, the council's strategy to promote the borough's heritage as one of the oldest parts of London;
- the Greater London Authority's new City Hall designed by Sir Norman Foster; and
- the redevelopment of London Bridge Station and surrounding environs.

Much of the residential redevelopment within North Southwark, especially along the river, has largely been of a private and upmarket nature (i.e. luxury apartments). Those in a position to consume such housing have mainly been young and established professionals. Furthermore, the types of leisure facilities (e.g. Shakespeare's Globe Theatre, the Tate Gallery of Modern Art and Vinopolis (a wine museum/restaurant) built have tended to be geared more towards the 'middle class' as opposed to the 'working class'. Nevertheless, Borough High Street, Borough Market and Bankside have become extremely vibrant areas and centres of employment opportunity. This socio-economic transformation, however, was perceived as holding relatively few benefits for 'local' people, especially in terms of employment prospects. Because of their generally low educational and skills profile, many local people could only expect to be employed in low-order, low-paid and part-time jobs (e.g. security guards, cleaners and retail assistants) (SBU, 1998; *Westside* Community Forum, 1996b). In other words, local people, interpreted to mean BMEs and the 'white' working-class to a lesser extent, were being left behind:

> What [the council] want to do is bring in lots of money and lots of capital money. They want to build Southwark to be a place for tourism instead of it being seen as a poor area! I THINK THEY DO VERY WELL! They do very well at getting money from central government! They have one of the biggest SRB projects, the PECKHAM PARTNERSHIP! They're very good at all that sort of stuff! In the north of the borough with all that work with the private sector – the Pool of London and Bankside – and all that stuff that is going on is REALLY good! But it's leaving people behind! It leaves local people behind!   (Interviewee 1)

Westside Community Regeneration: Conception and Evolution

The WCRP bid was 'signed off' by a total of twenty partners from the public, private, voluntary and community sectors when it was initially submitted to the GoL. Most of these partners had had nothing to do with constructing the bid nor did they any links with the *Westside* neighbourhood. The majority of these partners had in fact only been brought on board at the 'eleventh hour'. More importantly, the local community was a late joining partner and had also had minimal input into framing the content of the bid. In short, the WCRP was yet another example of 'imposed' regeneration, just as in *Northside* and *Southside*. Community activists were resentful of those who had come to their neighbourhood armed with what they saw as a ready-made plan. This resentment continued after the bid had been approved by GoL and was evident, albeit generally beneath the surface, throughout the fieldwork period amongst certain WCF members.

A Community-led Project?

The idea of the WCRP was born out of concerns from several agents involved in a separate DoE-funded partnership programme, operating in another part of the borough, concerned with tackling crime. These other agents included a housing association, LB Southwark's Equalities Unit (LBSEU) and, most interestingly, the Metropolitan Police. It was suggested during fieldwork that a senior local Police Officer and the then head of the LBSEU were the key agents behind an initially loose set of proposals aimed at tackling perceived crime and 'race' problems within the *Westside* area. The housing association partner assumed the role of 'lead body' in developing the formal bid. On the face of it, this seemed like a rather peculiar arrangement on account that it managed no stock within the *Westside* neighbourhood. It became apparent later that the housing association's involvement was in part due to it having established its own community development department and strategy to tackle social exclusion both in and outside its own estates.

The outline bid advocated a community-led approach to regeneration. Ironically, however, this initial bid had been constructed without any community consultation. Nonetheless, the bid was received positively by the GoL. The lead body was advised that the bid had been accepted in principle, but that it needed to be tightened up before being resubmitted. During this intervening period local community representatives were invited to have their input into the bid. Even at this stage of the process the local community were afforded little opportunity to have any 'real' input into shaping the content of the bid.

The first organization to be invited into the process by the three founding partners was not from the 'community sector' but the voluntary sector, the *Westside* Settlement Movement (WSM). The WSM was a medium-sized organization with a long history of voluntarism in the borough. It was the WSM, in fact, that contacted local community groups and informed them that funding had been provisionally secured and their involvement was being sought. As a result of its knowledge and links with *Westside* the WSM approached the two key community groups within the area: the Central *Westside* Community Centre (CWCC) and Central *Westside* Tenants Group (CWTG).

The sudden arrival of a set of regeneration proposals constructed by an 'outside' agency combined with a late, second-hand, invitation to contribute to the process proved irksome for community activists on a number of inter-related fronts. First, they were annoyed at not having been involved from the outset of the bid process, especially since several of them had been involved in drawing up their own community-led bid the previous year. Second, there was a feeling that the decision to involve the local community was tokenistic. Third, there was a concern that those behind the bid, especially the Police, had stereotyped the neighbourhood as a crime-ridden area. Finally, there were underlying suspicions as to the motives underpinning the housing association's involvement in the bid:

We came on board at the eleventh hour! [...] In hindsight a number of groups signed up without having been involved in the initial process of putting the actual bid together. [...] In retrospect, I CERTAINLY would have liked more time and CERTAINLY would have liked to have been involved in ALL stages rather than just sign up as a partner, albeit an active partner, at that eleventh hour! But, it HAS caused a few problems! That is, in not having been involved it could arguably be put forward that there was a degree of tokenism in that there was a different ethos between the housing association and the voluntary sector and us in the community sector. [...] I feel that if we had been involved during the initial preparation of the bid, then, there wouldn't have been so many minor problems that emerged later down the line.   (Interviewee 2)

They came here COMPLETELY with their OWN idea! They had their own proposals! So we expressed our concerns because the proposals were just a partnership between the housing association and the Police! They more or less based their proposal in terms of CRIME and things like that! We said that we were very concerned about that! You just can't label our estate with crime! It's just not CRIME! CRIME! CRIME! [...] We said that if you want to involve the *Westside* area then we should have been involved in the initial stages in the first place! We were not very happy! We told them that unless we were INVOLVED then we were not going to support the bid! Because our experience of PARTNERSHIP normally is that when they are asking for something – the Council or any agency – they USE community groups but after they have achieved what they want they abandon them!   (Interviewee 3)

Even the housing association representative, who had taken the lead in formulating the bid in the first instance, admitted that their whole approach had been ill conceived and it was not surprising that they encountered resistance from community activists:

> Quite frankly, we did everything WRONG! We then started to say that we better start talking to the local communities about this – hadn't we? The first organization that I contacted in the area – I don't even know how I got the name – was *Westside* Settlement who was far closer to any community activity than us because we didn't have any properties in that immediate vicinity! We had NO involvement there or activity there at all! But we did have a commitment to community regeneration in our business plan! So, it did FIT with some of our strategic objectives for me to take this forward! We then had a meeting in the CWCC, chaired by the *W*SM, with local community groups but the immediate reaction was – FORGET IT! WE DON'T WANT YOU COMING IN HERE ANY WAY!   (Interviewee 4)

This initial community antagonism was temporarily resolved in the run up to the bid being resubmitted to GoL. Community activists managed to get some of their concerns incorporated into the bid. Moreover, it was agreed that the local community would assume overall 'control' of the programme after it had been set up. That is, the proposed structure to oversee the implementation of the programme, the WCF, would be comprised mainly of representatives from local community and voluntary sector organizations.

Aims and Objectives

The WCRP sought to fulfil four SRB Strategic Objectives (*Westside* Community Forum, 1996a). These included:

- enhancing employment prospects, education and skills of local people and those at a disadvantage and promote equality of opportunity;
- promoting initiatives of benefit to ethnic minorities;
- tackling crime and improve community safety; and
- enhancing the quality of life and capacity to contribute to local regeneration by local people, including their health and cultural and sports opportunities.

More specifically, the project had six key aims:

- improving accessibility to growing local economic opportunities;
- improving school attendance and educational attainment and reduce exclusions;
- reducing crime and the fear of crime;
- reducing racist behaviour;
- ensuring that young people are stakeholders in the local community; and
- promoting civic pride and leadership.

The WCF faced a major uphill struggle in realizing these various aims and objectives in light of the relatively small level of funding it had received. For the GoL, the WCRP was very much a 'pilot' project on account that it was community-led and focused exclusively on social regeneration. The project's total funding regime amounted to £0.65m over three years (see Table 7.5). Despite this low level of funding, the long-term vision of the core partners on the WCF was to actively pursue additional sources of public and private funding.

Table 7.5 Regeneration Funding Regime for *Westside*

Funding Source	£m	%
SRB	0.2	31
Private Sector:	0.2	31
LB Southwark	0.25	38
Total	0.65	100

Source: (*Westside* Community Forum, 1997)

In terms of realizing the aforementioned objectives the WCRP was structured into a series of broad phases. The first phase entailed conducting a community audit in order to key problems within the neighbourhood. Next, an Open Day with the wider community was held to outline the strategic aims of the WCRP and for local people to meet WCF members and express their concerns and priorities. These two events constituted forms of action-oriented community consultation/participation. These events along with interviewees' experiences of the participation process are discussed later. The findings from the community audit and the Open Day were then to be used to draw up a suite of possible projects. Specific projects were to be democratically selected from this suite by WCF members in consultation with the WCC. Projects eventually implemented were to be overseen by a sub-committee made up of representatives from the WCF, WCC and ordinary members of the wider local community thereby reinforcing the programme's goals of enhancing community empowerment, control and ownership.

Despite the tensions between key local community activists and those agents who had constructed the bid, the former realized that it would be foolhardy not to get involved in the project once it was up and running. The local activists, however, were determined that they would play an instrumental role in decision-making once the programme officially commenced.

Organizational Structure of the Regeneration Process

The organizational structure of the WCRP was comparatively simplistic and leaner than in *Northside* and *Southside*. This was primarily a function of the small-scale nature of the programme and the fact that the local authority was not the 'lead body'. If this had been the case the WCF would have to have decisions ratified within the council thereby prolonging the decision-making process. As it was, the lead body on the WCF was a housing association whose representative had the delegated authority, due to being a senior manager, to make executive decisions within the WCF.

In short, there were only two tiers of decision-making (see Figure 7.1). The WCF had overall responsibility for both strategic and operational decision-making. The *Westside* Consultative Committee's (WCC) role was to act as a community sounding board, providing the WCF with information about issues within the wider neighbourhood and advising on project ideas. The long-term vision within the WCF was that WCC members would eventually play a more instrumental role in the regeneration process, providing employment and training opportunities and/or financial investment for projects set up within the neighbourhood under the guise of the WCRP.

As a bureaucratic organization with all the right resources it was only natural that the housing association assumed the role of 'lead body'. If the lead body had been a community-based organization it is highly unlikely that the project would have received the funding it had. The housing association also provided initial administrative support for the programme. It was keen, however, to disengage itself from this role as it did not want to be perceived as being the dominant or controlling agent within the project. Administrative functions were subsequently transferred to an external agency, Regeneration Support Service (RSS), some 5-6 months into the fieldwork period. As noted in Chapter 5, RSS was also involved in *Southside* where it acted as a consultant to one of the local community groups. In this instance, however, it played a neutral role servicing and organizing meetings of both the WCF and WCC.

Both the WCF and WCC were socially pluralistic forums in that their membership comprised agents from a diverse range of local interest groups – housing, education, children and young people, and BMEs. The WCF had set itself the objective, as outlined in the bid document, of becoming a more representative and democratic decision-making body. In other words, the WCF sought more direct involvement from 'ordinary' members of the wider community. There was a general desire to get more BMEs involved in local decision-making. And, more specifically, the WCF wanted to see greater involvement from the Bangladeshi and Somali communities.

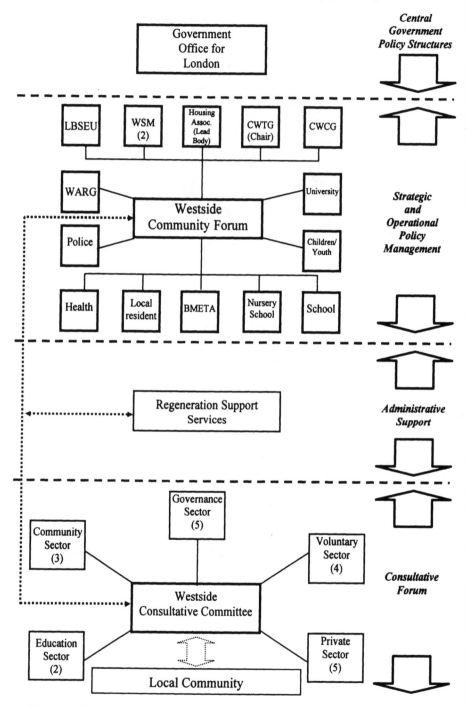

Figure 7.1 Organizational Structure of Regeneration Process (*Westside*)

Westside Community Forum

To reiterate, the WCF was responsible for strategic and operational decision-making within the WCRP. WCF committee meetings were held once a month. In essence, its essential responsibilities were 'prioritizing, procuring and monitoring projects' (WCF, 1996b: 17). Decision-making within the WCF was premised on a simple 'democratic' model. Ideas, issues and projects were all discussed openly amongst members with decisions and actions progressed via a majority vote mechanism. There was no power of veto. This simplistic approach was adopted in an effort to ensure that decision-making was a fairly efficient process.

In terms of membership profile, the WCF was very much a pluralistic forum. It comprised 12-15 members, the majority (64 per cent) of which were drawn from the voluntary and community sectors (see Figure 7.1). Additionally, in terms of ethnic and gender profile, both BMEs (including Irish) and women were significantly represented accounting for 47 and 60 per cent of members respectively (see Table 7.6).

The ethnic profile of the WCF was by no means representative of the wider community. There were, for example, no members of the Bangladeshi, Somali or Afro-Caribbean communities on the WCF. Similarly, there was no representation from the 'white' working-class community.

Table 7.6 Ethnic and Gender Profile of Community Forum (*Westside*)

WCF Member	Sector	Ethnicity	Gender
Housing Association	Voluntary	Black	Male
Westside Anti-Racist Group[1]	Voluntary	White	Female
WSM (x2)[2]	Voluntary	White/Black	Female
Westside Nursery	Voluntary	Black	Female
Community Health Services	Voluntary	White	Female
Westside Estate Play Group	Community	White	Male
BMETA	Community	Black	Male
CWTG	Community	Irish	Female
CWCC	Community	Mixed Race	Male
Independent tenant	Community	White	Male
Metropolitan Police	Statutory	White	Male
LBSEU	Statutory	Irish	Female
Westside School	Educational	White	Female
University	Educational	White	Female

[1] WARG representative resigned six months into fieldwork due to other commitments.
[2] The second representative from WSM, the Community Initiatives Manager, was a 'black' female who was appointed six months into fieldwork.

Source: Westside Community Forum (1998)

As a result of the composition and, more importantly, the vested interests of particular representatives, 'race' tended to feature as a frequent point of discussion and concern within the WCF. For example, the LBSEU displayed a keen interest in the Bangladeshi community. The reason for this was that the LBSEU and its representative had strong links with the Bangladeshi community by virtue of a council-run project for this ethnic group. Simultaneously, 'race' loomed large on the agenda due to the adversarial role played by the BMETA representative. His role was to act as the voice of the wider BME community. Notably, however, he seemed to champion the plight of the West African community, of which he was a member, more than the BME community in general.

In general terms, the two 'true' locally based organizations, the CWTG and CWCC, notionally 'represented' the wider local community. Yet, the representatives from both of these groups were noticeably more minded as to the plight of BME groups within the area.

Interestingly, the plight of the 'white' working-class community, nor the concept of 'whiteness', featured on the policy agenda or entered the racialized discourse within the WCF either at a collective and/or individualistic level. Over time it became apparent that the explicit and implicit significance attached to 'race' and particular ethnic groups within the WCF was somewhat misplaced. The role and significance of 'race' are discussed in more detail later.

Notably, the WCF lacked any representation from those super-structures within the council, the Regeneration and Housing Departments, with a direct remit for regeneration policy. Moreover, both of these departments were completely disinterested in the WCRP. Their lack of interest and involvement was somewhat discerning for the WCF first chairman, whose own organization had an otherwise good working relationship with these departments, especially in housing:

WE'VE BEEN IGNORED BY THE [COUNCIL'S] HOUSING DEPARTMENT! I've talked to the Director of Regeneration and said – "Aren't you interested in what we're doing? You're in charge of regeneration and nobody from your Department has had a single conversation with me or any of my colleagues about this project [but] GoL thinks it's a very interesting project"! [...] I think the reason for that is that Southwark is a highly departmentalized local authority in which individual departments do their own thing! I suspect that Regeneration and Housing are so busy arguing amongst themselves, that they've got no time for this STRANGE project. [...] I'm perfectly happy to say that the council is represented by the Equalities Unit, and it's up to their representatives to go back into the [council] machinery and to do all the liaison that's necessary with all the other departments! But, I do think that it's strange that the Regeneration Department hasn't had some sort of overview or asked to have the odd meeting! It would have been nice if they had offered us some support! But, they haven't done that!   (Interviewee 5)

The lack of interest from either the Regeneration or Housing Departments was grounded in the fact, as noted earlier, that they were both more concerned with being involved with large-scale capital projects. And, since the WCR programme did not fit this profile it was effectively deemed an insignificant project.

The Chairmanship of the WCF was assumed initially by the first representative from the lead body, a 'white' male and senior manager. This was intended to be a temporary expedient until the WCF had established itself. As intended, the Chairmanship reverted to one of the local community representatives some 3-5 months into fieldwork. Symbolically, this marked the tentative beginnings of the WCRP moving to being a community-led project. The representative from the CWTG, who rather reluctantly and nervously assumed the Chairmanship after being elected to the post by other WCF members, requested that the lead body's new representative, a 'black' male, be appointed Co-Chairman in order to allow her to adjust to her new position of authority. The WCF agreed to this request which prevailed for two WCF committee meetings before the CWTG representative became the full Chairman.

Despite being elected to this position of authority, the overall sense of control of the WCRP still tended to rest more with the housing association and the WSM. This was due to a combination of factors and is discussed later when attention turns to the issue of community power.

Westside Consultative Committee

The *Westside* Consultative Committee (WCC) was also a socially pluralistic forum that comprised between 18-20 members. These included representatives from the education (2), community (3), governance (5), voluntary (4) and private sectors (5) (see Figure 7.1). It should be stressed that the participation of these various representatives was largely due to the networking efforts of the CWTG representative. She had contacted a range of organizations and employers from within the borough in an effort to get them to sign up as 'partners' to the final bid prior to it being submitted to the GoL.

The motivation behind this was quite simple: the bid stood a much greater chance of being approved if it was seen to have the support of a diverse range of partners, particularly if they were from the private sector. A number of prominent organizations involved in the media, arts, business development and retailing all agreed to sign up to the WCRP bid. They did so under the premise that their role within the WCF would be as a passive partner role after the programme had commenced. The CWTG representative's decision to invite prominent organizations to support the WCRP bid demonstrated her astute understanding and, more importantly, ability to play the regeneration game:

> In fact, it was me that rang up all the big name organizations and asked them to be partners! They all said – Yes! […] At the time I said to them: Can you put your name to this and be one of the partners, as it would look quite good? I explained what it was and that we were trying to get money and the support would be very welcome and they didn't really have to get involved. [Their involvement] was VERY IMPORTANT in terms of getting money from GoL and to show that there WAS wide involvement! […] Because the whole raison d'être, if you like, of [the SRB] has been to create partnerships!   (Interviewee 6)

The primary purpose of the WCC was to act as a sounding board and provide strategic advice on policy ideas and programmes emerging from within the WCF. It was supposed to meet on a quarterly basis with meetings scheduled to take place at the CWCC. Meetings were held at this venue in order to stimulate greater community interest and a sense of community ownership and over the regeneration process.

Despite saying to those prominent organizations that signed up to the WCC that they wouldn't have to do anything other than lend their symbolic support, there was a latent desire, amongst WCF members, that they would become more intricately involved in the regeneration process. Specifically, there was an underlying hope that some of the private sector signatories would contribute financially to projects that emerged from the WCRP. This latent desire was never realized however. This was not because prominent organizations had expressed an explicit intention not to do so, although their lack of attendance at WCC meetings did suggest that they did not wish to become more than passive supporters of the WCRP. This non-attendance at WCC meetings combined with the WCF members not having enough time to develop links with WCC members also undermined the potential for greater involvement from these passive prominent organizations.

Interest in the WCC, as measured by who and the number of representatives in attendance at meetings, came mainly from community and voluntary organizations. The first WCC meeting was well attended and there was considerable enthusiasm around the table about the WCRP, its likely impacts on the local neighbourhood and the future of regeneration within the neighbourhood in general. This show of strength from community and voluntary sector organizations was an early encouraging sign for WCF members that they would realize their objective of creating a community-led regeneration project.

This enthusiasm was short-lived however. Interest and attendance at WCC meetings began to wane after the second of four scheduled meetings. In fact, the WCC failed to see through all of its scheduled meetings. As a result it became a defunct structure within the WCRP. Furthermore, the WCC failed to fulfil its role as a sounding board and strategic advisor to the WCF. This was largely because the role the WCC was supposed to play remained fuzzy. Moreover, there were no clear mechanisms or procedures in relation to how the WCC was supposed to feed into the decision-making processes of the WCF. Any advice or information provided by the WCC to the WCF seemed to be supplied on an informal and personal basis as opposed to a formal organizational one.

The demise of the WCC meant that the prospect of encouraging greater community involvement in the regeneration process was made all the more difficult. The WCC was the easier of the two decision-making structures within the WCRP for 'ordinary' members of the local community to access and join. In essence, the WCC was envisaged within the WCF as a stepping stone for 'ordinary' residents interested in community participation to becoming members of the WCF and thus involved in the 'real' decision-making processes of the WCRP. Power and responsibility was thus concentrated within the WCF. This placed additional pressures on the WCF and, in particular, its community representatives. These agents had little experience or time, due to their own personal commitments, to manage the project on a more regular basis. Also, they were not in receipt of any financial recompense for their efforts.

The WCF came to the realization, following the outcomes of the community audit and Open Day, that if the WCRP was to achieve its aims and objectives it had to employ someone on a full-time basis to manage the WCRP. The WCF duly created the post of Community Initiatives Manager (CIM). The successful applicant to the CIM post had two primary tasks. First, the CIM was to develop links with the wider community, especially BMEs, with the view to getting them more involved in the regeneration process. Second, the CIM was to identify projects and additional funding in order to sustain the WCRP and regeneration within the neighbourhood in general.

It was clear from non-participant observations of discussions about the CIM post and meetings in general that the WCF already had already decided the type of person they wanted for the job – a 'black' female. This outcome was predicted to a colleague who had worked on the community audit and also attended CWF meetings during the early stages of fieldwork. Sure enough, a 'black' female was duly appointed to the CIM post in mid 1998. It should be pointed out that although the CIM worked *for* and *with* the WCF the post was actually hosted and line-managed by the WSM. Again, this was the 'right' decision on the basis that the WCF was not legal entity *per se* and thus was not in a position to employ anyone. The post had to be hosted within a 'real' organization. The WSM agreed to act as the host organization arguing that it was important that the CIM was perceived as being located within the neighbourhood. This arrangement, however, had the (unintended) effect of accentuating the WSM's influence within the WCF. The complexities and dynamics of community participation and power are discussed in more detail below.

Community Consultation and Participation

A priority objective of the WCRP was to 'increase community and voluntary sector involvement in decision-making and service delivery' (WCF, 1996a: 6). In other words, it sought to be a more fully representative and pluralistic community-led regeneration programme. Specifically, the WCF wanted to encourage and facilitate more direct involvement from particular BME communities (Bangladeshis, Somalis and West Africans) who formed an increasing proportion of the local community and endured high levels of social exclusion (SBU, 1998).

There were two dimensions to the WCFs participation strategy. Within the first dimension, community consultation was conducted along a formal and explicit axiom. In short, the wider community was involved in the regeneration process through a combination of action research and traditional consultation techniques. In relation to the second dimension, the WCF consulted with the community, directly via 'behind the scenes' networking with smaller less developed, mainly BME, community groups that its members had pre-existing relationships with and/or a vested interest. The WCF also conducted indirect or second-hand community consultation via its links with WCC members.

Notably, concerns about involving BME communities within the regeneration process topped the agenda within both dimensions. Ironically, however, an overarching paternalistic culture within the WCF unwittingly inhibited BME organizations and representatives from becoming more directly involved in the process.

Community Consultation through Action Research

The first formal community-wide consultative exercise undertaken was a community audit. This was commissioned by the WCF and undertaken by a small team of researchers from South Bank University (SBU) between October-December 1997. The purpose of the audit was to develop a baseline of socio-economic conditions and identify community concerns and priorities. Furthermore, the findings would be used to inform the direction of the regeneration process in terms of the types of projects that should be developed (SBU, 1998).

A number of local tenants were recruited as interviewers to conduct the actual fieldwork on the community audit. Notably, almost all the interviewers recruited were from BME backgrounds. This was a deliberate intention of the WCF who, as noted, were (over)concerned with achieving BME issues. The decision to employ local people was part of the WCRP's overall objective of involving the local community in the regeneration process and instilling a sense of ownership over the project. It was hoped that by inducing local residents into the regeneration process in this, and other, ways some of them would eventually end up becoming WCF members and playing a more active role in decision-making.

Informal discussion with a few of the community audit interviewers revealed that they enjoyed the experience. The WCF considered the exercise a great success. Unfortunately, however, none of the fieldworkers became formally involved in the process, at least during the fieldwork period. A few of the community audit interviewers did attend the first two WCC meetings. But, they only played the role of passive observers. Furthermore, two or three of the fieldworkers had an indirect link to the regeneration process through their close links with the BMETA representative.

As a follow up to the community audit, an Open Day was held at the CWCC in early 1998 by the WCF. The aims of this event were threefold. First, it was set up to inform the local community that the neighbourhood had won regeneration funding and to explain the nature and purpose of the WCRP. Next, it was designed to explore and elicit tenants views, needs and priorities in terms of what they wanted to see happen to their neighbourhood. Finally, and most importantly, the Open Day was used as a means of trying to stimulate wider and deeper community involvement. In order to inform and consult with the local community the Open Day comprised a number of themed information stalls staffed by WCF members and other professional agents, mainly from the voluntary sector. These various information stalls included: *Support for Community Groups*; *Employment and Training*; *Bringing People Together*; *Information and Communication*; and *Environmental Projects*.

In short, the Open Day typified a form of 'traditional' participatory planning (Arnstein, 1969; Davidoff, 1982; Greed, 1999).

Racial Prejudice or Cultural Preference?

In an effort to stimulate attendance, the Open Day was widely advertised by way of a community newsletter. This was subsequently followed up with a leaflet drop throughout the Central *Westside* Estate and adjoining estates. There were concerns amongst WCF members about this approach. It was felt that it might not have the desired effect in light of the generally high levels of illiteracy and non-English speakers within the neighbourhood. So, to ensure sufficient participation from BME groups WCF members networked informally with members from BME communities with whom they had good links, chiefly the Bangladeshi and Somali communities.

As an extra incentive to attract as many people as possible to the Open Day a 'free lunch' was included. Again, to ensure the involvement of (particular) BMEs, a local women's group (i.e. the Bangladeshi Women's Project (BWP)) was invited, by the WCF, to prepare the lunch. The majority of foodstuffs (e.g. samosas, pakoras, bhajis) subsequently prepared were, for want of a better word, of an 'ethnic' nature. The free lunch did indeed prove to be a popular incentive given that most of the food was consumed. For a small group (i.e. 3-4 people) of elderly white tenants from one of the adjoining estates however, the 'ethnic' food was something of a disappointment. They were overheard complaining, "this food's too spicy" and "where's the ham and salmon sandwiches"? In other words, they were in search of more 'traditional' (i.e. English) food. The look on their faces at the lack of traditional sandwiches clearly demonstrated their sense of disappointment.

As well as being disappointed with the food on offer, this small group of elderly tenants also appeared to be uncomfortable with their surroundings. Observations of the group revealed that they shied away from socializing with other members of the local community, most of who incidentally were from BME backgrounds. Instead, the group systematically and hurriedly visited each information stall, asked one or two questions, picked up whatever printed information was available, quickly grabbed some fruit from the buffet table and then departed. On leaving they were overheard bemoaning that both the Open Day and WCRP seemed to offer *them* very little.

The comment that the WCRP offered *them* little combined with the groups' reactions to the food on offer and lack of interaction with other community members, raises the question as to whether their overall behaviour was racially prejudiced. Whilst it is impossible to discern with certainty that this was the case, it did seem clear from observations that the group were expressing, depending on where one is standing, a cultural preference (O'Keffee, 1986) or intolerance about aspects of the Open Day.

If this small group of elderly 'white' tenants were of the view that the WCRP seemed to be more concerned about BME groups and issues they were not far from the truth. Data gathered from non-participant observations clearly demonstrated that WCF members were almost exclusively preoccupied with participation from BME communities throughout the planning of the Open Day. At no stage during observed meetings did the WCF consider the need to ensure that disadvantaged 'white' tenants were in attendance. There appeared to be an inherent assumption that 'white' tenants would face few or no barriers to in relation to participating in the Open Day.

The Open Day was generally considered to be a 'success' by WCF members on account of the higher than expected turnout (i.e. 80-100 people). This success was qualified further by the fact that the majority of observed participants (approximately 65-75 per cent) were of BME origin. Notably, the Bangladeshi community was by far the largest represented group. Despite these successes there were some reservations amongst WCF members that the event had not been held earlier:

> I think that the last consultation day [i.e. the Open Day] was very good! A lot of people came! The CWCC representative said the feedback was really positive and people were saying that it was the first time that they had really been consulted about something and had been asked about something! That was very good!
>
> (Interviewee 6)

> The Open Day was very good! But, I don't know whether they gave it proper publicity! Another thing that people have got to understand is that before you even have an Open Day you must have what I call 'a bridging period', where you inform! Inform! The mix was okay but in a ward like this you would have expected more people than that! The turnout wasn't bad as such! I liked the Open Day but I wish that they had done it even earlier! I believe that even if you informed all residents at the start you wouldn't have a third of them turning up. I can guarantee you that! Regeneration is something that people don't understand easily!   (Interviewee 3)

> I would argue that a big motivating factor for the response we had at the Open Day was due to the fact that we had £107,000 for local community groups. I saw a different cross-section of people, some of them I didn't recognise or hadn't seen here before. [...] One of the mechanisms that we use to promote events is our informal network where we exchange information once a month at meetings. The Bangladeshi group, which has been here for a number of years, obviously encouraged and promoted the Open Day to their community and this was reflected in the good response or turnout from them!   (Interviewee 2)

There was a perception amongst past and present members of the WCF that there was some form of bias towards the 'Asian' community. One of the founding members of the WCR programme, for example, noted that within the wider community there was a feeling that the council had done more for 'Asian' youth than other communities within the estate:

> There was an element of resentment from 'white' and 'black' populations because there was a perception that a lot had been done for Asian youth in the area! Well, there are specific projects for Asian youth on that estate or in that area! There's the Asian YC and things like that! [...] I think that an officer from the Community Safety Unit at the council made an interesting point. When they analyzed where the

Youth and Leisure Services money had gone an ENORMOUSLY disproportionate amount went into the central *Westside* area! This area had actually done rather well over the years from the council from funding compared to other parts of the borough! And yet, it's perceived as being a deprived or poor area!   (Interviewee 4)

Similarly, the BMETA's representative, a 'black' African male, expressed concern that the WCF tended to over-concentrate on the needs and wants of the 'Asian' (i.e. Bangladeshis) community:

Well, the concerns that I had about the WCF were to do with when they were identifying ETHNIC GROUPS! My exact words were – "You always tend to look for the Asians! THE ASIANS! Just one segment!" I said – "What about Africans? What about Afro-Caribbeans"? That was the concern that I had!   (Interviewee 3)

These concerns of ethnic 'bias' were supported by data from non-participant observations. During observations of WCF meetings whenever discussions turned to issues of 'race' these tended to focus extensively on the needs of the 'Asian' community and projects, for example, the BWP and the Central *Westside* Asian Youth (CWAY) project. The prominence given to the Bangladeshi community was a direct function of the vested interests and close working relationships that several WCFs members had with this community. It, consequently, was through these relationships that representatives from the Bangladeshi community were kept informed about the WCRP and how their needs and concerns were mediated and filtered back into the regeneration process. Such 'behind the scenes' consultation also extended to other ethnic groups through the CWCC representative who had good links with a wide range of ethnic and other community groups within the neighbourhood. It was through this complex, but rather informal, community network as opposed to any formal consultation techniques that the wider community was kept informed about the WCRP.

Community Consultation through Community Networking

As noted in the last section, formal and informal community networking between WCF representatives and smaller community organizations was the primary means of informing tenants about the WCR programme. Again, the emphasis here was primarily on BME communities. A number of representatives on the WCF had varying degrees of contact with different BME communities within the area. For example, the BMETA representative was particularly well connected to the 'black' African community.   Conversely, representatives from WARG and LBSEU had well-established links with the 'Asian' community:

People know me in the area. Various different groups know me as I WAS councillor for 8 years and even after that I was still doing surgeries in the 1990s. I've been Chair on the Board of Governors at the local secondary school. I've been Chair of the local anti-racist group that arose out of young Bangladeshis being beaten up! I'm Chair of the Bangladeshi Mothers Group! And, when there was a

dispute in the Mosque some of the men came to me to sort it out!   So, I'm quite
WELL-KNOWN and well trusted by different groups!   (Interviewee 7)

I don't think that we've used any textbook methods of consultation!   We've simply
used networking and local contacts!   For instance, the CWCG is based in the middle
of the ward and it's used as a focal point!   The BWP is being used to get to people
from that community!   We've used individuals in other BME communities as well.
I think that other members such as BMETAs representative will target other 'black'
groups. And, the WSM has been making contact with people in the community as
well. I DO think that there is quite a good community network up there! It seems to
work quite well! Word does seem to go around the grapevine.   (Interviewee 1)

Ultimately, the CWCG was very much the lynchpin organization within this
informal networking process as it was the key community resource within the
neighbourhood.   The CWCG representative had regular contact and, most
importantly, a more intimate understanding of the needs and wants of the plethora
of ethnic (i.e. 'black' and 'white') groups within the estate. Notably, unlike other
representatives on the WCF, who tended to champion the needs of specific ethnic
groups, the CWCG representative talked about 'race' issues within a more rounded
context. The CWTG representative acknowledged the commitment of the CWCG
and other key WCF members to distilling information to the wider community:

I think that it is a very difficult thing to get information across! And, I think that
there are people on the WCF who have been particularly concerned that other
organizations – small organizations – get to hear about the money available and get
to put forward bids! In particular the LBSEU and WSM are very concerned about
the democratic process. That's quite good! These are people from entirely different
organizations. And, it makes you think: Why would someone like the person from
the Council bother with this? BUT SHE IS! The guy from the CWCG is obviously
very COMMUNITY-MINDED and he's very careful about spreading information
and so on!   (Interviewee 6)

Information, Consultation but No Invitation to Participation

Whilst this informal networking approach helped to keep smaller community
organizations informed about the WCRP, members of the WCF did relatively little
in the way of encouraging ordinary tenants to become more involved in decision-
making. In fact, smaller established and recently formed community organizations
such as the BWP and the Somali Self-Help Group (SSHG) were inadvertently
precluded from becoming full members of the WCF due to an inherently
paternalistic culture within it. Put simply, whilst certain WCF members advocated
the need to involve more ordinary tenants, especially BMEs, in the regeneration
process, they tended to follow this with assertions that particular communities were
either not ready or disinterested in participating in the formal processes of the
WCRP.

The LBSEU representative, for example, regularly argued that it was vitally
important for the Bangladeshi community to be empowered by the regeneration

programme and that they should be directly represented on the WCF. This standpoint was contradicted however by her claims that this community (even some its key activists) would find participating in the decision-making processes an alien and unrewarding experience. The WSM representative expressed an identical attitude. There was a perception that many, if not most, BME communities would be disinterested, lacked the knowledge and skills or not in a position to understand the machinations of decision-making within the WCRP. To support these assertions reference was also often made to the lack of English as a second language amongst elderly Bangladeshis and Somalis, the cohort deemed the most likely to want to participate in decision-making.

The perception that certain groups were not ready to become 'full' members of the WCF was true to a certain degree. The Somali community was arguably the least well ready group to participate within the WCF. A combination of inter-related factors underpinned this situation. First, the Somali community was a small and relatively new community made up mainly of refugees, many of whom spoke very little English. In short, this community was still acclimatizing to the formal and community structures, processes and mores within its new environs. The Somali community was in the early phases of building up its own social capital resources and networks via the recently formed SSHG. The leader of the SSHG, a male in his early forties expressed during a conversation at the Open Day a keen interest in joining the WCF. Unfortunately, he never received a formal invitation to join the WCF, during the fieldwork period at least.

The assertion that members of the Bangladeshi community were not in a position to comprehend the machinations of the WCF and the regeneration process in general were severely misguided. This attitude merely reinforced the overly paternalistic culture amongst WCF members.

Unlike the Somali community, the Bangladeshi community was relatively well established within the area and had become familiarized with its environs. This community had a fairly sophisticated social capital resource base that included the local mosque, the BWP, the CWAY and the Bangladeshi Community Development Project (BCDP). These various community structures were headed by a number of community activists, mainly males, who would have had relatively little difficulty in participating within the WCF. Yet, certain members of the WCF were adamant that even these agents were not ready to participate more directly in the regeneration process.

In overall terms, the paternalistic culture that prevailed within the WCF effectively kept small BME community groups at arms-length from the decision-making arena of the WCRP. It should be stressed, however, that this 'exclusion' was not in any way malicious. Paternalism blinkered the WCF's vision and prevented it from realizing the programme's core objective: a more representative community-led regeneration initiative. In addition, WCF members were not in a position, due to their normal work and personal commitments, to sustain a participation process that would ultimately lead to members from smaller community groups becoming more directly involved in decision-making. As already noted, the WCF appointed a Community Initiative Manager (CIM) to develop and oversee a sustainable community participation strategy. The need to appoint a community development professional was highlighted by the CWTG representative:

> I THINK INFORMATION IS A VERY DIFFICULT THING! That's why I think it is very POSITIVE that WE have decided to spend money on a Community Development Worker! You REALLY NEED someone like that! Somebody who is getting paid to spend their time on getting the community involved! Because, none of the organizations can do that! They can within their own little spheres! The housing association can bring in that woman who was doing the employment thing on the estates; The WSM can keep the youth organizations involved; and LBSEU can let people know in the Council. But, there's nobody there with the specific job or the training to actually get the community involved! The CWCG representative would probably be the best person at that! But, his job isn't really community regeneration! So, in a way, this community development worker is probably the best indicator that we regard community involvement and communication with the community seriously!
>
> (Interviewee 6)

Community Initiatives Manager: the Reification of Paternalism?

As already noted, in an effort to ensure that the local community became more involved in decision-making within *Westside* at a general (i.e. WCC) and specific (i.e. WCF) level a CIM was appointed.

The CIM post was shrouded in a racialized context from the outset of initial discussions about it through to the appointment of the eventual postholder. In short, it was envisaged, within the WCF, that the primary aims and duties of the CIM were to work closely, if not, virtually exclusively, with BME communities. This view was shaped by the fact that WCF members made no explicit reference to the CIM directly assisting 'white' tenants within the neighbourhood. Instead, discussions about the post amongst WCF members tended to focus on the need for the CIM to develop links with and projects for the Bangladeshi and Somali communities. Moreover, it was argued that the person eventually appointed should be both of BME origins and a female. Particular WCF members were of the view that a more successful outcome in relation involving BMEs could be achieved via 'ethnic matching'. That is to say, BME tenants were thought to be more likely to get involved in the regeneration process if they were being encouraged to do so by someone of BME origin.

There is clearly a case for ethnic matching to be used under certain circumstances. For example, when there has been a serious break down in trust and relations, due to the existence of racism, between BME communities and white-dominated bureaucratic institutions or community structures. This was not the case however in *Westside*. From observations, it seemed clear that the motivation(s) for wanting to appoint a BME female was grounded more in a shared feminist and philanthropic ideological standpoint amongst most WCF members.

It transpired after leaving the field that the person appointed to the CIM post was not in fact the first choice candidate. This had actually been a 'white' female applicant who had scored more points for the post based on the various job criteria. There was, however, quite significant resistance to this candidate from one of the

WCF members on the interview panel. This member was of the express view that the post had to be assigned to a BME applicant. During post interview deliberations amongst the interview panel this WCF member asserted their position of authority and managed to persuade the rest of the panel that the next best applicant (i.e. the 'black' female) should be appointed.

The ability of this WCF member to convince her colleagues to select the second choice candidate illustrated the extent of influence this agent had within the WCF. Moreover, such manoeuvring suggested that the WCF was more concerned with 'racial matching' than appointing the 'best qualified' candidate. This is not in any way to denigrate the skills and abilities of the candidate eventually appointed.

Whilst the CIM worked *for* and *with* the WCF the post was based within the WSM and directly line-managed by its Director. This arrangement had been agreed by WCF members on the grounds that it was the most pragmatic thing to do. This was indeed true. As the WCF was not a properly constituted organization it lacked all the necessary resources to act as an employer and host the CIM. As a bureaucratic organization with extensive experience of community development work and good links with community groups within *Westside* and surrounding neighbourhoods, the WSM was the only organization within the WCF to assume this role. The housing association partner could also have hosted the CIM, but it had ruled itself out of the role on the grounds that it did not want to be seen as an over-bearing partner within a project that aspired to be community-led.

The decision to house the CIM post within the WSM helped to enhance its position as the most influential partner within the WCF. In addition to managing the CIM, the WSM also effectively controlled WCF meetings. The fact that WCF meetings were held at the offices of WSM had the effect of raising other members' consciousness that they were 'guests' of the WSM. As so much of the real activities and management of the WCRP were going through the WSM its representative tended to assume a dominant role in overall proceedings. During meetings, for example, she would often set and steer the agenda; When the CWTG representative was either late or unable to attend meetings, the WSM representative automatically assumed the role of Chairperson. Hence, the paternalistic culture that was particularly evident within the WSM filtered down into the WCF and the CIM.

One of the CIM's first major tasks after being appointed was mapping and establishing contact with the various community organizations in the neighbourhood. Notably, particular attention was devoted to establishing links and developing proposals with and for BME groups. Yet again, the primary focus of these efforts tended to be on the Bangladeshi community. Very little attention, however, was given to explicitly inviting pre-existing community activists and/or encouraging 'ordinary' tenants from BME communities onto the WCF. In conducting this mapping and relationship-building exercise the WCF and/or the CIM displayed no explicit interest in involving more members of the 'white' working-class community in the regeneration process. It was almost as if the 'white' community was non-existent within the neighbourhood.

Instead of identifying and encouraging more local people to get involved in the decision-making processes of the WCRP, the CIM focused instead on developing localized initiatives aimed at enhancing job and life skills amongst BMEs so that they could enhance their employment prospects and self-esteem. Whilst such an approach was needed and admirable, the CIM and the WCF were still avoiding one of their primary objectives, the creation of a more representative community-led regeneration project. Put simply, the WCFs and CIMs attitude was still that certain (BME) groups were not ready to participate in what they referred to as the 'mundane experience of sitting around the decision-making table'. Additionally, such groups were thought to be in need of being 'trained up' before they could become more directly involved. There may well have been an element of truth to this in relation to tenants with no previous experience of community activism. But, the Bangladeshi and Somali communities had their own organizations (i.e. the BWP, BCDP, CWAY and SSHG) that were all headed by competent individuals who would have had little problem in participating on the WCF.

The CIM organized a seminar-type event designed to stimulate greater interest, understanding and, ultimately, participation in the regeneration process amongst BME communities. This event was criticized, however, by the CWCC representative. He was of the view that the whole approach and content of the seminar was 'traditional' in its approach. In other words it was both paternalistic and patronizing:

> Very often a local authority department or some other organization will come here with really good intentions and good project ideas. For example, one of the London wide voluntary sector organizations organized an Open Day for 'black' and ethnic minority communities. Their brief, or their remit, was to involve 'black' and ethnic minority groups in the urban regeneration process. They approached the WCF and said that they would run it and facilitate the meeting and they did! But, the feedback that I had was really poor! It was really the old traditional sense... we'll leaflet the estate; we will hold a meeting and we will get speakers in and they will talk to you! And, that was it! The feedback that I got was: "They were talking AT us". "We didn't understand what they were saying". It was that old-style meeting or set-up of [being] in the hall, a big row of chairs, five speakers throughout the day and that was it! I don't think that it achieved its aim! It may have achieved some OUTPUT figures and it may have had 50 people from here, but, the OUTCOME was arguably negative if anything as opposed to the Open Day that we've just had which was pretty good and were people felt that they could contribute!   (Interviewee 2)

It can be seen from the above comments that tenants who had participated in the seminar felt as if they had been treated like children in a classroom. In other words, the CIM had behaved paternalistically towards her client group. Moreover, organizing an event that treated tenants in such a manner points to a lack of understanding of the needs and wants of the local community. This is arguably often the case with paternalists since they assume that they know what's best for others.

Paternalistic Community Power

It would be somewhat unfair to state that the paternalistic culture within the WCF was *wholly* to blame for the lack of direct involvement in decision-making from particular communities. Paternalism, however, was the primary reason why so few tenants were involved on the WCF. And, this paternalism was borne out of the make-up of the majority of agents (professional voluntary sector agents) who dominated the WCF.

The paternalistic actions (and inactions) of the WCF in relation to generating community participation should not be perceived as being deliberately exclusionary or discriminatory. It was clear that WCF members were genuinely concerned about the needs of BMEs. Ultimately, the philanthropic legacy and the overall paternalistic mindset amongst members of the WCF meant that they tended to be overly interventionist in their approach to community participation. WCF members acted more as self-appointed representatives for those communities with whom they had close relations and/or vested interests. Consequently, the wider local community had no direct power or influence over the direction and nature of the WCR programme. Instead, their involvement was limited to being *informed* and *consulted* by representatives on the WCF and/or the CIM:

> Consultation? We had the community profile and we had the consultation day back in February or March. We've discussed newsletters. We've had a few people write in and ask to be part of the WCF and we've invited them to join. That's largely been it. Different groups working with different community organizations locally feed that back in via the WCF. And, now that we've got the CIM she's obviously out there in the community working day-in and day-out and identified a number of groups and individual that she's trying to support. Having said all of that though, I still very much get the sense that we're DOING things to people. We're still kind of doing things. Imposing solutions isn't the right phrase but people aren't involved in any changes that we're proposing. Decisions are not grassroots!   (Interviewee 8)

A combination of important secondary factors, such as establishment of sense of community, language barriers and cultural traits, also help to explain why key BME groups did not play a more active role in decision-making. The Somali community's absence, for example, was partly attributable to the fact that they were a relatively 'new' community the neighbourhood and many of its members spoke relatively little English. The Bangladeshi community's lack of involvement in the regeneration process can be partly explained by two key factors. First, like the Somali community, those most likely to participate in the process (i.e. adults) spoke little or no English and would thus have had difficulties participating in WCF meetings as these were conducted in English. Second, despite having quite an active women's group (i.e. the BWP), Bangladeshi females were effectively inhibited from participating in the regeneration process due to in-group cultural mores. WCF members recounted that within the Bangladeshi community women were expected to play a home-centred role, assuming full-time responsibility for domestic and childcare duties. Attending meetings and making decisions at them was seen very much as a male responsibility.

Ultimately, then, since virtually no members of the wider local community, particularly BMEs, had become members of the WCF it could not be said that there was an expression of community power *per se* within the decision-making processes of the WCRP. One person, a young 'white' male in his 20s, from the local community did join the WCF. He joined the WCF after hearing about it via his mother who had attended the Open Day. This young male, however, played an extremely passive role around the decision-making table at monthly WCF meetings. He did, however, become quite involved in a small local environmental group that was a member of the WCC and who were jointly developing an environmental improvement plan for the neighbourhood along with the CIM.

The lack of any wider community participation within the WCF meant that the local community's needs and wants were mediated and championed by a combination of well-meaning, but overly paternalistic, professional voluntary sector agents and a few locally-based tenant activists. The CWTG representative, for example, was there to represent the concerns of tenants from the Central *Westside* Estate. Similarly, the representative from BMETA had the responsibility for championing the needs of the BME community. It was clear from observations and comments made by the community representative that agenda-setting and interest filtration within the WCF was shaped by a small number of agents:

> I think that decision-making is FAIRLY collective really! I think that some people are better PLACED, for example, the WARG representative who has been in the community for years and years and knows more than anybody about what actually goes on! The WSM and LBSEU representatives, because of their positions, hear about groups that need things and so on! In fact, they are the people, more often than not, who raise concerns about projects who DON'T know about what's going on, for example, the Bangladeshi Women's Group.   (Interviewee 6)

Challenging Paternalism and Democracy within the WCF

In overall terms, the WCF made relatively few executive decisions that translated into policies or programmes, it owned or controlled, on the ground that benefited the local community. Of the few executive decisions taken (e.g. the Community Audit, the Open Day and the appointment of the CIM) these mainly served to benefit the WCF. The WCF committee spent considerably more time *discussing* rather than *deciding* what it could do to tackle the issues they were interested in. When decisions were taken, for example, inviting an employment and training organization to talk to local residents about how to enhance their job prospects, these were passed without any controversy. There, however, was one policy decision that provoked a major challenge from one of the community representatives on the WCF. This was the first (and only) attempt at an exercise of community power.

Pre-school education emerged as a particularly pressing issue within *Westside* with demand for nursery school places far outstripping local supply. The neighbourhood was served by two small nurseries that both had an ethnically diverse client base. The more established nursery was filled to capacity. The newer nursery had some spare capacity but it needed extra funding to make these additional places available. The WCF, keen to assist in reducing pressure on this issue, agreed at one of its monthly meeting via its majority vote decision-making system to allocate funding to the newer nursery. The BMETA representative, who had not been present at the meeting when this decision was made, vehemently objected to it at the next monthly meeting. At this meeting he levelled a number of allegations and threats against the WCF in an effort to overturn the decision.

First, he accused the WCF of acting improperly and undemocratically by arguing that because he was not present at the previous meeting he had been denied an opportunity to argue and vote against the decision. The WCF Chairperson, the CWTG representative, tried in vain to explain that the decision had been arrived at via the democratic process they had all agreed to. This failed to quell the protestations from the BMETA representative. He persisted in arguing that not only was the decision 'wrong', but also, that the voting system was 'unfair'. He sought to reinforce this point by noting that those who had made the decision were from outside the local community. This point seemed to have been used in an effort to make WCF members feel guilty.

After allowing the BMETA representative to outline his objections to the initial decision, the Chairperson called another vote on the matter. The outcome was the same: a majority, with the exception of the BMETA representative, in favour of allocating some funds to the newer nursery school. As the Chairperson moved to pass the vote, the BMETA representative, who was visibly displeased with the outcome, tried yet again to have the decision overturned by 'threatening' the WCF on two fronts.

First, he stated that he would report the WCF for acting improperly and undemocratically. The WCF Chairman viewed this claim with incredulity. She reminded the BMETA representative that all WCF members had agreed to the majority vote system. She reiterated that as he had been given an opportunity to outline his viewpoint on the matter and that a majority of members had voted a particular way he would have to abide with this decision. The BMETA representative was resolute in his position however. In a further attempt to make the WCF feel guilty and thus reverse its decision, he proclaimed that he would have no option but to resign from the WCF. This decision disappointed the other WCF members, especially the Chairperson, who, as the only other community representative, had had a good working (and personal) relationship with the BMETA representative. The Chairperson, and the other WCF members, stood her ground and argued that the democratic process of the WCF could not be held to ransom by a minority of one. The Chairperson repeated her position several times as the BMETA representative persisted in proclaiming that the process was unfair and that non-community members had no 'right' to be making decisions about *Westside*. Eventually there was a short silent stand-off before the BMETA representative announced his resignation and then left the meeting.

Whilst there was regret amongst WCF members at the BMETA representative's resignation, they did not try to coerce him to stay on. Instead, the remaining members pressed on with their meeting. As far as they were all concerned they had conducted their business properly and democratically and the majority view of the WCF was binding.

It was suggested later that the primary basis of the BMETA representative's objections to the newer nursery were grounded in two key inter-related factors. Neither of which had to do with any impropriety within the WCF. On the one hand, he was on the committee of the more established nursery. And, on the other hand, he had been involved in a dispute with a female member of the other nursery, who, in fact, had previously worked for the more established nursery. In short, vested interests and personal matters were thought to underpin the BMETA representative's standpoint.

In concluding this section, from a researcher-observer viewpoint the reactions and claims of the BMETA representative were wholly unjustifiable and unsubstantiated. The outright refusal to accept the 'democratic will' of the WCF reflected an image of the BME representative as an individual who was more important and knowledgeable than his colleagues primarily on account that he lived in the local area. There can be no denial that the BMETA representative may have had some special insights into the condition of his neighbourhood. But, he by no means had a monopoly on such insights. As a partner, within a partnership where decision-making is premised on a simple and universally agreed voting system, it is only 'right' that the will of the majority is at least respected.

The (Over-)Significance of 'Race'

'Race' featured as a significant issue of discussion and concern within the WCF. This was somewhat peculiar, in light of the findings of the community audit. The audit had been commissioned in order to identify key problems within *Westside* that were to be used to construct policy priorities. The audit revealed that racism was not deemed to be a particularly unproblematic issue. In fact, it was ranked eleventh out of fourteen major problems identified by survey respondents. The local community was more concerned about environmental issues. The top three major problems identified in the community audit included: a lack of parking facilities; litter and graffiti; and dog fouling. This, of course, is not to deny the existence of racism, historical and/or contemporaneous, endured by individuals within the neighbourhood.

In addition to the generally unproblematic nature of racism within the neighbourhood, the problem of 'youth racism' which had been a catalytic factor in the setting up of the WCRP in the first place had also subsided as a point of concern. The (perceived) youth racism problem, which centred on physical altercations between young 'Asian' males from *Westside* and young 'black' males from an adjacent neighbourhood, had been virtually forgotten within the WCF during the fieldwork period. A further indication of the declining significance of racism within the neighbourhood was the departure of the *Westside* Anti-Racist Group (WARG) representative from the WCF.

Why, then, in the face of the evidence above, did 'race' (and racism) remain high on the agenda within the WCF? A combination of inter-related factors was at play. First, the various WCF members all had a personal policy interest and/or historical background in 'race' issues. Next, key WCF members had strong organizational links and vested interests in certain BME groups and organizations. Finally, and, most importantly, there was a strong ideological commitment to the ideas of anti-racism and multiculturalism amongst WCF members.

Whilst good relationships with BME community groups and an adherence to anti-racism and multiculturalism may be honourable and admirable, the WCF displayed bias or favouritism towards particular ethnic groups. This was reflected, for example, in the high levels of interest shown in the plight of the Bangladeshi community (and the Somali community to a lesser extent) than other BME communities. The level of interest shown towards the Bangladeshi community by certain WCF members provoked an underlying resentment from the BMETA representative. Interestingly, however, he too was keen to promote the needs of a particular ethnic group – 'black' West Africans. This was despite the fact that he was supposedly there to represent the plight of BME communities in general. The relatively less explicit interest shown towards the West African community may also have been a contributory factor in the stand-off he had with the WCF over the funding allocated to the newer nursery.

More interesting, however, was the near complete lack of interest and/or even mention of the plight of the local 'white' working-class community within the WCF. Again, this was a function of the fact that WCF members were too consumed with the particular BME groups they had links to. Moreover, there was no representative from the 'white' working-class community on the WCF to champion their needs. The WCF never even considered trying to recruit someone from this community.

Ultimately, the over-significance attached to 'race' and racism meant that the WCF lost its focus and the opportunity to tackle the 'real' issues of concern within *Westside*. The wider community stood to benefit from the WCRP if the WCF had directly tackled the environmental problems identified in the community audit as opposed to championing particular ethnic groups. This would have been the more pragmatic route to have followed in light of the small budget of the WCRP.

Conclusions

This chapter has examined the nature of community consultation and power within a small-scale pilot project concerned with empowering tenants, developing a stronger community-led approach to regeneration and addressing the issue of racism. Ironically, the aim of getting people more involved in decision-making failed to materialize. This was largely a result of an overarching paternalistic culture within the key decision-making structure, the WCF, responsible for managing the regeneration process. Whilst the two decision-making structures, the WCF and WCC, that comprised this regeneration programme were socially pluralistic in terms of their membership profile, with representatives drawn from across the public, private, voluntary and community sectors, the balance of power within both, especially the WCF, rested with professional voluntary sector agents. It was this domination that underscored the paternalism within the overall regeneration process and particularly within the WCF.

Furthermore, although the programme had initially been set up to tackle youth racism within the local neighbourhood, 'race' and racism were not perceived to be that problematic amongst local tenants. Nevertheless, 'race' remained on the policy agenda within the WCF. This was a result of a combination of a policy commitment, but narrow understanding, of anti-racism and multiculturalism and vested interests that particular WCF members had with certain BME groups within the local neighbourhood. This bred resentment from some members within the WCF and the wider community. Furthermore, the regularity of the Bangladeshi community within the discourse of the WCF reinforced the perception that some form of 'positive discrimination' was being shown to this group. Interestingly, in all the discussions that centred on 'race' within the WCF the needs and wants of the 'white' working-class community were never discussed.

A strong pluralistic and community-minded spirit permeated the WCF. Unfortunately, the paternalistic mindsets of key WCF members, partly a function of the organizations they came from, inhibited the creation of a community-led regeneration project and any expression of community power within it.

Chapter 8

Conclusions: Reconsidering Community Power and the Significance of 'Race'

The current undiscriminating use of the word "democratic" as a general term of praise is not without danger. It suggests that, because democracy is a good thing, it is always a gain for mankind if it is extended. This may sound self-evident, but it is nothing of the kind.   (Hayek, 1960: 104)

To say that race is declining in significance, therefore, is not only to argue that the life chances of blacks have less to do with race than with economic class affiliation but also to maintain that racial conflict and competition in the economic sector – the most important historical factors in the subjugation of blacks – have been substantially reduced.   (Wilson, 1980: 152)

Introduction

It was argued in Chapter 2 that there had been a 'pluralistic turn' in British urban regeneration policy. Whilst urban policy has always been a partnership venture, primarily a dualistic one, it was not until the late 1960s/early 1970s that a more diverse range of interests became more directly involved in an increasingly 'democratic' policy process. This emerging pluralistic turn in policy was galvanized with the publication of the then Labour Government's White Paper, *Policy for the Inner Cities* (HMSO, 1977) which advocated a much broader partnership and 'democratic' approach to tackling urban problems. The 1977 White Paper, however, was shelved following the election of the neo-liberal/-conservative government of Margaret Thatcher in 1979. In its place a much narrower and privatized form of partnership between central government and property developers emerged creating a democratic deficit.

This privatized form of regeneration eventually gave way to what may be termed a 'pragmatic incrementalist' approach under John Major, who assumed leadership of the then Conservative Government in 1990 following the deposing of Margaret Thatcher. The competitive bidding regime introduced under Major, firstly, in the City Challenge initiative and, subsequently, the SRB programme ensured that urban regeneration policy retained a distinctly neo-liberal character. Simultaneously, urban policy became increasingly holistic in its focus and pluralistic in terms of who was entitled to participate in decision-making within local URPs. This 'pluralistic turn' was also complemented by a 'turn to community' (Duffy and Hutchinson, 1997). A more explicit commitment to pluralistic and democratic decision-making was then championed by Tony Blair's 'New Labour' government following its 1997 General Election victory (Tiesdell and Allmendinger, 2001a; 2001b).

This book, in light of the pluralistic and community turns in urban policy, has sought to address two key questions: (i) the nature of 'community power' within local URPs; and (ii) the significance of 'race' within local community forums and the regeneration process more generally. In order to address these two questions an ethnographic research methodology was adopted so as to 'get under the skin' of local URPs and community forums, the latter forming the primary locus of analysis. Furthermore, in an effort to generate some 'analytical generalizations' (Yin, 1984), a multiple case study strategy with analysis of three broadly similar locales was adopted.

The aim of this concluding chapter is to synthesize the theoretical (Chapter 3) and methodological (Chapter 4) frameworks used with the empirical data presented in Chapters 5-7 in order to advance a 'new' means of analyzing and understanding the pattern(s) of power and (in)significance of 'race' within urban regeneration policy. The role and potential of an ethnographic approach in analyzing URPs and community participation is briefly outlined in the first instance. Next, several key empirical issues – sense of community; the; participatory structures and processes; community power; and the significance of 'race' – within each case study area are outlined in order to illustrate how they compare with one another. This paves the way for the construction of a 'new' typology of community power and some concluding analytical generalizations.

Methodological Issues: The Case for Ethnography

As noted in Chapter 4, ethnography has traditionally been associated with anthropological and cultural studies where researchers sought to develop an understanding of the 'culture' (i.e. structures, networks, processes and relations) within 'less developed' societies and communities. Within the developed world and an urban policy context ethnography has had something of a chequered history. The Chicago School of Sociology, for example, produced a series of ethnographies during the 1920-40s (Saunders, 2001). Later, ethnography was central in the Community Studies tradition that emerged in the UK during the 1940s and prospered until the early 1970s (e.g. Young and Wilmott, 1957). Since the mid-1980s there has been something of a revival in the use of ethnography across the social sciences (Lofland, 1995). This has been especially true within the sub-discipline of the sociology of education, where considerable attention has been focused on analyzing the construction and significance of 'race' within schools, and between teachers and pupils (Connolly, 1998, 2001; Connolly and Maginn, 1999; Connolly and Troyna, 1998; Foster, 1990; Troyna, 1991).

In contrast to developments elsewhere, there has been relatively little modern use or explicit championing of ethnography within urban policy analysis. Notable exceptions, however, include Franklin (1986) and Greed (1994), who have both illustrated the strengths of ethnography and advocated that it should be used more frequently. Use of an ethnographic approach has also been stimulated by real world developments, because the greater fragmentation of actors in urban regeneration creates the need to investigate social interaction on a smaller scale than is feasible with most statistical analysis. In particular, this methodological approach offers an innovative means of studying tenants' involvement in formal decision-making structures. The approach is innovative, despite historical antecedents, because it represents a departure from the predominantly quantitative-based methodology used during the 1980s and 1990s. They used social surveys to generate statistically representative data to lay claims to objective and generalizable explanations of cause and effect (Franklin, 1989).

This is not to imply that ethnography is inherently superior to such quantitative research, as both approaches have advantages and disadvantages. Where an ethnographic approach has potential advantages is in very small sample situations, where measurement categories are hard to define in advance or to quantify in a way that enables simple aggregation. An ethnographic approach was adopted on the grounds that it was better suited to addressing questions and developing understandings of 'how' and 'why' (i) local communities exert their power and (ii) 'race' is constructed as an issue within and between agents and structures in the regeneration process. Ethnography necessitates researchers being located within their research settings for an extended period of time. Field research was conducted in *Northside, Southside* and *Westside* over a period of 12-15 months. During this period a total of 88 non-participant observations of community forum meetings and associated events and 69 in-depth interviews were conducted across all three areas (see Tables 4.1 and 4.2 in Chapter 4). The overall length of time spent in the three case study areas enabled the production of a theoretically informed 'thick description' (Geertz, 1973; Hammersley, 1992) of the nature and complexity of community participation and power in ethnically diverse localities.

These benefits of ethnographic research have also been used as a major criticism of it: as the research progresses ethnography produces biased, subjective and non-generalizable empirical research findings. This is because ethnographic research has concentrated on studying either a single or a small number of research cases as opposed to a statistically representative sample of cases. To an extent these criticisms can also be applied to statistical analysis as a whole. Measurement categories, even when chosen prior to empirical investigation, are still researcher influenced. The difference in the potential for researcher bias between statistical and ethnographic approaches, therefore, is partly a question of the effect of timing. Are prior categories necessarily more objective than ones that may change as a consequence of justifiable empirical observation? With regard to sample size, statistical analysis may encounter problems of sample representativeness as well. If populations are heterogeneous, it may be unreasonable to generalize from even large samples. The heterogeneity of urban regeneration schemes and the communities affected by them may consequently limit the applicability of the social survey approach. The difference between the ethnographic and social survey approaches, therefore, is not one between 'hard science' and 'soft observation', but rather one of different strategies to deal with different empirical contexts.

Mindful of the potential criticisms of ethnographic research, a comprehensive and holistic approach to data collection and analysis was adopted. This entailed using a multiple case study strategy, wherein three neighbourhoods undergoing regeneration with broadly similar socio-economic and political characteristics were selected in order to facilitate a comparative analysis and thus produce more credible 'analytical generalizations' (Yin, 1984). To reiterate, a range of research techniques was deployed so as to collate and triangulate primary data. First, non-participant observations from within the regeneration process were undertaken in order to observe and track the wider 'realities' and dynamics both within and between community forums, local URPs and other formal structures as the regeneration process unfolded in each neighbourhood. Second, in-depth semi-structured interviews (and casual conversations) with community forum representatives, local authority and housing association officers, councillors and consultants) were conducted in order to elicit people's historical and contemporaneous experiences and understandings of the local communities ability to influence decision-making and the significance of 'race'. Finally, focus groups were conducted as a means of triangulating the data collected via observations and in-depth interviews.

To summarize, the methodological approach used in this research was adopted in response to the greater emphasis by policy-makers on the need to involve the local community in formal decision-making, but without having sufficient understanding of the meaning, nature and complexities of what constitutes the local community. As Greed (1994) notes, ethnography provides researchers and, more importantly, policy-makers with an ideal means of 'investigating the dynamics of a spatially defined setting... and in evaluating the efficacy of a particular policy or initiative therein' (p.125-126).

Empirical Issues: Community, Participation, Power and 'Race'

This section provides an overview of the empirical findings of several key issues: (i) the meaning of community; (ii) community participation structures and processes; (iii) 'community power'; and (iv) the significance of 'race'. The condition of each of these issues within *Northside, Southside* and *Westside* are considered in turn.

In What Sense a Community?

The constitution of the 'local community' out of groups of people living in a local area has been at the core of debates surrounding community participation in planning and urban policy (Hill, 1994; Taylor, 2000a, b, 2002). There, however, has been a tendency amongst policy-makers to overlook this debate and assume that local communities can be readily conflated to a clearly defined cohesive entity. It was certainly true that during the initial stages of the regeneration process in each case study area policy-makers perceived and even sought to construct 'homogenous' communities via the drawing of regeneration boundaries and defining the membership of community forums. This seemed to be part of an overarching strategy to create a manageable community wherein antagonistic participants and other community problems could be contained and offset. As Cohen (1985), however, has highlighted who and what constitutes the local community is no easy task. Local communities are highly complex and dynamic phenomena and individuals may be members of many communities at any given time (Hill, 1994). Invariably, such complexity and dynamism may give rise to conflicts as individuals and groups within a local community compete with one another over scarce resources such as housing and socio-political power (Saunders, 1979, 1986). The empirical research outlined in Chapters 5-7 enables some evidence to be presented on the 'sense of community' within each case study area and the factors underpinning it. The evidence points to a different sense of community within each area thereby reinforcing the complexity nature and structure of local communities (Cohen, 1985; Hill, 1994; Jeffers *et al*, 1996).

Northside: A unified sense of community Of the three case study areas, the various community forums within *Northside*, especially the NCF, displayed a generally unified 'sense of community'. Of course, this is not to deny the existence of historical and contemporaneous tensions within and between community forums and the wider community. However, such problems tended to be of a comparatively minor, personal and temporary nature. The sense of community within *Northside* at the overall neighbourhood level and within the NCF had an organic feel to it. This was predicated on several factors. First, there was minimal intervention by policy-makers in relation to defining and managing membership of the NCF. The local authority's role on this front was restricted to putting in place policies and mechanisms designed to ensure that community forums were open to all groups within the area. Ultimately, the strong sense of community within the neighbourhood and the NCF was premised on tenants 'shared experience' in relation to their housing and social class situations. This unified sense of community was compounded as a consequence of the neighbourhood being perceived and labelled as a 'no-go area' and highly stigmatized by outsiders. This served to reinforce tenants' commitment to be an instrumental part of the regeneration process to ensure that when their new estate was completed the final outcome reflected, as much as possible, their image of their community and neighbourhood. This was clearly reflected in the camaraderie, diversity of membership and clear sense of direction within and between the various community forums that had evolved as the regeneration process unfolded.

Southside: A fractured sense of community By way of contrast, the 'sense of community' within *Southside* was highly fractured. This was true of both the community forum (the SCF) and the wider neighbourhood. This was initially a function of the local authority's failure to inform the wider community their neighbourhood had been earmarked for regeneration. This lack of consultation provoked a widespread community backlash and exacerbated pre-existing underlying tensions between a number of leading community activists who represented different community organizations and parts of the neighbourhood. To recap, the local authority had sought to 'impose' a number of distinct housing renewal proposals without consulting the local community, contrary to the fact that community participation was a stated strategic objective of the regeneration programme. Moreover, it transpired that the local authority was totally unaware, through a failure to initiate any form of consultation, of the existence of several discrete, yet distinct, housing sub-communities with clear and strong senses of community and territorial identity. The council had also failed to evaluate the significance and function of the local youth club, earmarked for demolition and relocation with the land it occupied be developed for housing, within the wider schema of community relations and politics in the area.

When the various housing sub-communities, tenant and other community-based organizations eventually became aware of the council's proposals to regenerate the area they all became highly self-protective and defensive of their assets, sense of identity and retreated from the regeneration process to consider their individual counter-offensives. This self-segregation within the wider community had negative knock-on effects in terms of the sense of community within the community forum. Despite the various sub-communities being wholly overlooked by the council, they had failed to recognize that they shared this common experience and could have utilized this fact as a means of constructing a unified sense of community. This strategy was rendered impossible however following efforts, mainly from the council, to manipulate membership of the community forum throughout the early stages of the regeneration process. In other words, the council sought to define the sense of community within the SCF in its own vision.

Specifically, the council, and indeed a few tenant activists, sought deliberately to exclude a prominent, yet controversial, community activist from the community forum and the regeneration process on the grounds that his involvement would impede and obstruct the development of both. Despite being a representative of one the borough's neighbourhood housing forums that had a strategic vested interest in the regeneration area, this militant activist was eventually excluded from any direct involvement on the community forum and the overall regeneration process. Subsequently, this community activist initiated a propaganda campaign designed to wreck the community forum and the regeneration programme. This entailed disrupting SCF meetings and slandering and intimidating members. This course of action fuelled suspicions and reinforced divisions amongst other community activists almost resulting in the demise of the SCF. Although it managed to survive, the sense of community within the SCF remained extremely fragile. This propaganda campaign also extended into the wider community where there were allegations of tenants also being intimidated in connection with a ballot on whether to demolish and redevelop or refurbish '*the Mall*'. This propaganda campaign created a sense of confusion within the local area, sustained divisions between community activists and strengthened historically cynical attitudes about the council's ability to deliver services.

Westside: An adversarial sense of community? There was no discernible 'sense of community' *per se* within the *Westside* Community Forum. This was based on the simple fact that the majority of the participants on the WCF were not local tenants. Instead, the majority of members were mainly 'white', middle-class female voluntary sector or local authority representatives, who worked within the wider local area and tended to have vested interests with particular BME groups, most notably the local Bangladeshi community. There were only two local tenant agents on the WCF, one from the local residents association and the other from a borough-wide BME organization. In overall terms, there was an adversarial sense of community within this forum.

Although the WCF was very community-minded, when members talked about helping or involving the 'local community' this effectively meant the 'BME community'. Furthermore, the sense of community was also structured by the fact that the regeneration programme was constructed around dealing with racism amongst the local youth within the area. Notably, the needs and aspirations of the local 'white' working-class community were effectively overlooked within the community forum. The issue of 'whiteness' *per se* never entered the discourses of the community forum or individual members. It was almost as if the 'white' community was not in need of any assistance or that they did not even constitute part of 'the local community'. As highlighted in Chapter Seven, community consultation events tended to be centred on trying to inform and involve BMEs in the regeneration process. Consequently, this led to a sense of exclusion being felt amongst some elderly 'white' tenants who attended the WCR Open Day.

The key conclusions that can be drawn on the issue of community include:

- There are distinct perceptions and constructions of who and what constitutes 'the local community' and this is structured by where people are socially located and how the urban regeneration process affects them;
- Communities may not be uniformly structured along particular socio-economic or cultural axes, such as class or 'race' or pertain shared motivations, values or interests;
- Communities are multi-faceted and dynamic entities and are constantly being reconstructed around social and political issues within the local neighbourhood; and
- Community politics can create perceptions of both community groupings and interests that may not necessarily be of continued relevance.

Community Participation Structures and Processes

The 'turn to community' in urban regeneration has necessitated structures and processes being put in place to facilitate meaningful participation with tenants. The general belief amongst central government policy-makers and academic commentators is that regeneration programmes are less likely to succeed if local communities are not directly involved in decision-making (Burton, 2003; Hastings *et al*, 1996; Taylor, 2002). It is important to note that this standpoint presupposes that successful regeneration programmes, and local communities' ability to influence decision-making can only be measured and considered valid if they are a formal component positively engaged in the regeneration process. This normative viewpoint is shown to have too narrow a conception of what constitutes success. Moreover, it completely overlooks tenants ability to influence decision-making from outside the formal confines of regeneration structures and processes. This section focuses on attitudes and commitment to community participation and the nature of structures and processes set up by the accountable bodies within each case study area.

Northside: progressive structures and processes LB Hackney claimed that is was committed to 'full' participation with the local community. This suggests that local tenants would be involved in *every* stage of the regeneration process. However, as highlighted in Chapter Five, the local community was not involved in the funding negotiations stage or the drawing up of the regeneration plan that was eventually presented to the local community and initially interpreted as a *fait accompli*.

The lack of participation during these embryonic stages of the process, especially during funding negotiations, was premised on a belief that the local community would revolt against the council for its apparent 'collusion' with the then Conservative government. If such a revolt had occurred the council feared that it would continue to be perceived by central government as a 'loony left' authority and subsequently lose out on obtaining much needed funding. Alternatively, if the council had involved the local community during this stage and had indeed lost funding as a consequence of community objections this would arguably have reinforced the wider community's already cynical and apathetic view of the council's inability to deliver services. The decision to side step the community during these stages of the regeneration process was understandable and, arguably justifiable, given the political risks underpinning the need to secure central government funding.

When the local community was eventually informed about proposals to regenerate their neighbourhood they were naturally suspicious and sceptical. The council and its development partners, however, were quick to embark upon a determined participation strategy. This witnessed the setting up of a new community forum, with clear equal opportunities policies, resourced with its own tenants' advisor, provided with office space and equipment and given direct access to both strategic and operational decision-making arenas within the council. The consultation process got off to a nervous and uncertain start as the various agents, especially 'old' and 'new' community activists, acclimatized to the various new and evolving structures and processes associated with the regeneration programme. As community forum activists acquired knowledge and an understanding of the nuances of regeneration they quickly became embedded within the decision-making process and demonstrated an ability to communicate and negotiate confidently with central and local government policy-makers.

These positive developments were also attributed to the progressive attitudes and culture towards participation amongst local authority officers and other professional agents. Furthermore, the ethnically diverse staff at the neighbourhood office boded well with the ethnic diversity within the estate and the community forum. All of this served to prepare the ground for the development of good working relations and an exchange of information and concerns between community activists, non-active tenants and local council officers.

In terms of community consultation by the various community forums within the area a combination of formal and informal mechanisms (e.g. AGM meetings and community fun days) was adopted in an effort to involve an even broader and more eclectic mix of people in the regeneration process. This had mixed success due to a combination of disinterest, apathy and a feeling that existing members were doing a good enough job already. Full membership of and/or simply attending community forum meetings in order to obtain information was open to any tenant within the area if they wished to do so.

Southside: bureaucratic structures and processes As with *Northside*, policy-makers in *Southside* also failed to inform or consult the wider local community during the formative stages of the regeneration process. This was despite the fact that participation was listed as a strategic objective. This failure to consult tenants was due to two key inter-related factors. On the one hand, policy-makers were apprehensive about losing central government funding as a consequence of a belief that there would be a community backlash towards proposals to regenerate the area. On the other hand, the council still retained an extremely bureaucratic approach in delivering services, a hangover of the 'loony left' days in the 1980s and 1990s, and was uncomfortable in sharing any sense of power or responsibilities outside its own structures. Moreover, this sense of bureaucracy pervaded the entire regeneration process and was reinforced in its human face. That is, the majority of officers involved in the regeneration process were 'white' professional males, from development or construction backgrounds, who held extremely technical views of urban regeneration.

This underlying technical culture within the SPB impacted negatively upon community participation. In short, policy-makers in *Southside* displayed relatively little knowledge, understanding or commitment to involving tenants in a meaningful and purposeful manner. In setting up the community forum, for example, an open day to recruit tenants into the process was held outside the neighbourhood in an environment, a hotel conference room, that was poorly attended and where 'ordinary' local people felt uncomfortable. A second attempt to set up the community forum proved more successful in that it attracted a greater number of curious and interested tenants. The council, however, attempted to exclude particular tenant activists from joining the community forum because of their radical standpoints and fundamental opposition to the regeneration programme. The council was essentially of the view that if these militant activists could be marginalized there would be minimal problems within the regeneration process. This strategy, along with the failure to consult the community backfired. It provoked a major political backlash within the local community that the council had hoped to avoid in the first instance and almost resulted in the demise of the community forum. The council did little to intervene and resolve the conflict within the community forum, preferring instead to keep at a critical distance and let community activists sort out the problem amongst themselves.

The council also failed to provide sufficient resources to enable tenants to accrue knowledge and understanding of the regeneration process to enable the community forum to participate effectively in decision-making. Finally, the SPB, the structure managing and delivering the regeneration on the ground, was effectively a part-time structure in that the Director only worked 2.5 days per week. Consequently, this added to the impression that the council lacked a serious commitment to community participation and the regeneration process overall.

Ultimately, then, the council lacked a sense of sincerity towards community participation and this was reflected in the ill conceived and ill-equipped structures and processes it had put in place. The council (and its development partners) came to the regeneration process with a rather fixed bureaucratic and technical mindset wherein they perceived their key objective to deliver project outputs (i.e. new housing) on time and within costs. Lastly, the council's attempt to massage membership of the community forum provoked a backlash from militant community activists that resulted in a fracturing of the local community, the near demise of the SCF and severe delays to the regeneration process.

Westside: paternalistic structures and processes Yet again, there was a near-complete absence of community participation during the initial stages of the regeneration process in this case study. Two community representatives, one who worked and the other who lived in the local area, were brought on board at the eleventh hour primarily to comment on the formal regeneration bid, which had already received provisional approval from the GoL. Moreover, although the final bid was signed off by a total of 20 'partners', some prominent and drawn from the voluntary, private, community and public sectors, the majority of these played no role whatsoever in the construction of the regeneration plan or executive decision-making within the actual regeneration process. Their inclusion was an astute piece of policy manoeuvring by a community representative nonetheless to illustrate to central government and thus secure funding that the project was supported by a wide range of agents and thus satisfied the criteria of setting up a partnership.

A two-tiered management and decision-making structure was set up in order to facilitate the execution of the regeneration programme. The first tier, the WCC, comprised representatives from the various organizations that had 'signed off' the bid document. This structure was initially set up to provide strategic advice and guidance to the second tier, the WCF, which was responsible for executive decision-making within the regeneration programme. Notably, there was a discretely held objective amongst members of the WCF that prominent members of the WCC would ultimately contribute some financial support to the regeneration programme. This objective was never realized. Ultimately, the WCC played virtually no role in the regeneration process. During the course of the year of fieldwork it only met two or three times, was poorly attended and dealt with superficial issues.

Although a diverse range of organizations was represented on the WCF, membership was comprised largely of professional voluntary sector agents who were mainly 'white' middle-class females who lived outside the local area but had close working relations with the neighbourhood. Consequently, an overarching paternalistic mindset and culture pervaded the WCF. This had impacts on community participation. In short, tenants were effectively kept at an arms-length from directly participating or influencing decision-making. The commonly held view within the WCF was that the 'average' tenant was not sufficiently interested or endowed to be constructively involved in the regeneration process. Hence, one of the key objectives of the programme was to 'train up' tenants so that it would eventually become a genuinely community-led initiative. This objective was never realized due to an unwitting reluctance amongst voluntary sector agents to relinquish power and responsibility down to the wider local community. Instead, voluntary sector agents continued to represent and lobby for particular ethnic groups whom they had close ties with. There, however, was a degree of bias in this adversarial representation. The needs of the Bangladeshi community tended to disproportionately dominate the discourse within the WCF. This provoked political and subtle racialized tensions within the community forum between one of the tenant activists, who, ironically, represented a borough-wide BME umbrella organization. This impacted negatively on the focus and pace of decision-making within the WCF.

Ultimately, there were no significant direct inputs from the wider community into the decision-making processes of the WCF other than the community audit and the Open Day that had attracted between 80-100 tenants of mainly BME origins. These two events only enabled the WCF to get a one-off fix on the community's main concerns, priorities and ideas for regenerating the area. Wider tenant involvement in decision-making was primarily articulated via adversarial representations and lobbying by well-intentioned, but overly paternalistic, professional voluntary sector activists.

The key conclusions from the empirical data on the issue of community participation structures and processes are:

- Tenants are unlikely to be actively involved in the embryonic stages (i.e. funding negotiations and bid preparation) of the regeneration process, as these stages are deemed to be too politically sensitive by institutional agents;
- Despite policy commitments to 'full' participation local authorities are likely to exhibit varying degrees of understanding and commitment as to what this actually constitutes. This is a function of the cultural mindsets carried by individual policy-makers and policy structures;
- Institutional agents will often, deliberately and/or unwittingly, seek to restrict radical tenants from accessing community forums and decision-making structures in an effort to minimize conflict and problems that pose a threat to their version of the regeneration process.

Community Power and Influence

Although tenants have been increasingly brought to the centre of the regeneration process and afforded the title of 'partner', questions and doubts remain about the nature of their power within decision-making arenas. On the one hand, there is a strongly held view that local communities command little or no 'real' power (Cooper and Hawtin, 1997b; Hastings *et al*, 1996; Smith and Beazley, 2001). Relatedly, government policy-makers tend to be of the view that power exerted by local communities can only be 'successful' and 'legitimate' if they are a formal component of the regeneration process. Consequently, this study sought to examine the nature of community power and the factors underpinning its structure. This was achieved via utilizing a combination of 'decisional' and 'reputational' approaches to measure power (Harding, 1996). In other words, community and institutional agents were asked to outline their interpretations and experiences of actual events of when, where and how community forums had affected change in decision-making.   These accounts were synthesized with non-participant observations of relations and interactions between community forum members and institutional agents in order to develop a composite picture of the nature of 'community power'. The main findings for each case study area are summarized below.

Northside: a pragmatic approach to influencing decision-making? Community forums in *Northside* were generally perceived to be powerful and influential structures within strategic and operational decision-making arenas. This was especially true amongst tenant activists who enthusiastically outlined during interviews that they had been given and negotiated direct access to decision-makers; had learned to speak the same language as policy-makers and were thus able to both understand and communicate more effectively within the regeneration process. This resulted in their concerns, needs and wants being listened to and heard.

The NCF managed to significantly alter several key strategic policies that the council (and central government) had initially tried to impose upon the local community. These included: (i) increasing the space standards of all new housing developments following criticisms of the size of homes built during the first phase of the regeneration process; (ii) increasing the bedroom space of homes allocated to households with two or more children of the same sex/gender; and, most significantly; (iii) reducing the proportion of new housing allocated to homeless households from outside the neighbourhood from 70/30 to 50/50. The change brought about on this latter policy in particular represented a clear indication of the nature of the NCFs power. The 70/30 policy was a central government policy that local authorities were obliged to implement in order to secure government funding for regeneration programmes.

The NCF managed to effect these changes due to a combination of factors. These included: asserting insightful knowledge and political nous of the objectives of regeneration policy at the national and local levels; developing positive working relations with professional officers at the local level; and adopting a pragmatic and professional approach to negotiations with central and local government policy-makers. The NCF's ability to execute these skills and thus secure the policy changes it achieved was grounded in three key factors. First, the unified sense of community enabled the NCF, and other community forums, to present a strong and representative voice within decision-making arenas. Second, the construction of positive and progressive participation structures and processes facilitated the development of mutual understanding and respect between community activists and professional officers. Finally, access to resources, especially technical expertise, enabled community activists to develop a sophisticated understanding of the political nuances of regeneration processes. In overall terms, tenants exerted a mix of 'persuasive influence' and legitimate pressure politics (Scott, 2001) in order to bring about change in the regeneration process.

Southside: a radical approach to influencing decision-making The SCF *per se* exerted practically no power within the decision-making processes of the SPB. Fundamentally, this was because it never really operated as a formal structure within the regeneration process. The various community organizations brought together to form this structure initially refused to engage in the process becoming self-protective of their own groups' or communities' interests following the council's attempt to impose proposals on the area. Furthermore, a complicated and protracted power struggle broke out amongst community activists following the exclusion of a prominent radical activist from the regeneration process. Community forum meetings were often inquorate preventing it from conducting any business and thus making any executive decisions as to what courses of action should be taken in the interests of the wider community who the SCF supposedly represented.

Although the SCF exercised no influence as such within the regeneration process, the various sub-communities represented on it were able to effect changes and/or delays in decision-making for their own ends. That is, those groups and sub-communities directly affected by the council's original proposals stepped outside the official decision-making process, breaking relations with policy-makers (i.e. the SPB) and effectively boycotted the regeneration process. A combination of pragmatic and radical strategies was deployed in an effort to influence decision-making.

On the one hand, both the OSTA and SHC, for example, adopted a pragmatic approach in devising alternative proposals. The SHC drew up its on counter-proposals independently whilst the SHC formed an alliance with a professional advocacy group. Both of these sub-communities were intent on re-entering the regeneration process in order to renegotiate with the council/SPB. On the other hand, the militant community activists took a radical approach totally objecting to the regeneration programme, refusing to offer any alternatives. This was grounded in their dogmatic opposition to the local council and a self-serving desire to accrue power within the local community. The regeneration process was severely halted. In particular, the centrepiece of the programme, the demolition and redevelopment of 'the Mall', was delayed for approximately 18 months by the propaganda-fuelled (re)actions of the small group of militant tenants who were supposedly excluded from the regeneration process. In addition, the refusal of a local shopkeeper to vacate his premises until he was adequately compensated also held up the redevelopment of 'the Mall'.

Both the council and SPB took an essentially bureaucratic view of the reactions by the various sub-communities represented on the SCF members and militant tenant activists. The delays to the regeneration programme, especially those created by the militant grouping, were perceived as adding costs to development proposals and denying the 'wider community' the chance to avail of much needed new and improved housing. As the regeneration process ground to a near halt, the reactions from all community activists impressed upon the council and SPB the ability of the 'local community' to influence decision-making and the need to take the issue of community participation more seriously.

In overall terms, the regeneration of *Southside* was hindered by community activists resorting to different forms of protest politics and devising radical counteractive strategies in an effort to exert influence over decision-making (Scott, 2001).

Westside: a paternalistic approach to influencing decision-making It was actually impossible to discern the nature of community power exerted by local tenants within *Westside*. There were two simple inter-connected reasons for this. On the one hand, the community forum, the WCF, was comprised mainly of professional voluntary sector agents as opposed to local community representatives. These professional agents acted as self-anointed adversarial representatives of the local community and, more specifically, particular ethnic minority communities from within the neighbourhood. In other words, decisions were effectively being made on behalf of the local community.

On the other hand, the WCF made very few executive decisions of a significant nature. Instead, decision-making, or to be more precise, discussion within the WCF regularly centred on two key issues. First, how best to take forward the Community Audit and translate it into a programme of action. And, second, the need to involve more tenants, especially BMEs, in the regeneration process in general and the WCF is particular. Ironically, however, this latter objective remained elusive because of the extremely paternalistic culture that prevailed within the WCF.

There was one tangible expression of community power by the 'local community'. This, however, actually occurred prior to the commencement of the programme when the local tenants' association representative, an Irish female, managed to convince a number of mainly private sector organization to lend their symbolic support to the bid document to be submitted to central government.

The key conclusions to be drawn from the empirical data on the issue of community power are:

- Local communities can effect significant change and secure major successes via the adoption of pragmatic and/or radical strategies that result in the construction of 'legitimate' and 'illegitimate' community power in the eyes of institutional agents;

- Changes in policy may be effected by the local community either from within and/or outside the confines of the formal structures of regeneration programmes;
- If 'true' community power is to be afforded the opportunity to flourish within regeneration programmes then local community representatives, as opposed to adversarial professional representatives, need to constitute the majority of members on community forums.

The (In)Significance of 'Race'

'Race' has traditionally been an ambiguous issue within urban policy (Young, 1983). It, however, has become a more explicit urban policy issue since its inclusion in two strategic policy objectives (i.e. SO1 and SO4) of the SRB programme in the mid 1990s (DoE, 1994). Nevertheless, concerns have remained about central and local government's commitment to ensuring 'race' stays on the policy agenda and enhancing BMEs active participation in decision-making within URPs and community forms (BTEG, 1995, 1997; Loftman and Beazley, 1998; Ouseley, 1997). In other words, there has been a call for policy-makers to acknowledge and ensure that 'race' *always* matters. This call is premised on the implicit and explicit claims that Britain is an institutionally racist society (Home Office, 1999). This study sought to explore how 'race' was structured and the significance of it within community forums and the overall regeneration process within three ethnically diverse neighbourhoods located in London.

As outlined in Chapters 5-7, 'race' was structured in different ways by different agents, for different motives and reasons and thus assumed varying degrees of (in)significance within *Northside, Southside* and *Westside*. The range of experiences as to the (in)significance of 'race' challenges the somewhat orthodox view within the British academic literature that racism is endemic, institutionalized and that 'race' must always be treated as a significant policy issue (Brownill *et al*, 1996; Brownill and Thomas, 1998; Cooper and Hawtin, 1997a; Lo Piccolo and Thomas, 2003; Munt, 1991). In many respects, the variability in the (in)significance of 'race' and racism within *Northside, Southside* and *Westside* paralleled those identified by Jeffers *et al* (1996). Ultimately, 'race' and racism were significantly less problematic issues in all three areas than what had been expected based on readings from the academic literature and discussions with colleagues. The individual and general conclusions about the significance of 'race' are outlined below.

Northside: the declining significance of 'race' As noted earlier there was a strong and unified sense of community within *Northside*. As a result of this, 'race' was effectively constructed as a 'non-issue' within the community forum and the regeneration process in general. Interestingly, and somewhat bizarrely, one or two local authority officers actually wished that 'race' had been more of an issue.

Both 'black' and 'white' community activists interviewed described 'race' relations within the wider neighbourhood as having been generally positive and unproblematic. There had been sporadic episodes of racial tension during the 1980s, primarily around the time of local political elections, when 'race' was problematized and politicized by the far-right political party, the BNP/NF. But, such processes failed to permeate and take hold within the local community. This was argued to be a function of several key inter-related factors.

First, on account of the extent of ethnic diversity within the local neighbourhood, and the borough generally, all ethnic groups laid claim to some form of minority status. This status generated an underlying sense of empathy between the various communities and precluded any one group from ascertaining or asserting a dominant position within *Northside*. Second, the council's historical commitment to anti-racism, albeit having varying degrees of success, had helped to galvanize a pre-existing sense of tolerance between the various ethnic communities within the borough. Finally, and arguably most importantly, the shared housing experience of both 'black' and 'white' tenants within *Northside* sealed their unified sense of community.

Further indicators of the unproblematic nature of 'race' were reflected in the membership profile of the different community forums, especially the NCF, and the absence of any antagonistic racialized discourse within them. In terms of ethnic profile, for example, BMEs constituted the majority of members, and were actually over-represented, within the various community forums on the estate. Furthermore, BME tenants held all but one of the positions of authority (i.e. Chairman, Vice-Chairman, Secretary and Treasurer) across all community forums. This situation challenges the traditionally held view that BMEs tend to be deliberately discriminated and excluded from joining, never mind playing an instrumental role in local decision-making structures. None of the 'black' community activists had encountered any problems in joining or participating in community forums and the regeneration process in general on account of their ethnic identity.

The over-representation of BMEs was not perceived as a 'new' form of colonization of community politics. Community forums within *Northside* operated a genuine open-door policy to any member of the local community and various steps and measures were undertaken to facilitate effective consultation and encourage participation from the wider population. Success on this front was not as great as hoped amongst long-serving community activists. This was due to a combination of disinterest in community politics and satisfaction with the achievements of existing community forum members amongst non-active tenants. The core group of activists involved on two or all three community forums were fundamentally motivated by altruistic goals, chiefly eliminating the stigmatized image of their neighbourhood and getting as good a deal as possible, in relation to housing, improved environment and other social resources, for the local community.

'Race' rarely featured as a topic of concern or debate within the discourse or agendas of community forums. To reiterate, it was a 'non-issue' primarily because of the shared housing experience of BME and 'white' tenants. Furthermore, the inclusion of explicit equal opportunities policies in relation to membership of community forums, housing allocations and a joint decision by community activists and institutional agents to have an ethnically mixed estate prevented any sense of territorialism evolving within the area. This all added to the diminution of 'race' as an issue within community forums, the overall regeneration process and the wider neighbourhood.

Ultimately, then, 'race' did not impact on the regeneration process on account that it was not deemed or experienced as a problematic issue within the local community. Moreover, the regeneration process had no discernible negative impacts on 'race' relations within the local community. This was largely due to policy-makers adopting a generally pragmatic and egalitarian approach to implementing proposals. To conclude, the significance of 'race' within *Northside* resonates loudly with Wilson's (1980; 1987) thesis that 'race', as a determining factor in explaining the marginalized position of 'black' groups, is one of declining significance.

Southside: the contested significance of 'race' Interestingly, 'race' was also very much a 'non-issue' within *Southside*. Unlike *Northside*, however, where the unproblematic nature of 'race' was a function of positive factors, within *Southside* 'race' was a 'non-issue' for negative reasons. In short, the actions and reactions of a small number of militant community activists, following their exclusion from the regeneration process, resulted in an acrimonious power struggle that suppressed any wider community issues from getting onto the agendas of the SCF or SPB.

Those SCF members (e.g. the OSTA and SHC) keen to see the regeneration of *Southside* proceed, but on their terms, as opposed to the militants who wanted to halt the programme altogether, became consumed with trying to save the continued existence of their own communities and the SCF. Similarly, the local authority and the SPB became pre-occupied with trying to assure central government that the regeneration process was moving forward in order to ensure that it did not jeopardize losing government funding. Despite the council's insensitive approach to community consultation, if the regeneration of *Southside* had been abandoned the council would have faced immense political humiliation from the local electorate and central government policy-makers. Put another way, the council would have lost the battle it had become embroiled in with the militant community activists.

There were some latent concerns about the significance of 'race' amongst a small number of SCF members. It was suggested that 'race' had failed to get onto the agendas of the SPB and SCF due to historical and contemporaneous structural and institutional racism within these structures. The USYC representative, for example, felt that his organization, which catered mainly for local 'black' youths, had been racially discriminated by the council, SPB and SCF. His position was premised on how he had been treated by these three bodies. First, the council and the SPB failed to properly inform or consult with him about proposals to relocate the youth club and redevelop the land it occupied. This was interpreted by the USYC representative as an indication of the council and SPB's disinterest in the 'black' community. Next, the USYC representative did not think that the SCF was sympathetic or supportive of his plight on account of the client group the USYC served (i.e. black youth).

The USYC representative's perception that his organization had been racially discriminated against was somewhat blinkered and inaccurate. This was due to a combination of factors: (i) a close relationship with the militant activists; (ii) a readiness to accept the militants version of events regarding attitudes and views within the council, SPB and SCF; (iii) and a refusal to attend SCF meetings due to factors (i) and (ii). The USYC representative failed to acknowledge that the council and SPB had treated *all* sub-communities within the neighbourhood indifferently in terms of informing and consulting them. Put simply, the entire local community had been 'discriminated' against by the council and SPB. This discrimination was premised on 'institutional incompetency and inexperience' within the council and SPB in relation to involving local communities in decision-making. Furthermore, observations and interviews revealed that the SCF, after individual members had recovered from the news that their own sub-communities were under threat from regeneration proposals and attempts to rebuild itself after the power struggle with community militants, expressed both concern and support for the USYC. But as they USYC representative attended SCF meetings on a highly irregular basis he was unaware of such sentiments.

Whilst there may well have been racialized events (e.g. mobilization of the NF during local elections in the 1980s) and structural racism within the area in the past, there was no explicit evidence to suggest that such processes were operating within the *Southside* regeneration programme. The local authority, SCF members and community militants were too caught up in trying to resolve their own specific problems that there was simply no time or interest for racism or racialized processes within the regeneration process. The local authority and SPB had adopted a bureaucratically colour-blind approach in relation to delivering the regeneration programme. That is, they took the view that their regeneration proposals were to benefit the 'whole' community, which was initially perceived as a homogenous entity. The council and SPB subsequently discovered, much to their cost, that *Southside* was a highly heterogeneous and fractured community. It is important to note, however, that the heterogeneous and fracturous nature of the local community was structured along spatial or territorial lines as opposed to racial ones.

To conclude, concerns expressed by some community activists that 'race' ought to be on the agenda of the SPB and SCF failed to materialize. The reason for this was not that policy-makers and others deliberately sought to keep it off the agenda. Instead, 'race' issues failed to get onto the agenda because it was not deemed or constructed as an issue of significance within the internecine conflict that pervaded the SCF and the regeneration process in general. Power was the only issue of concern. Historical experiences (and contemporary beliefs) in the existence of institutional racism (Peach, 1996; Peach and Byron, 1993; Wilson, 1980, 1987) reinforced contemporaneous perceptions amongst a small number of SCF members racism prevailed within the council, SPB and SCF. Local community reactions to regeneration proposals and the power struggle within the SCF did not fracture along racial or ethnic lines. Instead, the local community fractured along territorial and political axes. This explains why 'race' *per se* was essentially unproblematic and a 'non-issue' within the community forum and the regeneration.

Westside: the over-significance of 'race' 'Race' was very much at the heart of the policy agenda within *Westside*. Initial proposals for the area centred on perceived concerns, by a small group of professional voluntary sector agents and the local police, about youth racism and an apparent emerging gang culture within the neighbourhood and adjoining areas. Interestingly, these various actors, especially those from the voluntary sector, had vested interests in 'race' issues as a consequence of their professional and political agendas or advocacy relations with particular ethnic minority groups within the area. 'Race', subsequently, tended to feature as a constant issue within the discourse and overall mindset of the WCF. For example, when the community forum took the decision to appoint a community development officer, it was effectively decided before the job was even advertised that the successful appointee had to be of BME origins. Sure enough the job was offered to and taken up by a BME female despite the fact that another applicant, a white female, apparently scored more points at her interview. Moreover, despite constant reference by these community advocates of the need to involve more BME tenants in decision-making they were effectively kept at an arms-length from the process.

However, the significance of 'race' was somewhat over-emphasized within the WCF. A community audit conducted as part of the community consultation strategy of the WCRP in order to identify key problems within the neighbourhood revealed that the issue of racial harassment was generally unproblematic. The audit found that 56 per cent of total respondents (N=419) considered racial harassment to be 'not a problem'. Across different ethnic groupings a greater proportion of 'Asian' (57 per cent) and 'white' (63 per cent) respondents than Afro-Caribbeans (42 per cent) felt that racial harassment was 'not a problem'. In terms of racial harassment being a 'major problem' only 14 per cent of total respondents expressed this view. This increased to 17 per cent amongst 'Asian' and Afro-Caribbean respondents. A further indicator of the relative unproblematic nature of racial harassment was reflected in the fact that it ranked a lowly eleventh out of fourteen key problems identified by respondents. The local community's top three concerns, in order of preference, were car parking, litter and rubbish and vandalism/graffiti.

Despite these generally positive findings, 'race' continued to be constructed as *the* significant issue within the regeneration process as particular voluntary sector agents directly and indirectly lobbied that resources should be directed to particular groups, most notably Bangladeshi women and youth.

This *de facto* lobbying on behalf of the Bangladeshi community ensured that 'race' stayed on the agenda of WCF on account that it antagonized the BMETA representative who had his own highly personalized political and racial agenda. In short, he was motivated in assembling power for himself and would often resort to deliberately racializing issues within the WCF in an attempt to exercise influence. In particular, he was quite critical that the community forum was comprised mainly of voluntary sector agents, who were predominantly 'white', middle-class, females living outside the local area. For him, his WCF colleagues had no 'real' understanding of the structure, needs and wants of the local community. This led to personality clashes and underlying tensions within the community forum. So, when issues arose or when decisions needed to be taken these tended to be framed within some form of racialized context in an effort to influence decision-making by instilling a sense of guilt.

The over-significance attached to 'race' within the WCF was predicated less on the actual existence of any serious racial problems within the area and more on the personal and professional motivations and vested interests of particular representatives who followed and practised an anti-racist agenda. The form of anti-racism they espoused, however, was naïve and outdated (Bonnett, 1996; Gilroy, 1992, 1998). It managed to survive due to paternalism. The key conclusions from the empirical data on the issue of 'race' are:

• 'Race' does not always matter; and
• The construction of the significance of 'race' is determined by a combination of factors, most notably, the nature of race relations within the wider community and community forums and the political agendas of community activists.

A 'New' Typology of Pluralism

Pluralism has traditionally been used to explain the nature of (community) power within policy processes at the national, regional and city level (Dahl, 1961; DeLeon, 1992; Newton, 1976; Polsby, 1980; Stone, 1989; Waste, 1986; Waste, 1987; Yates, 1977). This emphasis has shifted to the sub-city (i.e. neighbourhood) level in recent years, within the local government literature, as a result of the increasingly diverse range of 'public, quasi-public, private and voluntary sector agencies now active in local service delivery' (Harding, 1996:646). Notably, Harding's conceptualization of 'community power' fails to recognize that 'real' local communities have become an increasingly formal structure within particular localized policy-making arenas with the potential to exercise power within decision-making processes. Relatedly, although there has been considerable attention devoted to the nature community involvement in urban regeneration (Taylor, 1995; Hastings *et al*, 1996) such analyses have overlooked the potential of pluralism as a theoretical framework to explain local communities abilities to influence decision-making.

The under-utilization of pluralism is surprising, especially in light of the increased pluralization and 'turn to community' in urban regeneration policy over the last decade. This book, consequently, has sought to conceptualize the nature of power or influence wielded by local communities involved in community forums by analyzing their reputations, positions, relations and abilities to influence decisions in local URPs. The neighbourhood was selected as the spatial object in which to develop a pragmatic perspective of this community power. Furthermore, an ethnographic methodology enabled an insider account of the complexities and dynamics of community politics in urban regeneration to be ascertained. Finally, using pluralism as the theoretical framework has enabled a typology of the overall nature of community power within the three areas studied to be constructed (see Table 8.1). These include 'pragmatic pluralism' (*Northside*); 'hyper-pluralism' (*Southside*); and 'paternalistic pluralism' (*Westside*). This typology extends the work of Waste (1986) who had previously pulled together the various strains of pluralist theory that had developed since the 1950s.

Table 8.1 A 'New' Typology of Community Power

Element	Pragmatic pluralism	Hyper-pluralism	Paternalistic pluralism
Power/ Influence	Negotiation	Confrontation	Advocacy
Structures/ Processes	Open/ Democratic	Restricted access/ Bureaucratic	Restricted access/ Adversarial
Officer-Community Relations	Positive	Conflictual	Patronizing
Community Forum Membership	Tenants	Tenants	Voluntary sector agents
Sense of Community	Strong/ Shared	Fractured/ Self-protective	Segregated
Community Politics	Apolitical	Power struggles	Suppressed by advocacy
Significance of 'race'	'Non-issue'	Varied perception	Over-emphasized

Community Power and the (In)Significance of 'Race'

To conclude, pluralism and ethnography provide an alternative and innovative means of analyzing how local communities are involved in the decision-making processes of local URPs. Specifically, both of these frameworks have enabled the development of a theoretically and empirically informed typology of community power at the local level. Relatedly, since the research was located in multi-ethnic localities the methodologies adopted have also helped to develop an understanding of the significance of 'race' within the urban regeneration process.

Community Power

The empirical data outlined in Chapters 5-7 clearly shows that 'community power' is stronger than often believed. The ability, however, of local communities to exert their influence on decision-making is dependent on them constituting the majority of members on community forums. Community forums dominated by professional officers, whether they are of a bureaucratic and/or adversarial persuasion, suppresses local communities from defining and articulating their needs, aspirations and having a powerful enough voice within decision-making arenas.

In order to realize change, community forums are likely to adopt one of two main strategies. On the one hand, community forums may adopt a 'rational' strategy wherein they enter URPs with the objective of developing rapport and positive relations with their professional counterparts. Consequently, when problems arise in the regeneration process these are resolved and decisions arrived at via direct negotiation and consensus-building. This is not to say that conflict and confrontations will not and do not emerge. Such conflictual situations are likely to be relatively short lived and muted as a result of mutual understanding and respect between community forums and bureaucratic agents. On the other hand, communities may assert what bureaucratic actors perceive as 'radical' or 'militant' strategies. In this context, communities distance or totally extract themselves from formal decision-making processes, as a mark of protest against imposed regeneration proposals, with the view that refusing to engage with policy-makers will influence decision-making and policies.

Those that merely distance themselves from the process ultimately have an eye on re-entering it with the aim of initiating discussions and (re)negotiations about their own sets of ideas and proposals. Conversely, those community activists who totally remove themselves from the process do so on the basis of wanting to severely disrupt or halt the regeneration process, proclaiming that their (re)actions are in the interests of the wider community.

The (In)Significance of 'Race'

'Race' *per se* was not as problematic an issue within *Northside, Southside* and *Westside* as was anticipated based on what is generally argued within the academic literature (Cooper and Hawtin, 1997a; Cross and Keith, 1993; Solomos, 2003; Solomos and Back, 1995, 1996). This is not to deny that 'race' in itself is not an important issue or that it can manifest or be deliberately constructed as such over space and time. Nevertheless, within two of the case study areas, 'race' never surfaced as a particularly problematic issue amongst and between officers and community forum members.

The relative unimportance of 'race' within *Northside* and *Southside* were a result of positive and negative processes respectively. In *Northside,* it was a 'non-issue' because of a combination of factors that included: tenants shared experience of poor housing and community struggle and action; generally positive 'race' relations within the local community; and open and democratic structures and processes within the regeneration process. Conversely, within *Southside,* it was a 'non-issue' because of the colour-blind and technical approach to urban regeneration. That is, professional officers perceived their role simply to be the development of new housing designed to benefit the whole local community, which was seen as homogenous. This homogeneity was structured along professional officers' perceptions that the local community shared identical attitudes and values about the condition of the area earmarked for regeneration and the need for it to be regenerated. This perception was based on the failure to profile or consult the 'local community'. There were mixed feelings about the importance of 'race' within the community forum. The more radically minded community activists expressed concerns about latent historical and institutionalized racism within society and the regeneration process. 'Race', and many other issues, was a non-issue on the basis that it was precluded from the agendas of both the SPB and SCF due to a series of power struggles being played out within and between community groups and professional officers.

Where 'race' is a significant issue within policy processes it is important to discern whether it is a 'real' problem or an artificially and politically constructed one (Foster, 1990; Hammersley, 1995; O'Keffee, 1986; Palmer, 1986). In *Westside,* 'race' was initially perceived as an emerging serious problem by a core group of concerned voluntary and public sector agents who, incidentally, due to a lack of consultation, failed to ascertain the local community's views on the significance of 'race'. This paternalistic attitude was carried throughout the regeneration programme despite 'race' being ranked an unimportant issue within the local community. The main reason for this was that paternalistic professional voluntary sector agents, with close relations to certain BME groups, dominated the community forum.

All of this should not be interpreted to suggest that 'race' and racism are never problematic and/or significant issues. Instead, what is being argued is that 'race' and racism do not *always* matter. Their significance, over space and time, will fluctuate, sometimes rising and at other times declining.

Conclusions

To conclude, if central and local governments continue in their pursuit of democratizing urban regeneration policy they must realize, as suggested in the abstract from Hayek (1960), that this agenda is not without danger. Having declared that they are committed to *full* community participation, policy-makers must realize that a failure to involve local communities from as early a stage as possible and any attempt to engineer the membership of community forums is likely to provoke conflict.   Such conflictual situations may prove politically, financially and temporally costly for local authorities, their institutional partners and the wider local community who stand to benefit from regeneration programmes.   The reactions, for example, of the 'local community' within *Southside* and other neighbourhoods such as Vauxhall, the Elephant and Castle and the Aylesbury Estate in London (North, 2003), are indicative of the 'dangers' that belie the democratization of urban regeneration.   In other words, URPs run the risk of delivering fewer outputs and outcomes and running over time and cost budgets if they become too pluralistic.   This, subsequently, raises interesting and difficult questions about what constitutes *successful* regeneration and community participation; limiting the extent and nature of community participation within urban regeneration; and streamlining decision-making in order to ensure that URPs retain their synergistic qualities (Ball *et al*, 2003; Ball and Maginn, *forthcoming a* and *b*).

Bibliography

Adler, P. A. and Adler, P. (1994) 'Observational techniques' in N. K. Denzin and Y. S. Lincoln (eds), *Handbook of Qualitative Research*, Sage: New York, pp. 377-392.

Allmendinger, P. (2003) 'From New Right to New Left in UK planning', *Urban Policy and Research*, **21**, 1: 57-79.

Allmendinger, P. and Tewdwr-Jones, M. (1997) 'Post-Thatcherite urban planning and politics: A major change?' *International Journal of Urban and Regional Research*, **21**, 1: 100-116.

Ambrose, P. (1986) *Whatever Happened to Planning*, Methuen: London.

Anastacio, J., Gidley, B., Hart, L., Keith, M., Mayo, M. and Kowarzik, U. (2000) *Reflecting Realities: Participants' Perspectives on Integrated Communities and Sustainable Development*, The Policy Press: Bristol.

Andersen, H., Munck, R., Fagan, C., Goldson, B., Hall, D., Lansley, J., Novak, T., Melville, R., Moore, R. and Ben-Tovim, G. (1999) *Neighbourhood Images in Liverpool: 'It's All Down To the People'*, JRF: York.

Anderson, N. (1961) *The Hobo: The Sociology of the Homeless Man*, University of Chicago Press: Chicago.

Arnstein, S. R. (1969) 'A ladder of citizen participation', *American Institute of Planners Journal*, **XXXV**, July: 216-224.

Atkinson, P. and Hammersley, M. (1994) 'Ethnography and participant observation' in N. Denzin and Y. Lincoln (eds), *Handbook of Qualitative Research*, London: New York, pp. 248-261.

Atkinson, R. (1996) 'Urban regeneration, community participation and social exclusion', *ESRC Seminar: Evaluating Policies to Combat Social Exclusion*, Bristol.

Atkinson, R. (1999) 'Discourses of partnership and empowerment in contemporary British urban regeneration', *Urban Studies*, **36**, 1: 59-72.

Atkinson, R. and Cope, S. (1997) 'Community participation and urban regeneration in Britain' in P. Hoggett (ed), *Contested Communities*, Policy Press, Bristol.

Atkinson, R. and Moon, G. (1994) *Urban Policy in Britain: The City, the State and the Market*, Macmillan, London.

Audit Commission (1989) *Urban Regeneration and Economic Development - the Local Government Dimension*, HMSO: London.

Bachrach, P. and Baratz, M. S. (1962) 'Two faces of power', *The American Political Science Review*, **56**, 4: 947-952.

Back, L. (1995) *Racisms and Multiculture in Young Lives*, UCL Press: London.

Baeten, G. (2001) 'Urban regeneration, social exclusion and shifting power geometries on the South Bank, London', *Geographische Zeitschrift*, **2**, 3: 103-112.

Bailey, N., MacDonald, K. and Barker, A. (1995) *Partnership Agencies in British Urban Policy*, UCL: London.

Ball, M., Le Ny, L. and Maginn, P. J. (2003) 'Synergy in urban regeneration partnerships: Property agents' perspectives', *Urban Studies*, **40**, 11: 2239-2253.

Ball, M. and Maginn, P. J. (*forthcoming a*) 'Urban change and conflict: Evaluating the role of partnerships in urban regeneration in the UK', *Housing Studies*.

Ball, M. and Maginn, P. J. (*forthcoming b*) 'The contradictions of urban policy: The case of the Single Regeneration Budget in London', *Environment and Planning C: Government and Policy.*

Bell, C. and Newby, H. (1971) *Community Studies,* Allen and Unwin: London.

Bennett, E. (2004) 'Camden chief: 'there's nothing we could have done differently'', *Housing Today.*

Ben-Tovim, G., Gabriel, J., Law, I. and Stredder, K. (1986) *The Local Politics of Race,* Macmillan: Basingstoke.

Bonnett, A. (1996a) 'Anti-racism and the critique of 'white' identities', *New Community,* **22,** 1: 97-110.

Bonnett, A. (1996b) ''White Studies': The problems and projects of a new research agenda', *Theory, Culture and Society,* **13,** 2: 145-155.

Bonnett, A. (1997) 'Geography, 'race' and whiteness: invisible traditions and current challenges', *Area,* **29,** 3: 193-199.

Bourdieu, P. (1991) *Language and Symbolic Power,* Polity Press: Cambridge.

Brindley, T. (1996) 'Popular Planning: Coin Street, London' in T. Brindley, Y. Rydin and G. Stoker (eds), *Remaking Planning: The Politics of Urban Change (2nd ed.),* Routledge: London.

Brindley, T., Rydin, Y. and Stoker, G. (1996) *Remaking Planning: The Politics of Urban Change,* Routledge: London.

Brownill, S. (1990) *Developing London's Docklands: Another Great Planning Disaster?* Paul Chapman Publishing: London.

Brownill, S. (1993) *Developing London's Docklands,* Paul Chapman, London.

Brownill, S. and Darke, J. (1998) *'Rich Mix': Inclusive Strategies for Urban Regeneration,* JRF/The Policy Press, York.

Brownill, S., Razzaque, K., Stirling, T. and Thomas, H. (1996) 'Local governance and the racialisation of urban policy in the UK: The case of Urban Development Corporations', *Urban Studies,* **33,** 8: 1337-1355.

Brownill, S. and Thomas, H. (1998) 'Ethnic minorities and British urban policy: A discussion of trends in governance and democratic theory', *Local Governance,* **24,** 1: 43-55.

BTEG (1995) *Invisible Partners: The Impact of the SRB on Black Communities,* BTEG, London.

BTEG (1997) 'A strategy for ensuring Black communities are involved in regeneration' in PLCRC/Docklands Forum (eds), *Urban Regeneration Partnerships for Success,* PLCRC/Docklands Forum, London.

Burns, D., Hambleton, R. and Hogget, P. (1994) *The Politics of Decentralisation: Revitalising Local Democracy,* Macmillan, Basingstoke.

Burns, D. and Taylor, M. (2000) *Auditing Community Participation: An Assessment Handbook,* The Policy Press/JRF, Bristol/York.

Burton, P. (1997) 'Urban policy and the myth of progress', *Policy and Politics,* **25,** 4: 421-436.

Burton, P. (2003) *Community Involvement in Neighbourhood Regeneration: Stairway to Heaven or Road to Nowhere?* ESRC Centre for Neighbourhood Research: Bristol/Glasgow.

Cairncross, L., Clapham, D. and Goodlad, R. (1994) 'Tenant participation and tenant power in British council housing', *Public Administration,* **72,** Summer: 177-200.

Carter, A. (2000) 'Strategy and partnership in urban regeneration' in P. Roberts and H. Sykes (eds), *Urban Regeneration: A Handbook,* Sage, London.

Cattell, V. and Evans, M. (1999) *Neighbourhood Images in East London: Social Capital and Social Networks on Two East London Estates*, JRF, York.

Chatterjee, M. (2002) 'Transfer defeat rocks sector', *Housing Today* http://www.housingtoday.co.uk/story.asp?storyType=7&sectioncode=306&storyCode=1017852

Chatterjee, M. (2002a) 'Birmingham takes stock', *Housing Today* http://www.housingtoday.co.uk/story.asp?storyType=7&sectioncode=309&storyCode=1017848

Clegg, S. (1989) *Frameworks of Power*, Sage, London.

Cochrane, A. (1993) *Whatever Happened to Local Government?* Open University Press, Buckinghamshire.

Cohen, A. P. (1985) *The Symbolic Construction of Community*, Routledge, London.

Cole, I. and Furbey, R. (1994) *The Eclipse of Council Housing*, Routledge, London and New York.

Colenutt, B. and Cutten, A. (1994) 'Community empowerment in vogue or vain?' *Local Economy*, **9, 3**: 236-250.

Connolly, P. (1998) *Racism, Gender Identities and Young Children*, Routledge, London.

Connolly, P. (2001) 'Qualitative methods in the study of children's racial attitudes and identities', *Infant and Child Development*, **10, 3**: 219-233.

Connolly, P. and Maginn, P. (1999) *Sectarianism, Children and Community Relations in Northern Ireland*, Centre for the Study of Conflict (University of Ulster), Coleraine.

Connolly, P. and Troyna, B. (eds) (1998) *Researching Racism in Education: Politics, Theory and Practice*, Open University Press, Buckingham.

Cooper, C. and Hawtin, M. (1997a) 'Community involvement, housing and equal opportunities' in C. Cooper and M. Hawtin (eds), *Housing, Community and Conflict: Understanding Resident Involvement*, Ashgate, Aldershot, pp. 245-272.

Cooper, C. and Hawtin, M. (1997b) 'Concepts of community involvement, power and democracy' in C. Cooper and M. Hawtin (eds), *Housing, Community and Conflict: Understanding Resident Involvement*, Ashgate, Aldershot, pp. 83-120.

Cooper, C. and Hawtin, M. (eds) (1997c) *Housing, Community and Conflict: Understanding Resident Involvement*, Ashgate, Aldershot.

Craig, G. and Mayo, M. (eds) (1995) *Community Empowerment: A Reader in Participation and Development*, Zed Books, Atlantic Highlands, NJ.

Crang, M. (2002) 'Qualitative methods: the new orthodoxy?' *Progress in Human Geography*, **26, 5**: 647-655.

Crang, M. (2003) 'Qualitative methods: touchy, feely, look-see? *Progress in Human Geography*, **27, 4**: 494-504.

Crawford, L. (1997) *The Crawford Report: An Inquiry into Employment Practices and Procedure in the London Borough of Hackney*, London Borough of Hackney, London.

CRE (1984) *Race and Council Housing in Hackney: Report of the Formal Investigation*, CRE, London.

CRE and GoL (undated) *Joint Report by the Commission for Racial Equality (London and South Region) and the Government Office for London - SRB: Round 1*, CRE/GoL: London.

Crook, T., Currie, J., Jackson, A., Monk, S., Rowley, S., Smith, K. and Whitehead, C. (2002) *Planning gain and affordable housing: Making it count*, JRF, York.

Cross, M. and Keith, M. (eds) (1993) *Racism, the City and the State*, Routledge, London.

Cross River Partnership (2000) *Cross River Partnership – Beyond 2000: Connecting Communities*, Cross River Partnership, London.

CUPS (1998) *The Impact of Urban Development Corporation in Leeds, Bristol and Central Manchester*, DETR, London.

Dahl, R. A. (1961) *Who Governs? Democracy and Power in an American City*, Yale University Press, New Haven.

Dahl, R. A. (1986) 'Rethinking who governs? New Haven revisited' in R. J. Waste (ed), *Community Power: Directions for Future Research*, Yale University Press, New Haven.

Davidoff, P. (1982) 'Advocacy and pluralism in planning' in A. Faludi (ed), *A Reader in Planning Theory*, Pergamon Press, Oxford, pp. 277-297.

Davies, J. S. (2001) *Partnerships and Regimes: The Politics of Urban Regeneration in the UK*, Ashgate, Aldershot.

Davies, J. S. (2002) 'Urban regime theory: A normative-empirical critique', *Journal of Urban Affairs*, **24**, 1: 1-17.

Davies, J. S. (2003) 'Partnerships versus regimes: Why regime theory cannot explain urban coalitions in the UK', *Journal of Urban Affairs*, **25**, 3: 253-269.

De Tocqueville, A. (1955) *Democracy in America*, Vintage Books., New York.

Deakin, N. and Edwards, J. (1993) *The Enterprise Culture and the Inner City*, Routledge, London.

DeLeon, R. E. (1992) *Left Coast City: Progressive Politics in San Francisco, 1975-1991*, University of Kansas, Kansas.

Dennis, N., Erdos, G. and Al-Shahi, A. (2000) *Racist Murder and Pressure Group Politics*, Institute for the Study of Civil Society, London.

Denzin, N. K. and Lincoln, Y. S. (1994) 'Introduction: Entering the field of qualitative research' in N. K. Denzin and Y. S. Lincoln (eds), *Handbook of Qualitative Research*, Sage, New York, pp. 1-17.

DETR (1997) *Involving Communities in Urban and Rural Regeneration: A Guide for Practitioners*, DETR, London.

DETR (1998a) *New Deal for Communities: Phase 1 Proposals - Guidance for Pathfinder Applicants*, DETR, London.

DETR (1998b) *Single Regeneration Budget Bidding Guidance: A Guide for Partnerships*, DETR, London.

DETR (2000) *New Deal for Communities: Race Equality Guidance*, DETR: London.

DETR (2001) *Local Strategic Partnerships: Government Guidance*, DETR: London.

DoE (1994a) *Bidding Guidance: A Guide to Funding Under the Single Regeneration Budget*, DoE: London.

DoE (1994b) *City Challenge: Partnerships Regenerating England's Urban Areas*, HMSO, London.

DoE (1994c) *SRB Bidding Guidance*, HMSO, London.

DoE (1995) *Involving Communities in Urban and Rural Regeneration: A Guide for Practitioners*, DoE, London.

DoE (1996) *Partners in Regeneration*, HMSO, London.

DoE (1997) *Effective Partnerships: A Handbook for Members of SRB Challenge Fund Partnerships*, DoE, London.

Dowding, K. (1996) *Power*, Open University Press, Buckingham.

Dowding, K., Dunleavy, P., King, D., Margetts, H. and Rydin, Y. (1999) 'Regime politics in London local government', *Urban Affairs Review*, **34**, 4: 515-545.

D'Souza, D. (1995) *The End of Racism: Principles for a Multiracial Society*, The Free Press, New York.

Duffy, K. and Hutchinson, J. (1997) 'Urban policy and the turn to community', *Town Planning Review*, **68**, 3: 347-362.

Duncan, S. and Goodwin, M. (1988) 'Removing local government autonomy: Political centralisation and financial control', *Local Government Studies*, Nov/Dec: 49-63.

Dye, T. (1986) 'Community power and public policy' in R. J. Waste (ed), *Community Power: Directions for Future Research*, Sage, London.

Evans, R. and Long, D. (2000) 'Estate-based Regeneration in England: Lessons from Housing Action Trusts', *Housing Studies*, 15, 2: 301-317.

Feldman, M. S., Bell, J. and Berger, M. T. (2003) *Gaining Access: A Practical and Theoretical Guide for Qualitative Researchers*, AltaMira, Walnut Creek CA.

Fetterman, D. M. (1984) *Ethnography in Educational Evaluation*, Sage, Beverly Hills.

Fetterman, D. M. (1989) *Ethnography: Step by Step*, Sage, Newbury Park CA.

Flyvbjerg, B. (1998) *Rationality and Power: Democracy in Practice*, University of Chicago Press, Chicago.

Foley, P. (1999) 'Competition as Public Policy: A Review of Challenge Funding', *Public Administration*, 77, 4: 809-836.

Foley, P. and Martin, S. (2000) 'A new deal for the community? Public participation in regeneration and local service delivery', *Policy and Politics*, 28, 4: 479-491.

Fontana, A. and Frey, J. H. (1994) 'Interviewing: The art of science' in N. K. Denzin and Y. S. Lincoln (eds), *Handbook of Qualitative Research*, Vol. 361-376 Sage, New York.

Forester, J. (1989) *Planning in the Face of Power*, University of California Press, Berkeley.

Forrest, R. and Kearns, A. (1999) *Joined-up Places? Social Cohesion and Neighbourhood Regeneration*, JRF, York.

Foster, P. (1990) *Policy and Practice in Multicultural and Anti-racist Education: A Case Study of a Multi-ethnic Comprehensive School*, Routledge, London.

Franklin, A. (1986) 'Ethnography and housing studies', *Housing Studies*, 5, 2: 92-111.

Geertz, C. (1973) *The Interpretation of Culture: Selected Essays*, Basic Books, New York.

Gibson, M. and Langstaff, M. (1982) *An Introduction to Urban Renewal*, Hutchinson, London.

Gibson, M. and Paice, D. (1999) *Brixton Challenge Impact Study: Final Report*, South Bank University: London.

Gibson, S. (2002) 'Ex-council worker to appeal against race ruling', *Inside Housing* (14/06/2002).

Giddens, A. (1990) 'Structuration Theory: Past, Present and Future' in C. Bryant and D. Jary (eds), *Giddens' Theory of Structuration: A Critical Appreciation*, Routledge, London.

Gilroy, P. (1992) 'The end of antiracism' in J. Donald and A. Rattansi (eds), *'Race', Culture and Difference*, Sage, London, pp. 49-61.

Gilroy, P. (1998) 'Race ends here', *Ethnic and Racial Studies*, 21, 5: 838-847.

GLA (2002) *Rebuilding London's Future*, GLA: London.

Goetz, J. P. and LeCompte, M. D. (1984) *Ethnography and Qualitative Design in Educational Research*, Academic Press, Orlando.

Goss, J. D. and Leinbach, T. R. (1996) 'Focus groups as alternative research practice: Experience with transmigrants in Indonesia', *Area*, 28, 2: 115-123.

Government Office for London (1994) *SRB Successful Bids: Round 1*, GoL, London.

Government Office for the Regions (1995) *Bidding Guidance: A Guide to Bidding for Resources from the Government's Single Regeneration Budget Fund*, HMSO, London.

Greed, C. H. (1994) 'The place of ethnography in planning: Or is it 'real research'?' *Planning Practice and Research*, 9, 2: 119-127.

Greed, C. H. (1999) *Social Town Planning*, Routledge, London.

Green, D. (Ed.) (2000) *Institutional Racism and the Police: Fact or Fiction?* Institute for the Study of Civil Society, London.

Guba, E. and Lincoln, Y. S. (1981) 'Criteria for assessing the trustworthiness of naturalistic inquiry', *Educational Communication and Technology Journal*, 29: 233-252.

Guba, E. and Lincoln, Y. S. (1982) 'Epistemological and methodological bases of naturalistic inquiry', *Educational Communication and Technology Journal*, 30: 233-252.

Hackney LBC (1996) *Urban Regeneration Strategy*, Hackney LBC, London.

Hague, C. (1990) 'The development and politics of tenant participation in British council housing', *Housing Studies*, 5, 4: 242-256.

Hall, S., Beazley, M., Bentley, G., Burfitt, A., Collinge, A., Lee, P., Nevin, B. and Srbljanin, A. (1996) *The Single Regeneration Budget: A Review of the Challenge Fund Round II*, Centre for Urban and Regional Studies (University of Birmingham): Birmingham.

Hall, S. and Mawson, J. (1999) *Challenge Funding, Contracts and Area Regeneration: A Decade of Innovation in Policy Management & Co-ordination*, The Policy Press/JRF, Bristol/York.

Hambleton, R. and Thomas, H. (eds) (1995) *Urban Policy Evaluation: Challenge and Change*, Paul Chapman Publishing, London.

Hammersley, M. (1990a) *Classroom Ethnography: Empirical and Methodological Essays*, Open University Press, Milton Keynes.

Hammersley, M. (1990b) *Reading Ethnographic Research: A Critical Guide*, Longman, London.

Hammersley, M. (1992) *What's Wrong with Ethnography: Methodological Explorations*, Routledge, London.

Hammersley, M. (1995) *The Politics of Social Research*, Sage, London.

Hammersley, M. and Atkinson, P. (1995) *Ethnography: Principle and Practice*, Routledge, London.

Harding, A. (1996) 'Is there a 'New Community Power' and why should we need one?' *International Journal of Urban and Regional Research*, 20, 4: 637-654.

Hastings, A. (1996) 'Unravelling the process of 'partnership' in urban regeneration policy', *Urban Studies*, 33, 2: 253-268.

Hastings, A. (1999) 'Analysing power relations in partnerships: Is there a role for discourse analysis?' *Urban Studies*, 36, 1: 91-106.

Hastings, A., McArthur, A. and McGregor, A. (1996) *Less than Equal? Community Organisations and Estate Regeneration Partnerships*, The Policy Press, Bristol.

Hayek, F. A. (1960) *The Constitution of Liberty*, Routledge & Kegan Paul, London

Healey, P. (1997) *Collaborative Planning: Shaping Places in Fragmented Societies*, Palgrave, London.

Hill, D. M. (1994) *Citizens and Cities: Urban Policy in the 1990s*, Harvester Wheatsheaf, Hemel Hempstead.

Hill, D. M. (2000) *Urban Policy and Politics in Britain*, Macmillan, London.

Hirst, P. (1990) *Representative Democracy and Its Limits*, Polity, London.

HMSO (1977) *Policy for the Inner Cities (Cmnd. 6845)*, HMSO, London.

HMSO (1991) *The Citizen's Charter. Raising the Standard (Cm. 1599)*, HMSO, London.

Holbrook, B. and Jackson, P. (1996) 'Shopping around: focus group research in North London', *Area*, 28, 2: 136-142.

Home Office (1999) *The Stephen Lawrence Inquiry: Report of an Inquiry by Sir William McPherson of Cluny (Cmnd. 4262-1)*, The Stationery Office, London.

Hughes, J. and Carmichael, P. (1998) 'Building partnerships in urban regeneration: A case study from Belfast', *Community Development Journal*, 33, 3: 205-225.

Hunter, A. (1993) 'Local knowledge and local power: Notes on the ethnography of local community elites', *Journal of Contemporary Ethnography*, 22, 1: 36-58.

Hunter, F. (1953) *Community Power Structure*, University of North Carolina Press, Chapel Hill.

Imrie, R. and Raco, M. (2003a) 'Community and the changing nature of urban policy' in R. Imrie and M. Raco (eds), *Urban Renaissance? New Labour, community and urban policy*, The Policy Press, Bristol, pp. 3-36.

Imrie, R. and Raco, M. (eds) (2003b) *Urban Renaissance? New Labour, Community and Urban Policy*, The Policy Press, Bristol.

Inside Housing (2003) *No to appeal on tribunal ruling*, http://www.insidehousing.co.uk/level1.phtml?sessid=5e08b3bdd2e0f0e39fd8d8d903b45 582ffa45852fdeaae31ab3a3ecd53b1f24f.

Jackson, B. and Marsden, D. (1962) *Education and the Working Class*, Routledge & Kegan Paul, London.

Jackson, P. (1985) 'Urban ethnography', *Progress in Human Geography*, 9, 2: 156-176.

Jackson, P. (1998) 'Constructions of 'whiteness' in the geographical imagination', *Area*, 30, 2: 99-106.

Jackson, P. (1999) 'Postmodern urbanism and the ethnographic void', *Urban Geography*, 20, 5: 400-402.

Jacobs, J. (1993) 'The city unbound: Qualitative approaches to the city', *Urban Studies*, 30, 4-5: 827-848.

Jacobs, K. (1999) *The Dynamics of Local Housing Policy*, Ashgate, Aldershot.

Jeffers, S., Hoggett, P. and Harrison, L. (1996) 'Race, ethnicity and community in three localities', *New Community*, 22, 1: 111-126.

Johnson, C. and Osborne, S. P. (2003) 'Local Strategic Partnerships, neighbourhood renewal, and the limits to co-governance', *Public Money and Management*, 23, 3: 147-154.

Jones, B. D. (1995) 'Bureaucrats and urban politics: Who controls? Who benefits?' in D. Judge, G. Stoker and H. Wolman (eds), *Theories of Urban Politics*, Sage, London.

Jones, P. S. (2003) 'Urban regeneration's poisoned chalice: Is there an *impasse* in (Community) participation-based policy?' *Urban Studies*, 40, 3: 581-601.

Jordan, G. (1990) 'The pluralism of pluralism: An anti-theory?' *Political Studies*, 38, 286-301.

Judge, D. (1995) 'Pluralism' in D. Judge, Stoker, G. and Wolman, H. (eds), *Theories of Urban Politics*, Sage, London.

Judge, D., Stoker, G. and Wolman, H. (eds) (1995) *Theories of Urban Politics*, Sage, London.

Junker, B. (1960) *Field Work*, University of Chicago Press, Chicago.

Karn, V. (1993) 'Remodelling a HAT: the implementation of the Housing Action Trust legislation 1987-92' in P. Malpass and R. Means (eds), *Implementing Housing Policy*, Open University Press, Milton Keynes.

Kearns, A. and Turok, I. (2000) 'Power, responsibility, and governance in Britain's new urban policy', *Journal of Urban Affairs*, 22, 2: 175-191.

King, D. (1993) 'Government beyond Whitehall' in P. Dunleavy, A. Gamble, I. Halliday and G. Peele (eds), Macmillan, London.

Lawless, P. (1988) 'British inner urban policy post 1979: A critique', *Policy and Politics*, 16, 4: 261-275.

Lawless, P. (1989) *Britain's Inner Cities*, Paul Chapman Publishing, London.

Lawless, P. (1996) 'The inner cities: Towards a new agenda', *Town Planning Review*, 67, 1: 21-43.

LB Hackney (1996) *Multi-ethnic Hackney: A Comprehensive Study*, LB Hackney, London.

LB Hackney (1998) *Northside 1998*, LB Hackney: London.

LB Southwark (1993) *Demographic Profile of Southwark*, LB Southwark, London.

LB Southwark (1994) *Peckham Partnership: A Bid for Single Regeneration Budget Funding*, LB Southwark, London.

Lees, L. (2003) 'Urban geography: 'New' urban geography and the ethnographic void', *Progress in Human Geography*, **27**, 1: 07-113.

Lewis, O. (1968) 'The culture of poverty', *Scientific American*, **215**, 16: 19-25.

Lo Piccolo, F. and Thomas, H. (2003) *Knights and Castles: Minorities and Urban Regeneration*, Ashgate, Aldershot.

Lofland, J. (1971) *Analysing Social Settings: A Guide to Qualitative Observation and Analysis*, Wadsworth, Belmont CA.

Lofland, J. (1995) 'Analytic ethnography: Features, failings and futures', *Journal of Contemporary Ethnography*, **24**, 1: 30-67.

Loftman, P. and Beazley, M. (1998) *'Race' and Regeneration*, LGIU, London.

LRC (1997) *Southside Partnership Baseline Survey*, LRC/Southside Partnership Board, London.

Lukes, S. (1974) *Power: A Radical View*, Macmillan, London.

Lyon, E. (1997) 'Applying ethnography', *Journal of Contemporary Ethnography*, **26**, 1: 3-27.

Mackintosh, M. (1992) 'Partnership: Issues of policy and negotiation', *Local Economy*, 7210-224.

Maginn, P. J. (2003) 'Towards more effective community participation in urban regeneration? The role and potential of 'applied ethnography'', *(mimeo)*.

Major, J. (1999) *John Major: The Autobiography*, HarperCollins, London.

Malpass, P. and Murie, A. (1990) *Housing Policy and Practice (3rd Edition)*, Macmillan, London.

Manley, J. F. (1983) 'Neo-pluralism: A class analysis of Pluralism I and Pluralism II', *The American Political Science Review*, **77**, 368-383.

Marris, P. (1964) *The Experience of Higher Education*, Routledge & Kegan Paul, London.

May, J. (1996) 'Globalization and the politics of place: Place and identity in an inner London neighbourhood', *Transactions of the Institute of British Geographers*, **21**, 194-215.

Mayo, M. (1997) 'Partnerships for regeneration and community development: Some opportunities, challenges and constraints', *Critical Social Policy*, **17**, 3: 3-26.

McArthur, A. (1995) 'The active involvement of local residents in strategic community partnerships', *Policy & Politics*, **31**, 1: 61-71.

McGregor, A., Clapham, D., Donnison, D., Gemmell, B., Goodlad, R., Kintrea, K. and McArthur, A. (1992) *Community Participation in Areas of Urban Regeneration*, Research Report No. 23, Scottish Homes: Edinburgh.

McLennan, G. (1995) *Pluralism*, Open University Press, Buckingham.

McLennan, G. (1997) 'The evolution of pluralist theory' in M. Hill (ed), *The Policy Process: A Reader*, Prentice Hall, London, pp. 53-61.

Ministry of Housing and Local Government (1969) *People and Planning: Report of the Committee on Public Participation in Planning*, HMSO, London.

Morgan, D. L. (ed) (1993) *Successful Focus Groups*, Sage, Thousand Oaks.

Mossberger, K. and Stoker, G. (1997) 'Inner-city policy in Britain: Why it will not go away', *Urban Affairs Review*, **32**, 3: 378-402.

Munt, I. (1991) ''Race', urban policy and urban problems: A critique on current UK practice', *Urban Studies*, **28**, 2: 183-203.

Murtagh, B. (1999) 'Listening to communities: Locality research and planning', *Urban Studies*, **36**, 7: 1181-1193.

Nevin, B., Loftman, P. and Beazley, M. (1997) 'Cities in crisis - Is growth the answer?' *Town Planning Review*, **68**, 2: 145-164.

Newton, K. (1976) *Second City Politics: Democratic Processes and Decision-making in Birmingham*, Oxford University Press, Oxford.

North, D., Stanworth, T. and Hotchkiss, G. (2002) *The Use of the Single Regeneration Budget in London, 1994-2000*, CEEDR Middlesex University: London.

North, P. (2003) 'Communities at the heart? Community action and urban policy in the UK' in R. Imrie and M. Raco (eds), *Urban Renaissance? New Labour, Community and Urban Policy*, The Policy Press, Bristol, pp. 121-138.

Oatley, N. (1998a) 'Restructuring urban policy: The Single Regeneration Budget and the Challenge Fund' in N. Oatley (eds), *Cities, Economic Competition and Urban Policy*, Paul Chapman, London, pp. 146-162.

Oatley, N. (1998b) 'Transitions in urban policy: Explaining the emergence of the 'Challenge Fund' model' in N. Oatley (ed), *Cities, Economic Competition and Urban Policy*, Paul Chapman, London, pp. 21-38.

ODPM (2000) *Our Towns and Cities: The Future (Urban White Paper)*, ODPM: London.

ODPM (2002) *Turning Areas Around - The Impact of SRB on Final Outcomes*, ODPM: London.

O'Keffee, D. (1986) 'Preference and prejudice: The mythology of British racism' in F. Palmer (ed), *Anti-Racism: An Assault on Education and Value*, The Sherwood Press, London, pp. 185-196.

OPCS (1991) *1991 Census Great Britain*, Crown Copyright, London.

Ouseley, H. (1997) 'Ethnic minorities and urban policy: The challenge experience', *Local Economy*, **12**, 1: 2-7.

Paddison, R. (2001) 'Communities in the city' in R. Paddison (ed), *Handbook of Urban Studies*, Sage, London.

Pahl, R. (1975) *Whose City?* Penguin, Harmondsworth.

Palmer, F. (Ed.) (1986) *Anti-Racism: An Assault on Education and Value*, The Sherwood Press, London.

Park, R. and Burgess, E. (eds) (1967) *The City Chicago*, University of Chicago Press, Chicago.

Peach, C. (1996) 'Does Britain have ghettos?' *Transactions of the Institute of British Geographers*, **21**, 216-235.

Peach, C. and Byron, M. (1993) 'Caribbean tenants in council housing: 'Race', class and gender', *New Community*, **19**, 3: 407-423.

Peck, J. and Tickell, A. (1995) 'Too many partners... The future for regeneration partnerships', *Local Economy*, **9**, 3: 251-265.

Pickvance, C. G. (1995) 'Marxist theories of urban politics' in D. Judge, G. Stoker and H. Wolman (eds), *Theories of Urban Politics*, Sage, London.

Pinto, R. (1993) *The Estate Action Initiative: Council Housing Renewal, Management and Effectiveness*, Ashgate, Aldershot.

Platt, J. (1971) *Social Research in Bethnal Green*, Macmillan, London.

Polsby, N. W. (1980) *Community Power and Political Theory*, Yale University Press, New Haven.

Power, A. and Mumford, K. (2003) *East Enders: Family and Community in East London*, The Policy Press, Bristol.

PPCR (1996) *Northside Skills Audit*, PPCR, London.

204   *Urban Regeneration, Community Power and the (In)Significance of 'Race'*

Quinn Patton, M. (1988) *How to Use Qualitative Methods in Evaluation*, Sage, Thousand Oaks.

Quinn Patton, M. (2002) *Qualitative Research and Evaluation Methods*, Sage, Thousand Oaks.

Ratcliffe, P. (1992) 'Renewal, regeneration and 'race': Issues in urban policy', *New Community*, **18**, 3: 387-400.

Ravetz, A. (1986) *The Government of Space: Town Planning in Modern Society*, Faber & Faber, London.

Rex, J. and Moore, R. (1967) *Race, Community and Conflict: A Study of Sparkbrook*, Oxford University Press, Oxford.

Rhodes, J., Tyler, P., Brennan, A., Stevens, S., Warnock, C. and Otero-García, M. (2002) *Lessons and Evaluation Evidence from Ten Single Regeneration Budget Case Studies*, DTLR: London.

Ricci, D. (1971) *Community Power and Democratic Theory*, Random House, New York.

Rist, R. (1984) 'On the application of qualitative research to the policy process: An emergent linkage' in L. Barton and S. Walker (eds), *Social Crisis and Educational Research*, Croom Helm, London.

Rist, R. (2000) 'Influencing the policy process with qualitative research' in N. K. Denzin and Y. Lincoln (eds) *Handbook of Qualitative Research* (2nd ed), Sage, Thousand Oaks, pp.1001-1017.

Rittel, H. W. J. and Webber, M. M. (1973) 'Dilemmas in a general theory of planning', *Policy Sciences*, **41**, 55-169.

Roberts, P. (2000) 'The evolution, definition and purpose of urban regeneration' in P. Roberts and H. Sykes (eds), *Urban Regeneration: A Handbook*, Sage, London.

Roberts, P. and Sykes, H. (eds) (2000) *Urban Regeneration: A Handbook*, Sage, London.

Robson, B. T., Bradford, M. G., Deas, I., Hall, E., Harrison, E., Parkinson, M., Evans, R., Garside, P. and Harding, A. (1994) *Assessing The Impact of Urban Policy*, HMSO, London.

Roger Tym and Partners (1998) *Urban Development Corporations: Performance and Good Practice*, DETR, London.

Russell, B. (1986) 'The forms of power' in S. Lukes (ed), *Power*, Blackwell, Oxford, pp. 19-27.

Salmon, H. (1992) Urban regeneration and the community: Birmingham Heartlands', *Local Economy*, **7**, 26-38.

Saunders, P. (1979) *Urban Politics: A Sociological Interpretation*, Hutchinson & Co., London.

Saunders, P. (1986) *Social Theory and the Urban Question*, Hutchinson, London.

Saunders, P. (1990) *A Nation of Home Owners*, Unwin Hyman, London.

Saunders, P. (2001) 'Urban ecology' in R. Paddison (ed), *Handbook of Urban Studies*, Sage, London.

SAUS (1983) *The Future of Local Government*, SAUS, Bristol.

Savage, M., Warde, A. and Ward, K. (2003) *Urban Sociology, Capitalism and Modernity*, Palgrave, Basingstoke.

SBU (1998) *Westside Community Regeneration Project: Community Profile*, South Bank University, London.

Scarman, L. (1981) *The Brixton Disorders, 10-12 April 1981: Report of An Inquiry (Cmnd. 8427)*, HMSO, London.

Scott, J. (2001) *Power*, Macmillan, London.

SEU (1998) *Bringing Britain Together: A National Strategy for Neighbourhood Renewal*, Social Exclusion Unit: London.

SEU (2000) *Minority Ethnic Issues in Social Exclusion and Neighbourhood Renewal*, Social Exclusion Unit, London.

SEU (2001a) *National Strategy for Neighbourhood Renewal: Policy Action Team Report*, SEU: London.

SEU (2001b) *A New Commitment to Neighbourhood Renewal: National Strategy Action Plan*, Social Exclusion Unit: London.

Silburn, R., Lucas, D., Page, R. and Hanna, L. (1999) *Neighbourhood Images in Nottingham: Social Cohesion and Neighbourhood Change*, JRF, York.

Skelcher, C. (1993) 'Involvement and empowerment in local public services', *Public Money & Management*, **13**, 13-20.

Skelcher, C., McCabe, A., Lowndes, V. and Nanton, P. (1996) *Community Networks in Urban Regeneration*, Policy Press, Bristol.

Smith, M. and Beazley, M. (2000) 'Progressive regimes, partnerships and the involvement of local communities: A framework for evaluation', *Public Administration*, **78**, 4: 855-878.

Smith, M. and Beazley, M. (2001) 'The community decides? Continuity and change in the involvement of communities in regeneration', *Area-based Initiatives in Contemporary Urban Policy: Danish Building and Urban Research and European Urban Research Association*, Copenhagen.

Smith, M. J. (1990) 'Pluralism, reformed pluralism and neopluralism: The role of pressure groups in policy-making', *Political Studies*, **38**, 302-322.

Smith, S. and Hill, S. (1992) 'An unwelcome home' in C. Grant (ed), *Built to Last*, ROOF, London, pp. 101-109.

Solomos, J. (1993) *Race and Racism*, Macmillan Press, London.

Solomos, J. (2003) *Race and Racism in Britain*, Palgrave, Basingstoke.

Solomos, J. and Back, L. (1995) *Race, Politics and Social Change*, Routledge, London.

Solomos, J. and Back, L. (1996) *Racism and Society*, Macmillan, London.

Southside Partnership Board (1995) *Southside SRB Delivery Plan 1995/96*, Southside Partnership Board, London.

Southside Partnership Board (1996) *Southside SRB Delivery Plan 1996/97*, Southside Partnership Board, London.

Sowell, T. (1994) *Race and Culture: A World View*, Basic Books, New York.

Spittles, D. (undated) *Five Years of the Challenge in Brixton*, London.

Stewart, M. and Stoker, G. (eds) (1995) *Local Government in the 1990s*, Macmillan, London.

Stewart, M. and Taylor, M. (1995) *Empowerment and Estate Regeneration: A Critical Review*, Policy Press, Bristol.

Stoker, G. (1995) 'Regime theory and urban politics' in D. Judge, G. Stoker and H. Wolman (eds), *Theories of Urban Politics*, Sage, London.

Stone, C. N. (1989) *Regime Politics: Governing Atlanta, 1946-1988*, University of Kansas Press, Kansas.

Taussik, J. and Smalley, J. (1998) 'Partnerships in the 1990s: Derby's successful City Challenge bid', *Planning Practice and Research*, **13**, 3: 283-297.

Taylor, M. (1995) *Unleashing the Potential: Bringing Residents to the Centre of Regeneration*, JRF, York.

Taylor, M. (2000a) 'Communities in the lead: Power, organisational capacity and social capital', *Urban Studies*, **37**, 5: 1019-1035.

Taylor, M. (2000b) 'Maintaining community involvement in regeneration: What are the issues?' *Local Economy*, **15**, 3: 251-255.

Taylor, M. (2002) *Public Policy in the Community*, Palgrave, London.

The Guardian (2002) *Hackney Race Row* (07/06/2002) http://society.guardian.co.uk/councilsincrisis/story/0,8150,492136,00.html.

Thernstrom, A. and Thernstrom, S. (eds) (2002) *Beyond the Color Line: New Perspectives on Race and Ethnicity in America*, Hoover Institution, Stanford, CA.

Thomas, H. (1994) 'The New Right: 'race' and planning in Britain in the 1980s and 1990s', *Planning Practice & Research*, **9**, 4: 353-366.

Thomas, H. (1995) "Race', public policy and planning in Britain', *Planning Perspectives*, **10**, 123-148.

Thomas, H. (1997) 'Ethnic minorities and the planning system: A study revisited', *Town Planning Review*, **66**, 1: 1-14.

Thomas, H. and Krishnarayan, V. (1994) "Race', disadvantage, and policy processes in British planning', *Environment and Planning A*, **26**: 1891-1910.

Thomas, H., Stirling, T., Brownill, S. and Razzaque, K. (1996) 'Locality, urban governance and contested meanings of place', *Area*, **28**, 2: 186-198.

Thomas, W. I. and Znaniecki, F. (1958) *The Polish Peasant in Europe and America*, Dover, New York.

Thornley, A. (1993) *Urban Planning Under Thatcherism: The Challenge of the Market*, Routledge, London.

Thrasher, F. M. (1963) *A Study of 1,313 Gangs in Chicago*, University of Chicago Press, Chicago.

Tiesdell, S. and Allmendinger, P. (2001a) 'The New Right and neighbourhood regeneration', *Housing Studies*, **16**, 3: 311-334.

Tiesdell, S. and Allmendinger, P. (2001b) 'Neighbourhood regeneration and New Labour's Third Way', *Environment and Planning C: Government and Policy*, **19**, 903-926.

Townsend, P. (1957) *The Family Life of Older People*, Routledge & Kegan Paul, London.

Triggle, N. (2001) 'Symbol clash', *The Guardian (28/11/2001)*.

Triggle, N. (2002) 'Blair flagship is sunk', *The Guardian (02/01/02)*.

Troyna, B. (1991) 'Under-achievers or under-rated? The experiences of pupils of South Asian origin in a secondary school', *British Educational Research Journal*, **17**, 4: 361-374.

Troyna, B. (1992) 'Ethnicity and the organisation of learning groups: A case study', *Educational Research*, **34**, 1: 45-55.

Vidich, A. J. and Lyman, S. M. (1994) 'Qualitative methods: Their history in sociology and anthropology' in N. Denzin and Y. Lincoln (eds), *Handbook of Qualitative Research*, Sage, New York, pp. 23-59.

Wallman, S. (1982) *Living in South London: Perspectives on Battersea 1871-1981*, Gower, London.

Wallman, S. (1984) *Eight London Households*, Tavistock, London.

Walsh, D. (1998) 'Doing ethnography' in C. Seale (ed), *Researching Society and Culture*, Sage, London, pp. 217-232.

Wanna, J. (1991) 'Community Power debates: Themes, issues and remaining dilemmas', *Urban Policy and Research*, **9**, 4: 193-208.

Ward, K. (1995) *A Rough Guide To... Regime Theory*, 5, University of Manchester: Manchester.

Ward, K. (1996) 'Rereading urban regime theory: A sympathetic critique', *Geoforum*, **27**, 4: 427-438.

Ward, K. (1997) 'Coalitions in urban regeneration: A regime approach', *Environment and Planning A*, **29**: 1493-1506.

Waste, R. J. (Ed.) (1986) *Community Power: Directions for Future Research*, Sage, London.

Waste, R. J. (1987) *Power and Pluralism in American Cities*, Greenwood Press, New York.

Weaver, M. (2001) 'Judge clears housing director after record race pay out', *The Guardian* (16/05/2001).

Weaver, M. (2002) 'Friction slows New Deal', *The Guardian*.

Wehner, P. (2002) 'Elephant just a memory', *Estates Gazette*, April pp. 42-43.

Westside Community Forum (1996a) *Westside Community Regeneration Programme*, Westside Community Forum, London.

Westside Community Forum (1996b) *Westside Community Regeneration: Bid Document*, Westside Community Forum, London.

Westside Community Forum (1997) *Westside Community Regeneration: Delivery Plan 1997-1998*, Westside Community Forum, London.

Westside Community Forum (1998) *Westside Community Forum Partners List*, Westside Community Forum, London.

Wilks-Heeg, S. (2003) 'Economy, equity or empowerment? New Labour, communities and urban policy evaluation' in R. Imrie and M. Raco (eds), *Urban Renaissance? New Labour, Community and Urban Policy*, The Policy Press, Bristol, pp. 205-220.

Wilmott, P. and Young, M. (1960) *Family and Class in a London Suburb*, Routledge and Kegan Paul, London.

Wilson, W. J. (1980) *The Declining Significance of Race: Blacks and Changing American Institutions*, University of Chicago Press, Chicago.

Wilson, W. J. (1987) *The Truly Disadvantaged: The Inner City, The Underclass, and Public Policy*, University of Chicago Press, Chicago.

Wirth, L. (1956) *The Ghetto*, University of Chicago Press, Chicago.

Wolman, H. (1996) 'Theories of local democracy in the United States' in D. King and G. Stoker (eds), *Rethinking Normative Theories of Local Government and Democracy*, Macmillan, London.

Wood, M. and Vamplew, C. (1999) *Neighbourhood Images in Teesside: Regeneration or Decline?* JRF, York.

Woodward, R. (1991) 'Mobilising opposition: The campaign against Housing Action Trusts in Tower Hamlets', *Housing Studies*, **6**, 1: 44-56.

Yates, D. (1977) *The Ungovernable City: The Politics of Urban Problems and Policymaking*, MIT Press, Cambridge MASS.

Yin, R. (1984) *Case Study Research: Design and Methods*, Sage, Beverly Hills CA.

Young, K. (1983) 'Ethnic pluralism and the policy agenda in Britain' in N. Glazer and K. Young (eds), *Ethnic Pluralism and Public Policy*, Heinemann, London.

Young, M. D. and Wilmott, P. (1957) *Family and Kinship in East London*, Free Press, Glencoe, Ill.

Zorbaugh, H. W. (1929) *The Gold Coast and The Slum*, University of Chicago Press, Chicago.

Index